New Directions in Te

D0117304

New Directions in Teaching Memoir

A Studio Workshop Approach

Dawn Latta Kirby
Dan Kirby

HEINEMANN
Portsmouth, NH

Heinemann
A division of Reed Elsevier Inc.
361 Hanover Street
Portsmouth, NH 03801–3912
www.heinemann.com

Offices and agents throughout the world

Library of Congress Cataloging-in-Publication Data
Kirby, Dawn Latta.
  New directions in teaching memoir : a studio workshop approach / Dawn Latta Kirby, Dan Kirby.
    p. cm.
  Includes bibliographical references and index.
  ISBN-13: 978-0-325-00668-0
  ISBN-10: 0-325-00668-7
  1. Autobiography—Study and teaching. 2. Biography as a literary form—Study and teaching. I. Kirby, Dan. II. Title.
  CT25.K47 2007
  808'.06692—dc22   2007007609

Editor: Lisa Luedeke
Production: Elizabeth Valway
Cover design: Bernadette Skok
Composition: SPi Publisher Services
Manufacturing: Louise Richardson

Printed in the United States of America on acid-free paper
11 10 09 08 07 EB 1 2 3 4 5

Contents

Preface   ix

1. **Memoir as Genre**   1
   Contemporary Memoir   1
   Types of Memoir   4
   Teaching Memoir   5
   Final Thoughts on Memoir   8

2. **Studio-style Teaching**   11
   Tenets for Teaching Contemporary Memoir   11
   Our Journey to the Concept of the Studio Classroom   13
   Applying Studio Methodology to Memoir   18
   Theoretical Grounding of *Work* Within the Studio Classroom   18
   Establishing Studio Classroom Values   21
   Final Thoughts on the Studio Classroom   26

3. **Explorations in Memoir Writing**   28
   Exploring the Territory of Memoir as Genre   28
   Exploring the Memoir Framework   29
   Getting Started with the Memoir Framework: The Pieces   34

4. **Further Explorations in Memoir Writing**   46
   The Snapshot Piece   46
   The Boundaries (or Map) Piece   51
   Adding to the Pieces on Your Own   56
   Principles for Reading like a Writer   56

5. **Writing Memoir Pieces**   59
    First Steps: Establishing Routines and Rituals in the Studio Classroom   60
    Drafting the Memoir Pieces   62
    Revising the Memoir Pieces   63
    Using Effective Writer's Groups   75

6. **Finding a Scheme**   80
    What Is a Scheme?   81
    Answering the "So What?" Question   82
    Determining a Personally Relevant Scheme   84
    Sample Schemes   91

7. **Exploring Forms and Formats**   92
    The Role and Message of Format in Writing   93
    Considering Stylistic Elements   93
    Final Thoughts   97

8. **Assembling the Memoir**   98
    Presentational Aspects of Finished Memoirs   99
    Layout Options for the Final Memoir   102

9. **Alternate Forms of Memoir and How to Write Them**   105
    Triptych   106
    "So What?" Stories to Illustrate a Personal Theme   117
    Multigenre Memoirs   117
    Memoir Blends   120
    Final Thoughts   121

10. **Tracking Memoir-writing Processes**   123
    Collecting the Invisible Information: Writers' Reflections   124
    Reflections Before Writing   124
    Reflections During Writing   129
    Reflections After Writing   134
    Final Thoughts   138

11. **Evaluating Memoir Writing**   140
    What Testing Is Not   141
    What Evaluation Can Become   142
    A Word About Grading   142
    A Bit of Terminology   143
    Mapping the Assessment Territory   144
    Tracking the Visible Information: Assessing, Evaluating,
        and Grading Work   146

Grading and Evaluating the Final Memoir Product   149
A Word About Portfolios   152
A Teacher's Reflective Log   154

12. Bibliographies in Memoir   **158**
Bibliography of Suggested Memoirs   159
Themed Memoirs and Memoir Pairings   165
Author Studies: Memoirs Plus   174
Memoir Blends   177
Memoiresque Books for Use with Younger Writers   179

Index   **181**

Preface

As the title of this book suggests, we want to take our readers in *new directions* for teaching and learning about writing and literature. One of those new directions includes enticing readers to explore the developing and changing genre of Contemporary Memoir (CM), both for your own intellectual pursuits and enjoyment and for use with your students. In Chapter 1 we chronicle some of the development of CM and how it is qualitatively different from mere storytelling and family tales. We talk about some of the key players in the development of CM. Throughout the book, we also offer a variety of strategies for engaging students in reading and writing CM, and we suggest ideas for responding to and evaluating their work. In Chapter 12, we present an extensive bibliography, suggesting possible pairings and groupings of CM that will help you decide which works might be appropriate for your own reading and thinking in the genre as well as for your instructional purposes and your students' interests.

We have written this book because for some time we have felt that the teaching of writing and writing practice in schools has too often been divorced from the study of literature. We have observed a kind of "I teach literature; *he* teaches writing" mentality among some English and language arts professionals. In fact, many English teachers have told us they see the study of literature through the reading and discussion of important works and the labor-intensive, sometimes grinding work of teaching writing as two separate enterprises. They have said that they find it difficult to be an expert in both kinds of instruction, and they experience problems trying to bring the two together in some integrated and meaningful way in their classes.

We suspect this problem has two sources. First, literature study has traditionally been based upon well-known works, works that have been critiqued, taught, and analyzed by scholars, teachers, and students over many years. If any writing accompanies traditional literary inquiry, it is often rehashed literary criticism and analysis: the kind of writing that asks students to rely on critical sources and generally accepted analysis rather than their own personal observations and interactions with the work.

Second, canonical works have been classified into genres that appear to have immutable characteristics and descriptors. The short story, for example, is taught as a genre with five essential elements. Similar characteristics of fiction and poetry are also taught to young people. Works the teacher knows well and genres with hard-edged definitions don't leave our students much room to engage in the discovery of how genres come to be formed and how they change over time. Similarly, writings that must be documented from research texts and critical sources leave students little room for original analysis. While the teaching of canonical works and of literary writing that has been deeply researched has its place in schools, we don't think that they are the only or even the primary type of reading and writing that helps us to grow quality readers and writers. And you don't need yet another book to tell you how to teach that genre. Instead, throughout this book, we hope to demonstrate how a dynamic genre like memoir can become an opportunity to teach essential literary concepts and to allow students to experience a literary genre that is changing while they study it, yielding writing that is personal, rhetorically sophisticated, audience aware, and moving toward skill and precision.

Another new direction we wish to explore with our readers is the possibility of creating studio classrooms for reading and writing. Many of us who teach writing now use some version of the writing workshop. While that pedagogy has substantially improved writing instruction in many classrooms, writing workshop methodologies are not an unqualified success. Too often students work at a superficial level in writing workshops, doing the tasks we ask them to do but failing to engage deeply and meaningfully in the writing work. For several years after we encountered Donald Schön's book, *Teaching the Reflective Practitioner*, we worked with artists and studio art teachers, visiting their studios and classrooms to see what we could learn from their work ethic and pedagogy. Schön's ethnographic rendering of the workings of an architectural studio were particularly exciting to us.

In fact, we enjoyed hanging out with an artist friend or two in their studios. One of our favorites is the talented Jerry Fuhriman, whose studio is in Logan, Utah. Jerry is an accomplished landscape artist capturing the scenic Cache Valley in stunning oils and watercolor. When we asked him about his work habits and mind-set as an artist, he said, "My studio is like [he pauses, seeking a word] kindergarten—like Mrs. Scott's kindergarten class: rich with possibilities. It is a statement of freedom. When I come here to work, I can wander around, play with the computer, move frames around, stretch canvas, stare at unfinished pieces, or sit down and talk to visitors. I can play music on the CD player or feed the dog or do my email or pay bills. But mostly I can work at whatever pace and with whatever intensity I am feeling. In this place, I don't have a schedule or a to-do list." Jerry's sense of freedom and creativity in his own space is exactly what we have worked to transport into our writing classes.

With all of these influences from artists in our psyches, we had originally thought about titling this book, *Of Painters, Potters, and Architects: Learning to Teach Writing from Artists*. As we continued to spend time with artists and potters, several observations impressed us. First, we came to appreciate how committed they were to their work. We noted artists working on multiple pieces, spending time on one piece and then putting it aside to work with another. We noticed their attitude toward pieces that didn't work, and how they were able to see failure as learning and growth. We wondered if we could transform our own sometime anemic writing workshops into studio-like experiences during which our students would find the work of writing and reading as compelling and engaging as the artists that we watched found their work.

We also found remarkable the artists' abilities to talk about their work and to share their particular vision or hope for a piece they were beginning or for a piece they had worked on for many days. Many of these artists were able to articulate their mental lives and their personal reflections of their growth as artists. We wondered if we might draw out of our students their thoughts and reflections about their reading and writing work during their response groups and during our conferences with them.

In studio art classes where students often worked intently for four hours, sometimes losing all track of time and place, we sensed a set of values embedded in a studio approach to teaching—values that would, when applied to the writing classroom, give students more freedom to write from their own experiences and also encourage them to develop more self-imposed discipline and care for the work they were doing. We experimented with instructional designs based on studio values that could serve to alter the balance of work and responsibility in our writing workshops. These musings and observations became central to a new direction in teaching for us, one that we have incorporated fully into our classroom practices and now into this book. We discuss and elaborate upon these values and our frameworks for instruction in Chapter 3.

Not unlike other books we have written, the ideas we offer in this text have been developed over a span of a dozen years or so. We have difficulty committing our ideas to books until we have put some miles on them in classrooms and workshops. Early explorations in memoir began for us in the mid-eighties as we held workshops with middle school–aged children around something we were calling personal narrative (PN). That form was popular both at National Writing Project sites and in many school classrooms; its use essentially led writers to tell the story of a significant incident or period in their growing-up years. These narratives often proved to be irresistible invitations to write for even the most reluctant writers, and process pedagogy was a great fit to support the creation of those stories. Students of all ages loved to write them. Everyone enjoyed hauling out their memorabilia and recounting poignant stories of the trials and tribulations of youth. And everyone enjoyed reading their tales aloud to each other in response groups. Personal narrative was an unmitigated feel-good experience.

As we continued to work with personal narrative in our classes and to have overall success with that form of writing, however, we began to notice some flies in the ointment and to question the extent to which those often facile and unreflective tales of youth really produced growth for our writers over time. Too often, students resisted our encouragement to craft and improve their narratives. They had told their stories and they liked them just as they were, thank you very much. Additionally, like many other teachers, we found that our students loved to write endless personal narratives, but they experienced great difficulty making a transition to any other form of writing. We also came to doubt the literary value of the students' writings and whether such writings were really teaching them anything about literature. Professional models for personal narrative were scarce outside of college textbooks, and we didn't really think PN met the criteria to be called a *genre*.

As we continued to work with PN, we began to read and deepen our knowledge of CM. In doing so, we came to see that memoir was both story *and* reflection. We began to encourage students to construct *life stories* rather than accounts of a simple narrative incident. We challenged students to consider their lives not as one story but as many. In order to complicate and intensify our student writers' work, we developed a series of short writings that we called Explorations and invited students to explore their lives from multiple perspectives. We then asked them to sort through their collected short writings to invent ways to weave them into longer, more complex narratives. In so doing, we were asking our students to work like memoirists even before we knew much about memoirists and how they worked.

Now that we have worked with memoir in our classrooms over several years, we have come to believe that memoir's essential function for both writers and readers is its ability to connect them to their pasts. Russell Baker calls the connecting process of memoir "braiding the cord" of human experience.[1] It is our firm belief that people, and particularly young people, need to be taught to come to know and understand their roots and origins. For this generation of young people we teach, life accelerates at warp speed. The past is a galaxy behind them. Far too many parents fail to tell family stories; they neglect to connect their children to family histories and cultural touchstones. We know from firsthand teaching experience that memoir can become a remarkable vehicle for leading young people to understand and perhaps even to celebrate their lives, however joyous or challenging they may have been. Memoir is a significant and powerful genre for chronicling bravery and suffering and for bringing to consciousness failures of the past. Memoir is worth teaching because it invites writers to remember, to reflect upon, and then to make sense of their lived experiences.

Perhaps more than any book we have written before, this book is authored for you as reader as much as for you as teacher. We know your reading time is scarce, carved out of other important times, but we think Contemporary Memoir is an especially appropriate genre for teachers. More than any other profession, teaching is a personal—even intimate—journey; teachers ultimately teach their *selves*, not their content. Reading and writing memoir can teach us to be more introspective. It teaches us to examine and reflect upon our lives as we support and care for other people's children. It helps us to see the work we have done in life-affirming ways. We hope it brings renewal for you, as it has for us.

Note

1. This metaphor is one of our favorites. It comes from Baker, Russell. (1982). *Growing Up*. New York: A Plume Book, New American Library, p. 8.

Work Cited

SCHÖN, DONALD. 1990. *Educating the Reflective Practitioner: Toward a New Design for Teaching and Learning in the Professions*. San Francisco: Jossey-Bass Publishers.

1

Memoir as Genre

Memoir is a well-traveled genre. Patricia Hampl dates the first Western autobiography to Augustine's thirteen-volume confessions in 397 A.D. (166). Since then, presidents, generals, tyrants, and movie stars have often had a need to tell the stories of their lives. Early memoir—or *memoirs*, as in, "I'm going to write my memoirs"—consisted primarily of personal accounts of the events and accomplishments of famous people, usually written near the end of their lives. The worst of these autobiographic recollections were rambling, unreflective tomes considered by the literati to be marginal forms of literature at best. Too frequently, these writings were adventures in self-aggrandizement, at least partially ghost written, depicting the subject as the protagonist of his or her own story. While the conventions of autobiography called for the authors to offer well-documented evidence of their exploits through diaries, notes, and historic documents, no doubt many of these larger-than-life early memoirists took license to make themselves look wise and heroic in their writings, regardless of the evidence. Because these life stories were often self-indulgent, poorly written, and lacking in literary merit, the audiences for such writings were frequently sparse. In many cases the readers were historians, biographers, detractors, family members, or unabashed fans of the well-known person, eager to read any crumb by the famous one.

Contemporary Memoir (CM)

Thankfully, something remarkable has happened to this genre during the last twenty years or so. Autobiography and the old *memoirs* discussed earlier have been reborn as literary memoir and transformed into a lively and highly readable genre, maintaining long runs on the *New York Times* bestseller list for nonfiction books. Contemporary writers of memoir, some of whom were completely unknown prior to the publication of their books, have begun to use the tools of the novelist and the poet, bringing to the genre such innovations as character development, scene setting, dialogue, figurative language, metaphor, symbol, and image. Even more important perhaps, as Patricia Hampl has pointed out, "contemporary memoir has reaffirmed the primacy of the first-person voice in American imaginative writing established by Whitman's 'Song of Myself'" (19). The best examples of this reborn genre read like good novels rather than dry accounts of historic or daily events.

Perhaps to distinguish the new, more literary and livelier memoir from the older writings, critics and writers have come to refer to these new versions of memoir as *Contemporary Memoir* (CM). No longer merely heroic epics of lives well lived, CMs explore both what writers can remember and understand from their lives and also take readers with them on journeys into unknown territory where writers use the form to try to understand and make sense of unexamined experiences they have yet to comprehend fully. CM has become a genre in which any reasonably reflective individual can construct a version of his or her own life.

CMs are often episodic and driven by short ministories of events and places. Many of these texts derive their continuity and sense of artistic unity through narrative structures. Through the author's recounting of the unfolding of family members' lives over time—sometimes over multiple generations—a larger, more compelling story emerges. CMs are reflective and often partially fictionalized creations that *reveal* truths and mysteries of lives we would never know if the author had not chosen to tell us.

We aren't sure of the birth date of this remarkable genre, but it came into its own in the early eighties. We first began to apply the term CM to these texts after reading Russell Baker's *Growing Up* in 1982. In interviews following the best-seller success of his memoir, Baker confessed that he wasn't sure why anyone would be interested in the details of his life. But, in the first chapter of the book, as Baker recounts the days of his mother's death, he has an epiphany that lights the spark for this new genre. He realizes that when his mother is gone, all of the stories of his growing up will go with her. He writes, "These hopeless end-of-the-line visits with my mother made me wish I had not thrown off my own past so carelessly" (8). In this tender moment, he realizes that he has not been a keeper of the family lore, nor has he shared any family history with his own children. He confesses this failing and offers, "We all come from the past and children ought to know what went into their making, to know that life is a braided cord. . .'" (8).

This metaphor of the braided cord and the realization that they, too, have done little to explore and preserve their own past has since seized many writers. They feel driven to create versions of their own lives and to share those quite personal and revealing stories with readers. Indeed, some critics and detractors of memoir, such as James Atlas, have labeled it a "confessional genre" in which writers tell all to "an audience of voyeurs" (26). To be sure, there are those out there who view CM as an opportunity to practice a kind of self-help psychoanalysis or to find redemption for their sins. Working as a memoirist can almost certainly take a writer to some tight spots, places of dark mystery, and uncomfortable self-discovery; but the effective memoirist can chose to *conceal* as well as *reveal*. The most well-crafted of CMs derive their power not from the narcissistic recounting of lurid detail, nor from a text version of reality television, but rather from the honest recounting of human struggles and triumphs. The best CMs do not read like pages from tabloids, but rather like the rich stories of literary novels.

William Zinsser's book, *Inventing the Truth: The Art and Craft of Memoir* (1998), also played an important role in the birth and development of CM. The book derives from a series of talks by well-known writers organized and hosted by Zinsser for the Book-of-the-Month Club and held in the New York Public Library. In *Inventing the Truth*, Zinsser points out that unlike autobiography, memoir is not the whole story of a life. He writes, "Unlike autobiography, which moves in a dutiful line from birth to fame, omitting nothing significant, memoir assumes the life and ignores most of it. . . . Memoir is a window into a life" (15). Annie Dillard (1998) echoed this notion of memoir as a selective genre when she asserted that "the memoirist must decide two crucial points: what to leave in and what to leave out" (143). Zinsser continues, "Memoir writers must manufacture a text, imposing narrative order on a jumble of half-remembered events. With that feat of manipulation they arrive at a truth that is theirs alone, not quite like that of anybody else who was present at the same events" (6). Selectivity, choosing just the right details, is one of the hallmarks of the CM.

Since the memory is an inevitably flawed instrument that is both unreliable and subject to interpretation, any memoir is at least in part an invention. Memory is quirky, partial, holding seemingly meaningless details and losing big moments and subtle nuances of relationships and events. Memoirs are often written at the very edges of a writer's memory where recollections are hazy and not known with certainty. Remembering can be impressionistic and partial, and writing memoir is an attempt to shape those images into story.

Another important and timely influence on the growth of Contemporary Memoir was the publication of Eudora Welty's *One Writer's Beginnings* (1983). Delivered originally as a series of three autobiographic lectures at Harvard, *Beginnings* was important not only for its literary quality but also because a writer of Welty's reputation and stature among the literati penned it. If Welty wrote in the genre, it was a clear endorsement of the relevance of the genre. Perhaps just as important as this publication was for the authorization of CM were the insights Welty offered into the value and purpose of writing memoir. She reminds us that "[w]riting a story or a novel is one way of discovering *sequence* in experience, of stumbling upon cause and effect in the happenings of a writer's own life" (90). We think her statements still hold true for memoirists of all ages.

Patricia Hampl has also been a significant player in the development of CM as a respected genre. In her seminal essay, "Memory and Imagination" (1999), she situates "memoir at the intersection of narration and reflection, of story telling and essay writing. It can present its story *and* consider the meaning of the story" (33). For us, that definition of memoir that locates it between story and essay is what also distinguishes it from biography and autobiography. The memoirist is not limited by a responsibility to scholarly accuracy as are biographers who must rely on factual documents, eye-witness accounts, and historical chronologies, though memoirists may certainly use those tools. Rather, it is the memoirist's responsibility to work with the partial information and inadequate data that the mind offers in order to construct a text. As Hampl (1999) states, "Memory is not a warehouse of finished stories, not a gallery of framed pictures" (26). Memoir is unique as a genre because the writer must try to find the relationships between mind pictures and feelings, seeking to reconcile through story the details of what is remembered and what has been forgotten. The memoir is ultimately a version of one's life constructed from facts and feelings, truths and inventions.

Types of Memoir

In many bookstores, memoir is still shelved in a section titled Biography. Take a casual stroll through that section, and you will be stunned by the proliferation of titles. Some will actually be biographies, but the great majority will be memoirs. You will know that fact because after the title, the publisher or author will offer as an explanatory subtitle, *A Memoir*. Just perusing titles, however, may not be a very sanguine way of coming to understand the breadth and diversity of this genre. In order to aid this process, we have extensive bibliographies of memoir titles in Chapter 12. Bibliographic information on all books we use as examples in the chapters that follow can be found there. If you are relatively unaware of this genre, let us suggest several possible schemas for classifying, cataloging, and ultimately selecting appealing examples of the genre. If you are an aficionado of the genre, you may enjoy comparing your favorites to our categories and bibliographies. Following are some of the subcategories of memoir that are interesting to us.

Cross-cultural

One of the most remarkable qualities of CM is the extent to which the genre crosses cultural, ethnic, and geographic boundaries. Writers of this version of memoir use the power of story and the uniqueness of their own cultural experiences to craft quite diverse accounts of their growing-up years in locations throughout the world. Some examples include African writers such as Ken Wiwa; African American writers such as Henry Louis Gates, Jr., James McBride, and Jamaica Kincaid; Chinese American writers such as Da Chen, Anchee Min, Li-Young Lee, and Maxine Hong Kingston; Vietnamese American writers such as Andrew X. Pham and Kien Nguyen; Cambodian American writers such as Chanrithy Him; Latino and Hispanic American writers such as Tiffany Ana Lopez, Flor Fernández Barrios, Marie Arana, and Jimmy Baca; Jewish writers such as Louise Kehoe and Michael Heller; and Afghani American writers such as Saira Shah.

Personal Journeys

Writers use CM to chronicle personal journeys, literal and metaphoric, that they have undertaken. Writers such as Tobias Wolff, Andrea Ashworth, and Frank McCourt preserve stories of their past, however painful and challenging. Steve Fiffer, Kay Redfield Jamison, and Stephen Kuusisto chronicle their journeys to overcome a handicap or physical disability. Frederick Buechner, Annie Dillard, Jane Goodall, Patricia Hampl, Annie Lamott, and Lauren Winner pursue spiritual journeys. Joan London and Nasdijj make sense of troubling and chaotic childhoods.

Multiple Memoirs

One might think that each of us has only one memoir book in us, but a number of writers of CM have written multiple memoirs, looking at their lives through a variety of lenses. In this category, try Mary Karr, Kathleen Norris, Alix Kates Shulman, Patricia Hampl, Jill Ker Conway, Homer Hickam, and Elie Wiesel, all of whom have written accounts of different periods in their lives.

Blurred Genre

Among the most interesting phenomena associated with the evolution of the Contemporary Memoir is the way in which writers have blurred the hard lines of genre distinction. One of the most successful examples of this genre hybridization has been created by writers who merge their ability to write about their observations in the natural world and at the same time, in the same one book, author memoir. One of the most unique examples of this genre experimentation is the work of Janisse Ray in which she alternates chapters of the natural history of her native Georgia with stories from her childhood growing up in a junkyard in south Georgia. Terry Tempest Williams, Thomas McGuane, and Barry Lopez also are adept at using landscape as character in their memoirs.

Collections

In addition to single, book-length examples of CM, collections of shorter life stories are emerging in themed books. Annie Dillard edits such a book, as does Henry Louis Gates, Jr., Alex Harris, and Claudine O'Hearn. One of our personal favorites in this category is Marilyn Sewell's *Resurrecting Grace: Remembering Catholic Childhoods*.

The subcategories in the genre of CM continue to develop as more memoirs are published, but our bibliographies in Chapter 12 will serve as a rather thorough introduction to the genre. Notice, however, that we have omitted the more traditional memoirs, such as those by Bill Clinton (2004) and Hillary Rodham Clinton (2004), that have been published in recent years. We have done so because our focus here is not on traditional memoir; it is, instead, on Contemporary Memoir as a genre, not just as a publication date.

Teaching Memoir

We have been teaching students to read and write memoir for the past fifteen years or so. We have used memoir with elementary, middle, and high school–aged young people. We have also used it in college-level freshman composition, and we use it in graduate English methods classes and with creative nonfiction writing classes. Throughout our experience of teaching memoir, our writers often become deeply engaged in journeys of memory, journeys in which they chronicle their struggles of growing up. Or these memoir writings may become explorations into the enduring family mysteries that writers still don't quite understand, with the writer struggling to come to some understanding or sense of resolution about the family puzzles.

Sometimes people ask us, "Should people, particularly students, be writing honestly about their life experiences? Aren't you playing psychiatrist—or worse, voyeur—to their lives?" These are questions we have thought about right from our earliest use of memoir. Dan remembers a writing workshop in a middle school in a coastal Georgia town. The school population was primarily African American children from poor and working-class families. As the students were working on their memoir pieces about family, an eighth-grade young woman drafted a piece that detailed why she wished she could live with her "real" (her word) mother instead of the woman with whom she was living. The girl's mother was serving time in the county jail for a drug offense, and the child had been placed in a foster home. The piece was so poignant and revealing that Dan was a little uncomfortable with her taking it public. He said that he was happy she had written such an honest piece, but asked her if she would prefer to keep it in a private place in her portfolio; he secretly hoped she would choose that option. "Oh, no," she said with a smile. "I have already shared it with my group, and they really thought it was cool. I want to post it on the Pieces in Progress bulletin board in the hall." Clearly, definitions of *private* and comfort zones will vary among writers.

From that early experience and many similar subsequent experiences in teaching memoir, we learned that our students are the best judges of what they should reveal in memoir, even if at times we may feel somewhat uncomfortable with their painful honesty. Our responsibility as teachers is to eschew the roles of psychologist and censor and to embrace the role of writing coach. With sensitive and caring attention to our students' stories, our job is not to fall into those stories with sympathy, hand wringing, or advice, but rather to help students craft their chosen stories with as much elegance and power as possible.

It has been our experience that student writers often seize upon a safe and supportive environment in which to explore difficult times and personal struggles. Abuse—both physical and sexual—neglect, divorce, gender confusion, alienation from family, and heart-wrenching losses may all become part of our students' memoirs. But it is our experience that the recountings of these difficult times in writing are often followed by healing, reconciliation, and awareness of personal growth for the student writers.

The stories are astounding. A thirty-something woman in Dan's writing methods class, returning to college to achieve her teaching license, wrote of her childhood among drunken and drug-using parents. The climate in her home became so volatile that she ran away as a junior in high school. As she was writing this story, she was moved to call her father to whom she hadn't spoken in twenty years. What followed that courageous phone call was a long-overdue reconciliation and an incredibly powerful memoir. In another class, several Vietnamese American teens recounted hair-raising stories of their escape from war-torn Vietnam in the mid-1970s. In another class, a mother with two teenage sons wrote the stories of growing up in her native India because she wanted to share her heritage with her boys. In a third-grade class, a boy wrote a memoir of his struggle to overcome epilepsy and to achieve his highest goal: "to be a normal kid," as he put it. In a middle school class, a girl chronicled the breakup of her family and the choices she had to make between parents and where she would live. In a high school composition class, a shy young woman's group responded so sensitively to her early drafts about growing up with a bipolar mother that she spent the entire semester crafting a remarkably literary account of those years. These may sound like stories from the *Oprah* show or Dr. Phil, but these vignettes are only a few examples of the power of memoir to heal and to transform painful memories into stories of triumph and growth.

Memoir as Literature Study

Contemporary Memoir is also an ideal genre for study as literature because its rules have not been set in concrete. Mercifully, there are not "five elements" to the memoir as traditionalists will claim about the short story. Rather, CM as a form continues to surprise and confound its readers. CM as a genre is in a constant state of change and development. Its conventions and constraints are seemingly challenged by the publication of each new memoir book. We think of the genre as dynamic and tectonic, shifting and changing, forming and reforming itself. Each reading of a new memoir adds to the possibilities of the form. Readers, who are teachers and students alike, are witness to an emerging genre that has not been overly dissected by critics or flattened by instruction. Here is an authentic opportunity for students to share in the process of literary criticism and in the analysis of an emerging genre.

Of course as English teachers, we always feel a little more comfortable when we are teaching genres that we have read and studied in graduate school, but toss out those stale college notes on literary criticism. This is a fresh genre and an innovative teaching framework to study *with* your students.

DIVING INTO MEMOIR

We like to take a very inductive approach to the introduction of memoir into our classes. Most students have read very few memoirs and have only the vaguest notions about the genre. We want them to feel the sense of discovery and license that an emerging genre like memoir affords them. We try to *tell* them as little as possible about the genre at the beginning, knowing instead that as we read and write memoir with our students, we and they can begin to understand its power and identify its features.

We usually begin by finding out what students already know about genre and genre studies. Do they know what the word *genre* means and how it is used in literature?

What genre can they name (short stories or poetry or essays, for example) and what exemplars (titles and features of one genre that distinguish it from the next, for example) can they list of that genre? When they read a poem or a novel, what kinds of unique expectations do they have for that specific genre? Teachers of younger children may want to begin by asking a more age-appropriate series of questions centering on how students might catalog or classify the different kinds of books they read, such as fairy tales, nursery rhymes, or fantasy. What kinds of expectations do they have when they read a particular kind of book or text?

We then read excerpts of CMs with our students and engage in some unrehearsed, cold turkey critical theory and homegrown scholarly explanations of this emerging genre. Again, we ask key questions. What is the tone of the passage? Is it written in first-person or in third-person omniscient point of view? Does it sound like a textbook or a novel or something in between? What is the topic of the passage, and how will that topic relate to us, the readers? What is appealing about the passage?

One of our favorite activities for beginning a study of memoir as genre is what we call Examining Contemporary Memoir Texts or, more simply, Book Examination. For this activity, we bring in a stack of CMs and lead students through an inspection of these texts. We use the guide in Figure 1–1 titled Examining Contemporary Memoir Texts to engage students in an anthropological dig in the artifacts of the genre. We use this guide with our high school and college students. For middle school and elementary students, you may need to reword or simplify the form. Of course, not all memoirs contain all of the features we list on the guide, but most memoirs will have some of these elements with which the aspiring memoirist will want to be familiar as possibilities and options that enhance the genre, theme, and purpose of the author's writings.

Final Thoughts on Memoir

What we've tried to do in this first chapter is to provide a brief overview of Contemporary Memoir, both as a genre and as an option for teaching. We like memoir because we can use it to develop a large, inclusive framework that gives us the opportunity to work with our students as readers and as writers. Memoir offers possibilities for in-depth literary study and analysis and for connecting literature to personal experience through writing. We've worked with this genre for over fifteen years with students in kindergarten through graduate school and still find it to be engaging, versatile, and dynamic. In the following chapters, we'll detail how we teach memoir in our classrooms, how we use it as a literary form, and how we devise a framework for writing based on memoir.

As you read this book, you might want to make notes in your own Idea Notebook for how these activities will work for your students, or how you want to pursue some of these readings and teaching ideas in a discussion group with your colleagues. Adaptation is the key to inventive teaching, so we encourage you to think, plan, jot, and discuss as you read this text.

Examining Contemporary Memoir Texts

Directions: Use this guide for examining how contemporary memoirs are organized and what interesting features appear in these texts. Examine at least three of the memoirs that are in our classroom today. Discuss the texts and the prompts below in your Writer's Groups. Jot your responses on your individual sheets in the spaces provided below.

Title: What is the title of the memoir? What is its significance? Does it seem to be literal, or does it seem to have a symbolic or metaphoric meaning? How do you know? How does the title serve the text?

Front Material: What is on the pages that appear before the opening page of text? Is there an introduction or dedication? Are there quotations, graphics, pictures, or maps? Is there a prologue or an explanatory essay? If so, who wrote it and what is its purpose? How do the front materials enhance the memoir?

Table of Contents: Is there a table of contents? How is the book divided: by chapters, sections, or in other ways? How many of each type of division exists? Do the divisions have titles or numbers? List some examples. What seems to be the overall effect of the divisions on the organization of the memoir?

Visual Material: Does the author use pictures, maps, drawings, photographs, or any other visual aids in the text? If so, what is the impact of the visual materials on the text?

Textual Material: Does the author use dialogue? If so, how is it punctuated? In what tense is the text written—past, present, future? Does the author insert phrases in a language other than English? If so, how are those passages incorporated into the text? Is there anything unusual about the typeset or about how the book is laid out? How do these textual features impact the overall memoir?

End Material: How does the book end? Is there an epilogue? Is there any documentation at the end of the book? Does the author take any parting shots? What is the impact of the end materials on the memoir?

May be copied for classroom use. © 2007 by Dawn Latta Kirby and Dan Kirby, from *New Directions in Teaching Memoir* (Heinemann: Portsmouth, NH).

Figure 1–1. *Examining Contemporary Memoir Texts*

We also find that we can easily devise grades for multiple written pieces, writer's group activities, and responses to literary selections within this framework; and that we can easily meet many state and national standards and practice state-mandated writing forms within the framework of memoir. In the following chapters, we'll highlight some of those strategies that we use, and we specifically discuss assessment in Chapters 10 and 11. Additionally, as you read this book, we encourage you to jot notes in your Idea Notebook of the ways in which you can meet state standards and district guidelines as well as your personal goals for your students' progress in literacy as you teach memoir.

While you're at it, try picking up a few of the memoirs that we list in Chapter 12 that sound interesting to you and start reading in the genre, looking for excerpts that are suitable for use with your students. Relax, read, enjoy, think, and create as you join us on this exploration of a compelling and contemporary new genre.

Works Cited

Atlas, James. May 12, 1996. "Confessing for Voyeurs; The Age of Literary Memoir Is Now." *New York Times Magazine*.

Baker, Russell. 1982. *Growing Up*. New York: Plume Books.

Clinton, Bill. 2004. *My Life*. New York: Alfred A. Knopf, Inc.

Clinton, Hillary Rodham. 2004. *Living History*. Nan Graham (Ed.). New York: Scribner.

Dillard, Annie. 1998. "To Fashion a Text." In *Inventing the Truth: The Art and Craft of Memoir*, edited by William Zinsser, 141–61. Boston: Houghton Mifflin.

Hampl, Patricia. 1999. *I Could Tell You Stories: Sojourns in the Land of Memory*. New York: W. W. Norton.

Welty, Eudora. 1983. *One Writer's Beginnings*. Cambridge, MA: Harvard University Press.

Zinsser, William, ed. 1998. *Inventing the Truth: The Art and Craft of Memoir*. Boston: Houghton Mifflin.

2

Studio-style Teaching

In Chapter 1, we introduced you to Contemporary Memoir (CM) and described its unique features and the appropriateness of using that emerging genre to engage and energize student writers. In this chapter, we make the case for the marriage of CM and studio pedagogy. Much of our past teaching, even in writing workshop mode, has required that we assume the roles of assignment designer and writing task manager. Teaching CM well requires that we explore new, more complex roles as teachers, roles beyond merely assigning work, responding to papers, and grading that work. We find that a coachlike stance and a supportive environment are essential to cultivate the birth of our students' life stories. In this chapter, we explore a richer, more complex metaphor for creating a unique environment for memoir study.

Tenets for Teaching Contemporary Memoir

When we teach CM, we ask our students to construct narrative versions of their lives, to remember events and people from their past, and to invent additional detail and dialog as necessary. We ask them to consider the "So what?" of their remembered stories. As we discuss in detail in Chapter 6, the "So what" idea is a direct way of capturing student writers' intentions and of asking them to consider how their life events and meanings will resonate with readers. Barbara's parents divorced when she was ten; why will readers want to hear about that part of her life? What did she learn as a result, how does she now view marriage and family, and what character traits developed within her as a result of her experience? In short, your parents divorced; so, what's the resulting personal learning, and how can you share that insight with an audience?

When we teach CM, we also ask students to come to some understanding of why they remember specific events, people, and places, and what those remembrances tell them about who they are now. When we teach CM, we are upping the ante for our students' writing, asking them to take more risks and assume more authorial responsibility for their final products. Doing so requires us to accept the fact that these are our students' life stories, and that they may often be quite personal and unique. That's part of the point; in order to resonate with readers, student writers will strive to find experiences that stand out in some manner, that speak of their individual lives and perspectives, and that sound a familiar—but not trite—chord with an audience.

Memoir writing requires that students write about their lived experiences, which they know far better than we. We can neither tell our student writers exactly how these stories should go nor what meanings they should ultimately make of them. That's because the knowledge of their experiences resides within our students, not with us as omniscient teachers. Therefore, to teach memoir writing well, we have found that we cannot respond to these writings in the same manner that we might respond to their expository pieces. Life stories are too close to the bone—the student cares about them deeply—and we need to let the student writer work a while on discovering meaning and on communicating that meaning to an audience. It serves neither the development of the student writer nor the development of the genre of memoir for us to be prescriptive in our advice or judgmental in our criticism. Instead, we have found success by teaching memoir from a more interactive, shared, and communal stance in which we ask more questions of our student writers and give far fewer answers. We encourage them to find their own answers through writing and through rendering their stories.

Reworking Workshops

We suspect that many of you reading this book have used traditional writing workshops as one of the cornerstones of your writing instruction techniques. Perhaps many of you have struggled with workshop pedagogy and found it to be something less than the penicillin of writing instruction as it may have been sold to you—as have we. Certainly, you—and we—have experienced occasional magical workshop *days*, when all of your students were productive and even enthusiastic about writing in community. And there have no doubt been the occasional moments of epiphany when individual students made remarkable discoveries for themselves as writers. But many teachers tell us that productivity in their writing workshops is inconsistent, and in some classes, workshop pedagogy fails to engage any students in meaningful work. So, if traditional writing workshops aren't the key to effective writing instruction, what is? Why aren't writing workshops functioning quite so well for us instructionally? Why aren't writing workshops promoting the development of our student writers?

Reworking Work

We think that one reason that writing workshops aren't delivering more instructional and learning impact may be that for many of our students, the workshops themselves do not always provide meaningful work. Notice that we used the expression *meaning-*

ful work. Work. That word has always haunted thoughtful teachers. In the past, we—and perhaps you, too—heard ourselves saying to our students admonitions such as, "Finish your work," "Turn in your work," or the dreaded "You're not working up to your abilities," and "Some of you are just not working in this class." The results of such pronouncements weren't very satisfying. We were frustrated and our students often seemed unconcerned. Even though we knew writing workshop pedagogy well, even though we worked hard as teachers, went home tired most nights, and spent too many weekend hours planning workshops and minilessons and grading and responding to students' papers, we were quite certain that we were spending far more time on our students' papers and *work* than they were. We resolved that something essential needed to change so that students were engaged and learning and progressing. We resolved that our students needed to work productively and to work at least as hard as we were. We began experimenting, reading, studying, writing, and thinking. Now, after years of work and after dramatically changing our approaches to instructional delivery and pedagogy, we think we have some resolutions to this issue of *work* that are effective for us and for our students.

We are convinced, and have been for quite a while, that the *something* that had to change is the balance of work and responsibility in our workshops. Somehow, we had to assist and enable and maybe even demand that students take more responsibility for their own writing, that they experiment and try new ideas, and that they solve their own writing problems as they work through a piece. Naturally, we realized that mere lip service wouldn't be effective or productive, so we set out to create instructional strategies and to reorient our thinking about pedagogical techniques so that the *work* associated with writing and writing well in our classes would become more apprentice-like, with students retaining artistic control and decision-making authority over that work, and with students assuming more responsibility for how to shape and complete their writing projects. As teachers, we set out to learn how to better mentor and coach the work of writing rather than simply assigning, managing, and regulating work like a factory supervisor.

Our Journey to the Concept of the Studio Classroom

We began this redefinition and transformation of our approaches to teaching by examining our metaphors for the act of teaching. Over the past fifteen years or so, we have spent a good deal of time searching for a metaphor that would help us redesign our writing instruction for the purpose of helping students develop as skilled writers. At the same time, we were committed to achieving a better balance of work and responsibility in our classes.

The Power of Metaphor for Redefining Teaching Pedagogy

Early in that search, we were in need of some kind of miracle insight to explain to ourselves how to accomplish such a radical reinvention of our classes. As readers of research associated with literacy, we were fully aware of the early work of Vygotsky

(1986) indicating that thought and language are reciprocal, so that what we call something affects how we think about it and the attitudes we have toward it. As literature teachers, we knew the power of metaphor in that medium. So we resolved to develop fresh metaphors for the classroom and the workshop.

Because we have been teaching for many years, we were familiar with some of the old metaphors that had been adopted by schools and teachers. There was the medical metaphor: Our students come to school with deficiencies that we *diagnose*, for which we then develop a *remedial plan* (notice the close relationship to the word *remedy*), place them in *labs*—such as reading or writing labs—to work on their skills, and then make a *prognosis* for their reentry into mainstream classes. Or, there were the factory models and the business models. Quality Based Education, a sanitary and wrongheaded notion of effective teaching, comes to mind: Specify outcomes, create tight organizational structures, monitor progress, and assess results. None of those instructional models worked too well or for too long, and none addressed the central problem we faced of redefining the role of *work* in the contemporary classroom.

After rejecting these old metaphors, we searched for a contemporary metaphor to capture a fresh view of our role as teachers and of our students' roles as workers and learners within an instructional atmosphere. Our favorite metaphor came from nature: classroom as ecosystem, a place where the environment is delicate and too much of almost anything can destroy the balance and harmony of the place— too much teacher talk, too little direction and coaching; too much structure, too little organization and modeling. Indeed, the classroom ecosystem needs a healthy balance of student and teacher work and responsibility. Once this nature metaphor occurred to us, we considered adopting a kind of hands-off philosophy, thinking of our classrooms as nature preserves where our primary responsibility would be to drive around in our Range Rovers, keeping out the poachers—such as school-mandated writing prompts designed to "teach to the state-mandated tests" in rather mindless ways, or students' aggregate writing scores that were published in the newspaper and that publicly rated us from first to last within the district based on those scores—as best we could, and checking on water supplies and the health of the—aaahhh—animals. We decided that the last part of the analogy was a bit unfortunate. Still, it had potential.

The Studio Classroom: Pedagogy and Metaphor for Teaching

It was our encounter with Donald Schön's (1987) book, *Educating the Reflective Practitioner: Toward a New Design for Teaching and Learning in the Professions*, that finally gave us a strong push in the right direction and suggested to us a rich metaphor by which we might reinvent our writing pedagogy. Schön's primary gift to us in that book was his ethnographic look at various kinds of studio-based instruction. In the book, he takes readers on a visit inside an architectural studio classroom where beginning architecture students were admonished by the studio master, "I can tell you that there is something you need to know, and with my help you may be able to learn it. But I cannot tell you what it is in a way you can now understand. I can only arrange for you to have the right sorts of experiences for yourself. You must be willing, therefore, to have these experiences. . . . If you are unwilling to step into this new experience without knowing ahead of time what it will be like, I cannot help you. You must trust me" (93). That quote struck us as precisely the key to a new direction in teaching writing that we sought.

Schön, who was closely associated with John Dewey, also reminds us that Dewey postulated that "[s]tudents cannot be taught what they need to know, but they can be coached: They have to see on their own behalves and in their own ways the relations between means and methods employed and results achieved. Nobody else can see for them, and they can't see just by being told, although the right kind of telling may guide this seeing and thus help them see what they need to see" (17). Those two tenets together—Schön's on having the right experiences and Dewey's on coaching—grounded our work and sent us in the new directions for teaching writing that we had been seeking.

But how were we to get students to pursue and even enjoy such "work"? How were we to enact these new ideas in real classrooms? We returned to the concept of *studio* from Schön.

What images does the word *studio* provoke for you? For us it is images of light, space, creative energy, works in progress, experimentation, and engrossing work. It was a metaphor that resonated for us. We wanted a classroom full of engaged students, pursuing their own work with commitment and passion.

We were absolutely taken by Schön's idea of teaching as artistry, and we saw immediately the value of redefining our concept of writing workshop so that our classrooms could become more studio-like environments in which to teach writing. We came to understand that effective coaching requires enormous patience and adroit timing. We came to see that we were too much given to *telling* our students how to solve their writing problems. Our failing was that we had been entirely too helpful and too quick to jump into the middle of a piece of student writing. Schön's investigations of studio instruction convinced us that studio-style teaching was an excellent fit with CM because memoir, by the very nature of the genre, will always belong to the writer.

A Brief History of the Studio Classroom: Controversy and Modern Applications

Since that encounter with Schön's writings and throughout our work of the past decade, we have been repeatedly drawn to artists, potters, and architects both to observe them at work and to question them about the environments in which they work. We knew that studio pedagogy had been around for centuries in the arts and continues to play an important role in contemporary arts education. We began to do some research and reading about the studios and salons of Paris in the late nineteenth century. We discovered that great controversy existed even then as to how studios and studio masters should prepare aspiring artists.

The more conventional notion of the period was that novice artists should spend their time in the Louvre copying the masters whose work hung on the walls of that famous museum. This notion, one held by many of the masters themselves, was, of course, that copying good work would develop in young artists both an aesthetic sensibility and the rudimentary skills they needed to find their place in a studio of an important artist. Others, many Impressionists among them, contended that art was about individual visions, not replication of the masters.

Obviously, these two polar opposite views of art instruction are analogous to some of the polar opposite views about writing instruction. Students were once told to read the literary masters and then write like Hemingway or Faulkner. As ideas about writing as a process entered our pedagogical conversations, we began to focus less on master writers and more on the processes of successful writers: drafting, revising, and publishing writing. The clashes among artists about how to learn to be an artist and among teachers about how students best learn to be skilled writers are not very dissimilar, and they illustrate well parallel conflicts in philosophy and in pedagogy.

These conflicting viewpoints raised interesting questions for instruction. What should be the role of a studio master? Should he work in front of his students, modeling with his own artistic creations, or should he remain in the background as critic and coach? As writing teachers, we have asked ourselves a similar question: Can we encourage originality and freshness in our student writers and still develop essential writing skills?

Another continuing controversy among nineteenth-century studio masters was a spirited disagreement about the level of criticism one should use with developing artists. In many cases, the harshest studio masters literally took brush or charcoal in hand to alter a student's emerging work. Such heavy-handedness is not unlike what any teacher has done whenever she has rewritten a sentence on a student paper and handed it back as if to say, "Here is what you really meant to say; it's better if you word it as I did." Other studio masters looked to praise the good in their students' work, ask writerly questions, and to *suggest* specific technical alterations that the young artist might consider.

Observing Contemporary Studio Classrooms

To further our understanding of studio work, we began to observe studio instructors to help us construct our own version of that pedagogy. As we spent time in studio art classes, observing studio instructors working as artists, coaches, critics, and mentors, it became apparent that what was at the heart of studio instruction was not the orchestration of performances but the cultivation of experimentation; not the assignment of highly specific, corporate creations but the encouragement of students to form individual visions and versions of the work. We were always impressed with the work ethic of students and the coaching/mentoring stance of the instructors. Studio instructors alternately demonstrated new ideas and techniques, worked on their own projects, and quietly visited students at work, offering coachlike suggestions. "Oh, I like the proportion on this hand," or "Try a lighter wash on that tree in the background," we heard them say.

Students worked with such intensity during those studio classes that the instructor had to interrupt their work—literally—to inform them that the class period had ended. We were stunned to observe classes of students, even very young students, who were so engaged and so actively at work that the time flew by. We wanted our classes to be so engaging for students that they would be still hard at work at the bell and in no hurry to pack up and leave.

The studio classes we observed fostered an approach to instruction that sponsored experimentation, aesthetic choices, decision making, collaboration, self-awareness, and reflection. Taken together, those studio values convinced us that we could never have the kind of classroom we wanted until we could fashion a new definition for the idea of *work*.

Evidence of Studio Work: Observing Products and Processes

At about this time as we still contemplated how to translate these newfound insights in our classroom, two fortuitous experiences with artists and art occurred for us. First, we traveled to the National Gallery in Washington, D.C., to the *Helga* exhibit, a staggering collection of work by Andrew Wyeth arranged in such a way as to reveal the artist's process and actual studio work over a fifteen-year period. The path through the exhibit literally enabled the audience to trace Wyeth's artistic journey from preliminary sketches to finished works. In that exhibit of over 500 pieces, only seven or eight were actually finished: several oils, three or four egg temperas, and several signature dry-brush watercolors. All of the other 500 pieces were essentially prefatory work: sketches, compositional studies on a hand or face, adaptations of perspective and hue, explorations of subject and background. During that productive period, Wyeth said he often papered the floor with failed trials and false starts in hopes that walking over failures would improve future efforts.

The Wyeth exhibit helped us understand the amount and variety of practice and prefatory work in which artists engage in order to find their way to finished products. We realized that we had expected our students to move too quickly to finished pieces, and for the first time we caught a glimpse of how a new version of a writing workshop should be structured.

Second, several months later, the National Gallery staged an exhibit of John Singer Sargent's massive work *El Jaleo*, one curated in similar fashion to the *Helga* exhibit. The exhibit showcased Sargent's prefatory work of research and fieldwork, of sketchbook and tedious studio trial and error that brought forth the stunning finished piece of artwork. Seeing the artists' prefatory work helped us realize that was precisely the kind of commitment to practice that we needed to create within our students if we were to realize a true studio classroom. We began restructuring our teaching, our workshops, and our students' work in earnest.

The Final Piece in Redefining Work

Enter an extraordinary middle school teacher at Amphitheater Middle School in Tucson, Arizona. Ernie Galaz and Dan were collaborating in a program for student teachers when Ernie heard Dan talking one day about studio-based instruction and our effort to redefine *work* in our classes. "Oh, you need to look at Matthew Fox's new book, *The Reinvention of Work: A New Vision of Livelihood for our Time*," said Ernie. And Ernie was right. Among other things, Fox helped us think more clearly about the notion of *authentic* work and the importance of *inner desire* in the classroom environment we were trying to create. We came to see that *inner desire*, the love of writing and the passion to do one's best, grows in our students as they do *authentic* work, real writing for real purposes. We recommend that book to you, along with the works of Schön.

As we began implementing our ideas on redefining work in our classes, we designed our version of a studio portfolio, marking the boundaries for our inquiry and developing a series of explorations that would engage students in meaningful work. We redefined and created evaluation tools (see Chapter 10 and 11 for our ideas on evaluation of CM) to suit our new approaches, and we incorporated students' reflections on their writing processes, products, and learning as a central role of the class's writing-teaching-learning processes. The reflective thinking of our students, which we solicited through their portfolios both for the continued development of our own thinking and for their metacognitive benefits to our students, taught us much about what we were doing right and what we still needed to change. But, at last we and our students were working more effectively, having more fun, sharing the balance of work and control in the classroom, and learning from our reflections and discussions. We were well underway.

Applying Studio Methodology to Memoir

CM is a genre uniquely suited to studio methodology because students are writing from life experience, and they know that subject matter better than the teacher. Creating a writing environment in which students work from expert knowledge leads writers to see their work as meaningful work. I know what was special about my fourth Christmas; you don't—unless I tell you. I know how my sixth birthday is emblematic of many of my social interactions and of my mother's efforts to be a so-called *good mother*; you don't—unless I tell you. When the balance in the classroom shifts a bit so that students know that they are working from a stance of expertise, they are motivated to work well and to work honestly on producing quality writing, engaging storytelling, and meaty substance within their writing.

Naturally, teachers are always pleased when students *work*, but the type of work to which we're referring is not work for the sake of work; it is not mere seat work or busywork. It is the type of work that all real artists, writers, naturalists, medical interns, and even novice teachers undertake—that of working like the professional that you are striving to become. It is work that embodies the theories and values underpinning the studio writing classroom.

Theoretical Grounding of *Work* Within the Studio Classroom

This pedagogical approach to teaching and learning writing is based on the three main theories of phenomenology, epistemology, and constructivism. We have found that when the preservice and inservice teachers with whom we have conducted various consulting workshops and programs understand fully the theoretical tenets of these philosophies, they are better equipped to understand how this approach is distinctive and different from ordinary approaches to the teaching of writing. With such grounding, teachers also see how frameworks like memoir are uniquely suited to this pedagogical approach to the teaching of writing.

A Brief Overview of Phenomenology

Phenomenology asserts that events that occur within the real world have significance and meaning; the term *phenomenon* is related to this theory that looks for real occurrences in the real world and then posits meaning based on interpretations of those events. It is a theory that seeks grounding in reality rather than one that supports merely formulating ideas and hypotheses that have no authenticity in actual practice.

For teachers, students, and writers of memoir, the idea of phenomenology means that you are teaching, studying, and writing a genre that exists in reality. Just take a look at our bibliographies in Chapter 12, peruse the *New York Times* bestseller list in nonfiction, or stroll through any bookstore to see the explosion of publishing in this genre. Memoirs exist; they are real. Real people read and write memoir. In contrast, we challenge any teacher or student of writing to find an authentic five-paragraph theme in published literary sources outside of those especially created for the English classroom. It doesn't exist; it has no basis in reality. The five-paragraph theme does not occur in the real world that lives and breathes outside of the rather protected and somewhat isolated world of school. Therefore, phenomenologists would assert that the five-paragraph theme is not a legitimate genre, while memoir is.

A Brief Overview of Epistemology

Epistemology has some grounding in religious studies, but most certainly is not limited to that field. Epistemology holds that in order to learn to conduct any endeavor well, the learner must think and work and behave like the professional she wants to become. Under this philosophy, those who want to become artists must work and live as do real artists; they must engage in the activities of real artists. They must have the mind-set and the values of artists. The same would be true for basketball players, skateboarders, teachers, and writers. Simply reading and studying about a field is not enough to learn the field—though such study may certainly help. But in addition to *knowing about* a field of study or an endeavor, one must *live the life*, as Anne Dillard (1989) reminds us, of one engaged in that endeavor. A basketball player can read about historically great games and players, she can read about how to make a hook shot or a slam dunk, but that is not enough. The basketball player must work and practice as do real players. The dedication to living the life of the professional player and to working as hard as do pro players is not an easy task, but the learner—the player wannabe—must undertake such disciplined work if she is to excel.

We have long made the case that the same is true for teachers and for writers. Teachers candidates cannot merely read about and conduct enlightened discussions about teaching—though such *knowing about* activities may provide useful background information to the aspiring teacher. Instead, it is not until the teacher candidate meets real students in real classrooms and begins dealing with the many challenges and demands of teaching that he sets in motion the work, learning, and tasks necessary to become eventually, after much practice, an expert in the field of teaching.

For writers of memoir, the same is true. Students must become *memoirists*—even if it is memoirists-in-training—who are reading, writing, thinking, and living as do published memoirists. Reading memoir is helpful. Talking about your memories is helpful. But no single intellectual activity is enough. The writer must submerge in the full range of activities lived by actual memoirists before he can hope to produce an authentic piece of writing. In this process, the role of the teacher is to create a conducive, safe environment within which a community of writers can think, work, practice, experiment, and learn. Teachers can help construct numerous opportunities—which we call *Explorations*—for students to work and engage in the activities of memoirists. When teachers provide such opportunities and when student writers engage in such work, they are implementing the philosophy of epistemology—and of sound writing pedagogy.

A Brief Overview of Constructivism

Constructivism surmises that all knowledge is essentially personal and created by the learner and enhanced and enriched when those constructions are shared in a social setting. The word *construct* is key here. The learner builds, or constructs, individual knowledge. Then the learner shares her individual constructions of knowledge with other learners within a trusted community in order to refine her ideas, compare them to the ideas of others, build a body of shared experiences within the community, and otherwise benefit from the sounding board and reality check that fellow learners can provide. Constructivists posit that our knowledge is based upon our perceptions, experiences, and interpretations of the world as we know it, personally and individually, and that those perceptions are improved through social interactions.

For teachers, such a philosophy would hold that learning must be active and individual. Lecture may provide useful background information or instructions, but it is not until the learner is personally and *actively engaged* with the information to be learned that she is able to learn and retain it in any meaningful way. The philosophy would also hold that students need class time to interact with their peers in learning-based social engagements such as writing workshops, crit sessions, literary circles, critical friends groups, and other such activities in order to refine and clarify their thinking.

Taken to its logical conclusion, this theory would suggest that *writers must actively build knowledge by thinking and writing in the genre they are trying to learn.* Such a statement seems absurdly simplistic, but think about it for a moment. Too often we have merely *assigned* writing, and done too little *teaching of* writing. We have structured writing assignments rather than scaffold writing activities. Assigning a memoir as a reading or writing project does little to help students comprehend and undertake the tasks and steps involved in understanding, producing, crafting, and structuring such a product.

Instead, teachers *teach* when they model for students the activities that the students need to learn, and writers learn when they have class time to engage actively in those activities within a community of writers. Teachers *teach* literary genre when they read with and to students exemplars of the writing to be created, and students learn when they have class time to delve into discussions of what is appealing about the writing and what specifically is expertly crafted within the written piece. Teachers *teach* writing when they write with their students and when they work as writers in front of their students, and writers learn when they talk about the challenges and rewards of writing within a community of writers that includes the teacher, sharing experiences and stories together.

In these ways, teachers and students are actively constructing their personal and individual knowledge. They are applying the theories of constructivists.

Approaching the teaching and writing of memoir from a studio methodology incorporates tenets of phenomenology, epistemology, and constructivism. It is real. It focuses on *working like* a memoirist. It provides guidance and modeling for the student writer to build personal knowledge and apply that knowledge to a specific genre and literacy task. It provides a strong interactive and social component for learning. These are the theoretical reasons behind this approach to teaching memoir that give it validity and power.

Next, let's examine the reasons why memoir, specifically, is a powerful genre for these theoretical and pedagogical approaches to literacy and why the studio approach is a compelling methodology for teaching memoir.

Establishing Studio Classroom Values

The work of transforming your classroom into a more studio-like environment for teaching contemporary memoir may seem like a daunting task. You will probably not be able to move your students to a loft or a cavernous studio space with windows and natural light. You won't be able to do much with the physical arrangement of your classroom, but you can do a great deal about altering how your classroom *feels* to students. As we have spent time in studio environments of all kinds, we have come to believe that it's the values you establish in your classroom that create the feel of a studio.

Studio Value #1: Work

We believe that authentic work is the central value of the writing studio. Without work, students don't learn, engage, and progress. Without work, our classrooms are dull places. The main work of the memoir-writing studio is threefold:

- reading memoir,
- writing memoir, and
- thinking like a reader and like a writer about memoir.

We see authentic work as *apprenticeships in a context of making and doing*. Because students must read extensively in the genre that they are to learn, we read and discuss numerous excerpts from published memoirs in our class activities and discussions. Students read entire published memoirs that appeal to them, not in order to complete a book report but in order to converse knowledgeably about what they see happening in the genre and to share examples from their chosen text during class discussions. We bring boxes of memoirs into our classrooms and give minibooktalks about several memoirs each day in order to pique interest in specific books and in the genre. We explore our own memories and the stories that might be interesting for us to write and that might connect with other readers. We study the craft of writing memoir, which we'll discuss at length throughout this book. We read. We write. We discuss. We think. We work. We live the reading and writing life of memoirists. As you continue to read this chapter and this book, you'll see numerous examples of the ways in which our students and we engage in work and in *apprenticeships of making and doing* during the memoir-writing studio.

Studio Value #2: Practice and Experimentation

Perhaps first and foremost, the studio is a place for practicing and experimenting. Writers need to try out their voices and their writing techniques in multiple settings, contexts, and genres in order to flex and develop their writing muscles. Within the framework of memoir, writers engage in teacher-sponsored, but not teacher-owned, explorations of their ideas and writers' techniques. Think again of the studio art classes. Student artists work in front of other student artists. If we are student artists in the studio, we can see each other's work, but I don't stop my work to tell you how yours should take shape. I own my work; you own yours. We both are looking at the same model, perhaps, or trying to sketch the same still life, but no one expects that our finished products will be identical.

The same principles hold true for the writing studio. The idea here is for writers to explore their memories, their voices, and various approaches to their craft in order to see what works for them. They do so by trying out lots of explorations in writing. (We discuss several of these Explorations, or minipieces, in Chapters 3 and 4.) Teachers lead the explorations but do not require the typical standard polished papers in the early stages of the writing. They expect and encourage student writers to turn out unique pieces that represent their individual writing styles and life experiences. And like the prefatory pieces of Wyeth or Sargent, these are experiments, not finished products early on. Smaller pieces of writing may lead to a larger, connected piece of writing, but the connections may not be the typical sequential or numeric transitions of more formulaic writing. We don't encourage students to rush to some organizational scheme for the larger piece too quickly. We believe the final structure of their memoirs will suggest itself in due time. The connections that emerge to unify the piece can be as unique as the use of white space or as complex as the application of an extended metaphor or as simple as the use of a song lyric or a line of poetry.

These written explorations are also related—but not sequential. Just because a particular piece is written before another short piece does not mean that the two pieces will appear in that order in the finished memoir—or even that they will appear in the finished memoir at all. Such work is consistent with the principle that students—not teachers—own and operate, organize and manage their writing.

All of the written exploratory pieces are filed in students' Writer's Notebooks or in their portfolios for future consideration and for possible future work, or the pieces may be left in the Writer's Notebook as a representation of work conducted on an idea that didn't fit with the finished memoir piece. *No writing is wasted writing* in the practice and experimentation stages, but not all writing will be worth polishing and including in a final memoir piece.

Such experimentations are surrounded by reading memoir excerpts and then engaging in *representational talk*. Student writers benefit from hearing themselves and others talk about what they think, what they have experienced that relates to the memoir excerpt being read, what they know that they might write about, and how they might approach a piece of writing—all done *before* they are ready to write.

In the studio classroom, we take our time and explore. We think and wonder and ponder and talk with fellow readers and writers. We don't rush to finished product—though the time and the deadline for the finished product will most assuredly come, but within a few weeks or months, not within a few days. As teachers and as writers, we plant the seedbed of ideas and then engage in the coaching and mentoring activities that will help students to grow those ideas through planning, experimenting, crafting, practicing, and polishing their writing.

Studio Value #3: Individual Visions and Versions

Just as all artists represent their artistic visions in varying and unique ways in their paintings and artwork, so do all writers. Here, individual and personal voices, writing styles, writing emphases and foci, and presentational styles for the finished products all come into play. Our memoir will not look or sound like yours, and that's how it should be. In the memoir-writing studio, we read numerous excerpts from published memoirs not in order to use those texts as templates and directly copy an author—not so we can write as did that author—but so we can study the craft and technique of individual writers in order to see what we can learn about writing to then apply to our own writing. All authors have distinctive writing voices and writing styles, and that's exactly one of the hallmarks of polished writing that we hope to develop in our students' writings, but such distinction does not come easily.

Recall our discussion earlier in this chapter of the various *compositional studies* that artists use to try out the various positions and poses of something as seemingly minor as a hand that will appear in a portrait. For the *Helga* exhibit alone, Wyeth drew enough sketches of the same two hands in different poses to fill an entire wall in the gallery. Similarly, writers need to practice, experiment, and try out which of their versions of a memory will work within which version of a finished piece of writing. They will experiment with which vision—or perspective—of their topic that they want to present to their audience. They will test first one finished format and appearance for their memoir, and then another. Like the artists Wyeth and Sargent, student writers need the time and coaching, encouragement and support to find what version will work for them within their finished memoir.

Studio Value #4: Decision Making About Options and Choices

Because the writing studio is teacher-sponsored but not teacher-owned, student writers find that they are faced with many options, choices, and decisions to make. Which experimental pieces will work in the final version of their memoir? Which voice will they use? Which presentational techniques will they include? Where will the memoir begin, and where will it end? Which details will be included and which excluded? The writers' choices are almost endless, but learning to make wise decisions in these areas is part and parcel of what real writers do for each published piece. These are the types of decisions with which student writers need to experiment and grapple if they are to learn actively and to develop their writing techniques and craft.

Giving up so much control over the final product may be challenging for some teachers, but remember that as the constructivists that you now are, you know that students have to engage in that decision making for themselves in order to grow substantially as writers. We may suggest to student writers that we like a particular piece and would like to see more work on that writing, but it is the students who decide whether to continue experimenting and crafting a piece. It is the students who decide if and in what order a piece appears in the final memoir. We certainly coach and mentor those decisions, but the students ultimately make the decisions. Students know what they are trying to convey in their writing; we want to help them to reach their individual goals.

Such an approach to writing clearly flies in the face of regulated and prescribed formulas for writing such as accordion paragraphs, five-paragraph themes, or anything else with lockstep rotes and instructions to follow precisely and exactly. We have long maintained that writing is a creative act of the mind, an artistic endeavor to be nurtured by informed intuition and knowledge of technique, but not one to be boxed and packaged, not one to be chopped and diced into meaningless color-coding, counting, or typecasting.

Such a stance may take some practice on your part. Students are quick to sniff out any reluctance or phoniness in your attempts to convey this message about who's in charge of the writing. When you say, "I *really* like this piece," to a student, is your subtext, "And it better show up in the final memoir product if you want an A on the paper!" If it is, work on letting go of that control and of that subtext. Work on helping the student writer to improve the pieces that *she* likes and values, not just the ones that you like.

Artists know various painting and sculpting techniques, and they use that knowledge to enhance their works of art. But, there is no one prescribed right way to draw or sculpt a hand, as you can see in the works of Andrew Wyeth and other artists. Such is also true of writing. Informed decision making about options, choices, and possibilities enhance and enrich students' writings, just as they do the works of professional artists.

Studio Value #5: Working and Writing Within a Community of Learners

Within the writing studio, the word *community* connotes something much more than just *cooperation* or merely a nice group of people, though those factors are certainly to be desired. The word *community* implies a group of writers and learners who do the following:

- · share common values,
- · conduct themselves according to agreed-upon standards of behavior,
- · support each others' efforts and work,
- · praise and support experimentations and risk taking even when those experiments and risks don't entirely work, and
- · project genuine interest in each others' work and pieces of writing.

Teachers foster the development of such a community of writers, thinkers, readers, and learners when they seek divergent strains of thought, various answers and options to questions and problems, and multiple avenues to success. Teachers also encourage community when they work as readers, writers, and thinkers in front of and along with their students, sharing their struggles and decision-making processes, their interpretations of texts, and their insights as one of the many voices that are valued in the discussion. Certainly, teachers are more informed about writing craft and technique than are most students, but students' insights are often rich with meaning and with fresh creativity that will be lost if the teacher's voice and knowledge are the only ones valued and heard. If such is the case, you will have merely a group of students doing your assigned work, not a true *community*.

Studio Value #6: Reflection and Self-Awareness

Contrary to the opinions of some, the studio-based writing classroom is not a willy-nilly, feel-good-without-standards kind of place. Standards for conduct, for response to writing, for work, and for productivity are very much in place, are clearly detailed at the outset of each new studio class, and are incorporated throughout the time that the group spends together, whether that is a semester or a year. These standards become part of the fabric of the community, part of the accepted modus operandi of the class, and students learn how to point out to each other a consistent lack of effort or of progress. Such self-awareness and group accountability does not come naturally or easily to student writers and learners. It has to be nurtured and encouraged, fostered and developed by the teacher as mentor and coach.

One of the ways in which students can monitor their own progress, growth, and development as thinkers, readers, and writers is to keep a reflective log as part of their Writer's Notebooks with weekly entries on their work and progress that week. How much did they write that week? What was the quality of their writers' experimentations? How much did they read, and what was the quality of their responses to those readings? How well were they prepared for their writers' workshops, and what was the quality of their responses to their group members' writings? We refer to these reflective logs as *Audits*, and we discuss them further in Chapter 10.

Further, at the end of the memoir-writing process, we ask students to reflect upon their processes throughout the framework, on the types of writings and techniques that they tried, and on the extent of their success with those practices. We ask them to talk about what they have learned about this genre of writing that they can apply to other genres of writing, and we ask them to reflect upon what they can do better within the next framework for writing in order to continue to grow as readers, writers, and responders to texts, including both published texts and those produced by students. We explore this concept further in Chapter 10, giving specific examples of the types of reflections that we encourage from our student writers. But we are firm believers that without self-monitoring, self-awareness, and self-reflection, the cycle of learning that can occur within a framework for writing does not achieve its full potential.

Final Thoughts on the Studio Classroom

We think that the studio approach is appropriate for teaching all types of writing, kindergarten through college, and it is the primary methodology that we use in our own teaching. We encourage you to begin now to adapt studio methodology to your teaching not only of memoir but of all that you teach. You'll have some ups and downs, but we believe that the effort is worth the outcomes in learning and in self-efficacy for our students.

Now that you have a basic understanding of the values and work ethic, theories and theorists behind the studio approach to writing, let's examine in Chapters 3 and 4 how those studio values apply specifically to memoir.

Works Cited

DEWEY, JOHN. 1974. *John Dewey on Education: Selected Writings*. R. D. Archambault, Ed. Chicago: University of Chicago Press. In Donald Schön. 1987. *Educating the Reflective Practitioner:*

Toward a New Design for Teaching and Learning in the Professions. San Francisco: Jossey-Bass Publishers.

DILLARD, ANNIE. 1989. *The Writing Life*. New York: Harper & Row, Publishers.

FOX, MATTHEW. 1994. *Reinvention of Work: A New Vision of Livelihood for Our Time*. San Francisco: Harper San Francisco.

SCHÖN, DONALD. 1987. *Educating the Reflective Practitioner: Toward a New Design for Teaching and Learning in the Professions*. San Francisco: Jossey-Bass Publishers.

VYGOTSKY, LEV S. 1986. *Thought and Language*. Alex Kozulin, Ed. Revised Edition. Cambridge, MA: MIT Press.

3

Explorations in Memoir Writing

The following eight chapters are the *how to do it* chapters. They are designed to help you enact the values of the studio into your teaching repertoire. They are written as a guide to step you through the process of teaching your students to write powerful Contemporary Memoirs. We will share the instructional framework we have created and offer examples of the kinds of reading and writing explorations in which our students engage. We hope these chapters will also encourage you to establish a studio-style classroom and to expand and deepen your practical knowledge of process pedagogy.

Exploring the Territory of Memoir as Genre

Because we have found teaching memoir to be an excellent invitation to teach students about literary genre, we urge you to begin your work with memoir by reviewing the concept of genre with your students. Because of the way genre has too often been taught in schools, students have acquired some narrow understandings of how works of literature end up classified as a particular genre. "If it rhymes or has meter, it's poetry." "If it ain't true, it's fiction." "All short stories have five main features." As you read and write memoir with your students, you will have opportunities to debunk all of these conventional myths and to help them acquire the more sophisticated understanding that many works of literature cross the boundaries of several genres.

One of the key ways in which we initially explore memoir as a genre is to examine some of the observations that memoirists have published about the genre. See Figure 3–1 for several quotes about memoir that we use as a handout to share and discuss with our students in order to prompt their thinking about the genre.

We like these excerpts for the insights they give us about writing and reading memoir. Based on these passages, we infer that memoir is *not* the same as autobiography. Memoirs validate our lives and those of others, but memoir does not attempt to capture all of the details of a life. A memoir is a selective collection of life stories, an attempt to create a "braided cord of humanity" (Baker 1982). Memoir can help writers discover sequence and importance in their lives. Writing memoir gives the writer an opportunity to find threads of meaning and untangle them to form a "clear line" (Welty 1983). Discussing these points with students will help them understand what memoirists do and think; it will also help your students understand what they will be trying to do and think throughout the entire Memoir Framework.

Exploring the Memoir Framework

We believe in an approach to teaching memoir that is comprehensive, carefully planned, and fully orchestrated. That distinction, as you will see, is part of what separates our idea of a *framework* for writing from mere assignment-giving. Other key features of our framework follow:

1. The student writer is also a careful *reader* of memoir, reading both whole memoirs and a plethora of carefully selected excerpts from published memoirs. Each excerpt is selected in order to illustrate a specific technique that student writers will then discuss and attempt in their own writing.
2. The student writer attempts many short exploratory pieces, which we sometimes call *Spider Pieces* (see the following section). After a student has written twelve or more such short pieces, the writer culls them, looking for powerful language, potent expression and emotion, apt metaphor, and a premise that resonates with both the writer and her readers.
3. Finally, the student writer extensively revises three to five (sometimes more) of the short pieces to craft a final memoir piece.

Let's examine how our framework plays out in actual practice.

Overview of the Memoir Framework

Following the philosophical tenets discussed in Chapter 2, we read and discuss exemplars of each short piece that students will then explore in their own lives and writing.

Observations on Memoir as Genre

<u>Directions</u>: **As you read these excerpts from writers of memoir note how they define the genre. Jot any surprising phrases that describe memoir in the spaces provided.**

1. "Memoir" is defined as some portion of life. Unlike autobiography, which moves in a dutiful line from birth to fame, omitting nothing significant, memoir assumes the life and ignores most of it. The writer of a memoir takes us back to a corner of his or her life that was unusually vivid or intense—childhood, for instance—or that was framed by unique events. By narrowing the lens, the writer achieves a focus that isn't possible in autobiography; memoir is a window into a life.

    —William Zinsser, *Inventing the Truth*

2. Ego is at the heart of all the reason why anybody writes a memoir, whether it's a book or a pamphlet or a letter to our children. Memoir is how we validate our lives.

    —William Zinsser, *Inventing the Truth*

3. The best memories, I think, forge their own forms. The writer of any work, and particularly any nonfiction work, must decide two crucial points: what to put in and what to leave out.

    —Annie Dillard, in *Inventing the Truth*

4. These hopeless end-of-the-line visits with my mother made me wish I had not thrown off my own past so carelessly. We all come from the past, and children ought to know what it was that went into their making, to know that life is a braided cord of humanity stretching up

Figure 3–1. *Observations on Memoir as Genre*

from time long gone, and that it cannot be defined by the span of a single journey from diaper to shroud.

—Russell Baker, *Growing Up*

5. Writing . . . is one way of discovering sequence in experience, of stumbling upon cause and effect in the happenings of a writer's own life. This has been the case with me. Connections slowly emerge. Like distant landmarks you are approaching, cause and effect begin to align themselves, draw closer together. Experiences too indefinite to outline in themselves to be recognized for themselves connect and are identified as a larger shape. And suddenly a light is thrown back, as when your train makes a curve, showing that there has been a mountain of meaning rising behind you on the way you've come, is rising there still, proven through retrospect.

—Eudora Welty, *One Writer's Beginnings*

6. It seems to me, writing of my parents now in my seventies that I see continuities in their lives that weren't visible to me when they were living. Even at the times that have left me my most vivid memories of them, there were connections between them that escaped me. Could it be that I can better see their lives—or any lives I know—today because I'm a writer? . . . . Writing has developed in me an abiding respect for the unknown in a human lifetime and a sense of where to look for threads, how to follow, how to connect, find in the thick of the tangle what clear line persists. The strands are all there: to the memory nothing is ever really lost. . . .

—Eudora Welty, *One Writer's Beginnings*

Figure 3–1. *Continued*

Our explorations consist of paired readings and writings in memoir surrounded by thought, discussion, and experimentation. Our framework for memoir generally looks something like this:

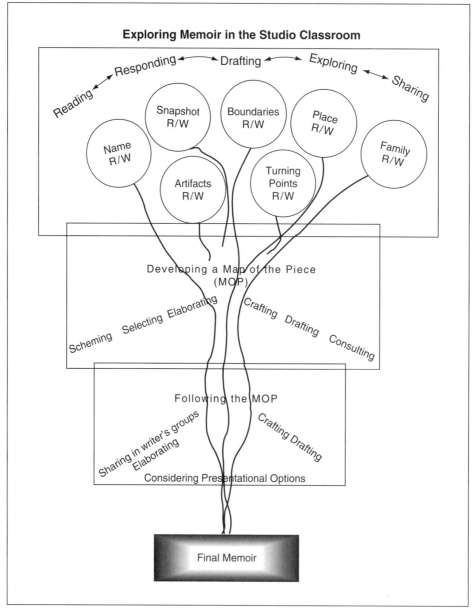

Figure 3–2. *Exploring Memoir in the Studio Classroom*

Once our students and we have accumulated some writings of our own, our written texts become part of the readings that we share and discuss alongside the published memoir excerpts. In this manner, we explore the territory of *reading like a writer* and of *writing like a reader*, both for ourselves and our emerging craft, and for those who are published in the genre. We discuss the principles for reading like a writer and writing like a reader at the end of this chapter.

The idea of pairing the readings and written pieces serves to create a wealth of layered and multifaceted memories in writing from which to draw for our final, woven-together memoir piece. Too often, inexperienced writers struggle precisely because they try to write from an impoverishment of ideas; they have nothing to write because they have neither read nor thought deeply about the subject on which they are to write. Our Memoir Framework goes a long way toward alleviating that deficit.

SPIDER PIECES (EXPLORATIONS)

In his poem "The Noiseless Patient Spider,"[1] Walt Whitman writes of the process and tenacity that a spider uses to weave its web. The spider throws out filament after filament until, finally, a single thread attaches securely. This anchor filament forms the guiding thread—the anchor—around which the remainder of the web is woven. Extending this metaphor to writers, we encourage student writers to work like patient spiders, trying out lots of pieces of writing before they find the one that can anchor their memoir piece. We offer students many triggers to memory and to writing for their exploration. They try these *Spider Pieces*—these short, exploratory writings—to see which ones work, to delve into connections among their memories, and to find metaphors, key characters, and strong voices within their life stories that can enhance the telling and interpretation of those stories in the here and now. They are looking for their *hook* or *anchor piece* and all of the other pieces that will attach to it in order to form the final memoir piece.

The Spider Pieces are teacher-sponsored; that is, we don't instruct students merely to "Write about what you remember." Vague advice doesn't do much to help writers. Rather, we carefully choose published memoir excerpts that illustrate a specific subject or technique that we want our students to explore in their own thinking and writing. We read and discuss the selected excerpts, and students write a Spider Piece using the excerpts to trigger their own remembered experiences. Such work is not quick, nor is it easy. It requires the tenacity and assuredness of eventual success inherent in the weaving work of the spider.

By writing exploratory pieces, students discover meanings within their tellings that they didn't necessarily know existed. These short pieces are sometimes multifaceted, related, and guided by reading and discussing published exemplars from existing memoirs. Student writers are encouraged to follow emerging connections and tangents, weaving memory webs that eventually yield a storyline—the hook—to follow.

AN ENVIRONMENT FOR AUTHENTIC REVISION

As this process unfolds, it presents a powerful tool for authentic revision. Too often, student writers equate revision with a retype-it-and-fix-the-commas type of activity rather than a true re-seeing (re-vision) of the piece. The processes for engaging in writing that we use within our framework encourages real revision for several reasons:

1. Not all of the short Spider Pieces that a student writes will appear in the final memoir. Some will be discarded as either too vague or as not fitting with the overall premise of the memoir.

2. The writer may find that she needs to write new pieces and new sections of existing pieces to weave into the final memoir paper.

3. The writer will need to work on transitioning, ordering, and organizing pieces that began as separate entities in order to have a coherent final piece of writing.

4. The writer will need to weave together the perspectives and tones of the original short Spider Pieces around the central *hook* or *anchor piece* to help unify the final memoir piece.

SUMMARY OF KEY POINTS OF THE MEMOIR FRAMEWORK

Approaching the teaching of writing, specifically of memoir, from within our Memoir Framework solves several of the dilemmas faced by teachers who want to motivate student writers.

- It is consistent and grounded in theory.
- It connects reading and writing in meaningful ways.
- It helps student writers to derive a wealth of knowledge from which to write.
- It provides multiple opportunities for practicing writing.
- It encourages and practically demands that students engage in authentic revision.

So, what are the texts that student memoirists read and write? Several examples with which we have had success are detailed in the next section.

Getting Started with the Memoir Framework: The Pieces

We have developed this set of exemplars, or Explorations, throughout the last decade or more by working with memoir. Nonetheless, this list is far from exhaustive. We add and delete from this list of memoir exemplars almost every time we teach the Memoir Framework to our students, pulling what seems to meet our particular students' needs and interests. We encourage you to do the same, finding readings that suit the ability level and interests of your students, exploring new techniques with which you want your student writers to experiment, and using exemplars from the most current memoirs available at the time that you teach.

Our students typically read and write these Explorations in pairs, though we have not necessarily found a professional published exemplar for each Exploration listed in Figure 3–3. That's at least one of the times when our writings and those of former and current students become the texts of our class. We find that having students read and write approximately eight to twelve of these paired Explorations provides them with a wealth of memories and of studied writers' craft from which to weave together their final memoir paper. Depending on your time frame, interest level, and objectives for instruction, you may elect to engage your student writers in more or fewer of these Explorations. We suggest trying several combinations, however, to see what resonates most for you and your students.

Overview of the Pieces

Figure 3–3 indicates several of the Explorations in which our students engage as they read and write memoir. Based on the motif for each Exploration, students read a memoir excerpt and write their own Spider Piece. We explain our teaching of several of these Explorations in detail in the next section. For others, we invite you to find excerpts from published memoirs and explore them with your students. We also invite you to add to our ideas by creating ideas of your own that are triggered by your readings in the genre and by your students' original ideas and memories. In no particular order, here are several Explorations with which we have had success:

Name Piece	Snapshot Piece	Firsts Piece	Boundaries or Map Piece	Artifacts Piece
Family Secrets Piece	Difficult Times Piece	Mysteries Piece	Home Piece	Family Perspectives Piece
Holidays and Celebrations Piece	Ethnicity or Culture Piece	Eating, Cooking, or Favorite (or Despised) Food Piece	Parent Piece	Pet Piece
Dialect, Dialogue, or Favorite Sayings Piece	Favorite Transportation Piece: Skateboards, Bikes, Cars, etc.	Conscious Artist Piece	Family Trip Piece: Car Behavior, Airport Behavior, Packing Routines	Personal Portrait Piece
On the Day I Was Born Piece	Sibling Piece	Teachers or School Worries and Woes (or Joys and Triumphs) Piece	Grandparent Piece	Hiding Places and Hidden Treasures Piece
Place or Spiritual Home Piece	Family Lore Piece	Epiphany or Turning Point Piece	I'm This Way Because. . . Piece: Inherited Behaviors and Tendencies	Futuristic Piece: What I'll Be Like in 10 Years (or 5, 15, 20, etc. years)

May be copied for classroom use. © 2007 by Dawn Latta Kirby and Dan Kirby, from *New Directions in Teaching Memoir* (Heinemann: Portsmouth, NH).

Figure 3–3. *The Memoir Pieces*

Remember, the paired readings and writings are important here, not the order of the pieces.

Using the Memoir Framework to Evoke Short Writings

Let's walk through a sample Exploration to show you how we implement the Memoir Framework with short exploratory or Spider Pieces. As you read through this example, try to look at it not as an instant lesson plan but rather as a kind of model for you to use to develop your own age- and student-appropriate Explorations.

THE NAME PIECE

We often begin our memoir Explorations with the Name Piece. It is an unabashed favorite of ours and of our students. All kids have names and usually they have some stories or memories associated with their names. In the early stages of talking about their names, if some students don't know much at all about their names or why they have a particular name, encourage them to talk to parents and grandparents about their names. Such conversations among the generations are an added bonus of this Exploration. Many published pieces on names exist in memoirs and in fiction. We invite you to look for examples to add to our suggestions.

Because this Exploration has been consistently successful for us and our students, we illustrate it in some detail here. Once we present the general principles of reading, discussing, writing, and thinking that are associated with this Exploration, we think that you will be able to apply them readily to the additional Explorations in this chapter.

Readings   We begin by initiating class discussion about names: the importance of names, how names connect us to our families, and how names can be culturally or ethnically based. Then, we introduce students to excerpts from several professional memoirs and novels, discussing the similarity in writing technique in both fiction and nonfiction for this motif of names (see Figure 3–4 on page 38).

For each excerpt, students are to notice how writers do what they do in this genre. Our discussions are not literary critiques per se, but rather writerly discussions based on what our writers' eyes see about the author's techniques in the excerpts. Students might notice information such as what the author tells us about names in the piece, how the names are important, whether the names are liked or disliked by those who hold them, the voice employed by each narrator—child's voice, adult-looking-back-in-time voice, third-person omniscient detached voice—vocabulary, and other relevant writer's craft features of the piece. Because we have deliberately chosen pieces here in order to appeal to the cultural and ethnic diversity of the students in our classes, we urge readers also to notice the cultural connections in these particular pieces.

We cannot emphasize enough that locating excerpts that are suitable for your students from sources that are suitable for your school's constituents is paramount for success when using excerpts in the classroom. Although the excerpts we have chosen, we think, are generally rated G, or sometimes PG, the books from which they are taken are sometimes rated R—or more. We offer these exemplars only as guides, not as the only excerpts that will work for each pair of readings and writings.

Also, for each excerpt included in this book, we give only a small sampling of the more complete excerpt that we use with our students. We encourage you to obtain each of the memoirs and novels that we discuss in these sections and to use excerpts of a length and content that is appropriate for your students. Of course, do observe all relevant copyright laws, as we do.

Writings   Once students have read several published excerpts like the ones in Figure 3–4 and discussed the key features of each, comparing the excerpts to each other and to their own life experiences, it is time for students to begin writing about their own names. First, we ask students to complete a Name Chart on which they write their names—full names, nicknames, whatever names they want to include—across a sheet of paper. Then, under each individual name, they jot what they know about that specific name.

As a guide, we write our names and jottings on the board or on the LCD display-equipped computer at the same time that students are writing their jot lists. Or, sometimes we give students the handout shown in Figure 3–5 to model for them what we want them to accomplish. Remember, students may not know much about their names at first, so these jottings may have to be filled in further once students have talked to their parents and grandparents.

Both of us have written many name charts over the years while working in front of our students. Here is a sample chart from Dan.

Daniel	Ralston	Kirby
From the Bible?	Richard Ralston (grandfather) RRK initials on his sample cases Dry goods salesman in west Texas	Formerly O'Kearby Irish
"Dare to be a . . . ."	Ashamed of that name as a kid	Who? Where?
Brave in the lion's den	Kids called me "shredded" and "Purina" and "hot"	"Kirb"

We encourage you to create your own name chart and to share it with your students. Doing so is a fabulous icebreaker and a way for you and your students to get to know each other better.

Once students have written and discussed their Name Charts with partners or writing groups and completed the family research that they may need to conduct in order to add more detailed information to their Name Chart, they draft a first attempt at a name piece.

The idea here is to write a first draft—a Spider Piece, an Exploration—based on their names. This Spider Piece is not a finished product at this point, but it may reveal the potential for further work at some future date.

Name Piece Excerpts

Excerpt #1: From *My Name* in Sandra Cisneros' *The House on Mango Street*

In English my name means hope. In Spanish it means too many letters. It means sadness, it means waiting. It is like the number nine. A muddy color. It is the Mexican records my father plays on Sunday mornings when he is shaving, songs like sobbing.

It was my great-grandmother's name and now it is mine. She was a horse woman too, born like me in the Chinese year of the horse—which is supposed to be bad luck if you're born female—but I think this is a Chinese lie because the Chinese, like the Mexicans, don't like their women strong. . . .

At school they say my name funny as if the syllables were made out of tin and hurt the roof of your mouth. But in Spanish my name is made out of a softer something, like silver, not quite as thick as sister's name—Magdalena—which is uglier than mine. Magdalena who at least can come home and become Nenny. But I am always Esperanza.

I would like to baptize myself under a new name, a name more like the real me, the one nobody sees. Esperanza as Lisandra or Maritza or Zeze the X. Yes. Something like Zeze the X will do.

Excerpt #2: From *This Boy's Life* by Tobias Wolff

I didn't come to Utah to be the same boy I'd been before. I had my own dreams of transformation, Western dreams, dreams of freedom and dominion and taciturn self-sufficiency. The first thing I wanted to do was change my name. A girl named Toby had joined my class before I left Florida, and this had caused both of us scalding humiliation.

I wanted to call myself Jack, after Jack London. I believed that having his name would charge me with some of the strength and competence inherent in my idea of him. The odds were good that I'd never have to share a classroom with a girl named Jack. And I liked the sound. Jack. Jack Wolff. My mother didn't like it at all, neither the idea of changing my name nor the name itself. I did not drop the subject. She finally agreed. . . .

My father got wind of this and called from Connecticut to demand that I stick to the name he had given me. It was, he said, an old family name. This turned out to be untrue. . . .

My mother was pleased by my father's show of irritation and stuck up for me. A new name began to seem like a good idea to her. After all, he was in Connecticut and we were in Utah. . . . We were barely making it, and making it in spite of him. My shedding the name he'd given me would put him in mind of that fact.

Excerpt #3: From *The Names: A Memoir* by Scott Momaday

My name is Tsoai-talee. I am, therefore, Tsoai-talee; therefore I am.

The storyteller Pohd-lohk gave me the name Tsoai-talee. He believed that a man's life proceeds from his name, in the way that a river proceeds from its source. . . .

Figure 3–4. *Name Piece Excerpts*

You know, everything had to begin, and this is how it was: the Kiowas came one by one into the world through a hollow log. They were many more than now, but not all of them got out. There was a woman whose body was swollen up with child, and she got stuck in the log. After that, no one could get through, and that is why the Kiowas are a small tribe in number. They looked all around and saw the world. It made them glad to see so many things. The called themselves **Kwuda,** *"coming out."*

—*Kiowa folktale*

. . . . The names at first are those of animals and of birds, of objects that have one definition in the eye, another in the hand, of forms and features on the rim of the world, or of sounds that carry on the bright wind and in the void. They are old and original in the mind, like the beat of rain on the river, and intrinsic in the native tongue, failing even as those who bear them turn once in the memory, go on, and are gone forever: Pohd-lohk ["Old Wolf" in Kiowa], Keahdinekeah ["Throwing It Down" in Kiowa, the name of the author's great-grandmother], Aho [meaning unknown; the name of the author's grandmother].

Excerpt #4: From *The Namesake: A Novel* by Jhumpa Lahiri

As for a name, they have decided to let Ashima's grandmother, who is past eighty now [and living in India], who has named each of her other six great-grandchildren in the world, do the honors. When her grandmother learned of Ashima's pregnancy, she was particularly thrilled at the prospect of naming the family's first sahib. And so Ashima and Ashoke have agreed to put off the decision of what to name the baby until a letter comes, ignoring the forms from the hospital about filing for a birth certificate. Ashima's grandmother has mailed the letter herself, walking with her cane to the post office, her first trip out of the house in a decade. The letter contains one name for a girl, one for a boy. Ashima's grandmother has revealed them to no one.

Though the letter was sent a month ago, in July, it has yet to arrive. Ashima and Ashoke are not terribly concerned. After all, they both know, an infant doesn't really need a name. . . . Names can wait. In India parents take their time. . . .

Besides, there are always pet names to tide one over: a practice of Bengali nomenclature grants, to every single person, two names. In Bengali the word for pet name is *daknam*, meaning, literally, the name by which one is called, by friends, by family. . . .

Every pet name is paired with a good name, a *bhalonam*, for identification in the outside world. Consequently, good names appear on envelopes, on diplomas, in telephone directories, and in all other public places. . . . Good names represent dignified and enlightened qualities. Ashima means "she who is limitless, without borders." Ashoke, the name of an emperor, means "he who transcends grief." Pet names have no such aspirations.

Figure 3–4. *Continued*

Memoir Exploration #1: The Name Piece

<u>Directions</u>: Now that you have read several pieces by writers about their names, see if there are some memories floating in your head about your own name. On a sheet of paper, print your full name, leaving plenty of space for jottings. Each part of your name will head a separate column. Think about these questions as you stare at your name. Then, when you are ready, jot information that you can recall about each specific name. Be prepared to share your Name Chart with members of your Writer's Group.

<u>Key Questions</u>:

· Who named you? Why? What is the significance of your name, if any? Does your name have a special meaning?

· What are some of the names that you almost had? What are some of the names that you've always wanted to be called?

· How does your name connect you to other members of your family?

· What troubles or opportunities has your name afforded you?

· What are some altered versions of your name? What are some of your pet names or nicknames?

First name	Middle	Last	Variations

May be copied for classroom use. © 2007 by Dawn Latta Kirby and Dan Kirby, from *New Directions in Teaching Memoir* (Heinemann: Portsmouth, NH).

Figure 3–5. *The Name Chart*

The following is a Spider Piece—an Exploration—written by Dan and based on his Name Chart as shown in Figure 3–5.

Daniel Ralston Kirby—Danny—then Dan when I insisted in the seventh grade. Kirby to my school friends or Kirbs as in, "Hey Kirbs, let's go down to Bargers Drive-in for lunch." Dan, Daniel—Biblical, I'm sure. Daniel in the Old Testament in the lions' den and unafraid. Refused to tell the king what he wanted to hear. Funny, I've never really connected that Bible story to my name before. My parents never told me much about my name. I don't remember them telling me to "Dare to be a Daniel" or "We named you Danny because. . . ." Now, my middle name, the one that has since become an initial, was always an embarrassment. Junior high was the worst, eighth grade. "Ralston" . . . "Purina" . . . "Dog Chow." I tried to hide it from my friends. My grandfather's name was Richard Ralston Kirby. I remember seeing the initials "RRK" embossed on his sample cases and his briefcase as he packed his car on Monday mornings. He was a traveling salesman—a dry goods salesman who traveled the back roads of west Texas in the 1920s and 1930s. He died of leukemia at the age of fifty. I was maybe ten years old. Maybe if he had lived and I had been his grandson longer, the one who helped him pack his cases into the old black Buick, I would have been proud of my middle name, but mostly I hide that name with an R.

—*Dan Kirby*

Dan feels that this name motif has potential for him, so he tries a second exploratory piece on the same subject. Sometimes an idea will resonate for a student, so that she wants to try the technique of *looping*, of taking a key idea from one piece of writing and then writing a second piece based on the idea from the first piece. Dan does that here, as you'll see. He's still working on details and on sorting out his feelings about his name; he tries a new opening and addressing the reader directly this time. His grandfather is still clearly an important figure in this exploration and in his family connections to name.

I have always tried to hide my middle name. Sometimes behind the initial "R" or sometimes by leaving it blank on all those forms. Sometimes I have lied, writing "Robert" or "Richard." I've tried to hide my middle name because my friends loved to torture me about it. We moved a lot when I was a kid. I was a semi-permanent new kid in school. At each new school, I begged my mother to hide my name, to leave it off of the school forms. But someone always gave me away. Ralston, that's the name I've hidden, yes, Ralston like the cereal. See? You think it's funny, too. You would tease me, too. My friends called me "Shredded" for short in the second grade. And "Hot." I think I had a short career as "Hot Ralston" and "Purina." And yes, I was always Purina. So I hid my name.

For some reason my parents never explained the significance of the name. If I had known it was my grandfather's middle name and his mother's maiden name, I might have borne the humiliation with some sense of family purpose or pride. But it was at my grandfather's death that I learned the significance of Ralston. I read it on the In Memoriam leaflet, "Richard Ralston Kirby." Born 1898. Died 1952. I was ten or eleven at the time. I sat there in the church staring at the leaflet—Richard Ralston—and I felt ashamed for hiding my middle name.

—Dan Kirby

Once a student has tried one or two explorations based on his names—or on any Exploration we discuss here—the student needs to decide if the piece has potential. Maybe it's such a strong piece that he can use it to build other short pieces around it. Maybe it could be the *anchor piece* for the whole memoir. Or, if the piece isn't going all that well—perhaps because the student doesn't have enough strong memories to make the piece powerful—the piece needs to be filed in the student's Writer's Notebook for possible future consideration and as an example of the work in which the student is engaging.

Student Examples of the Name Piece   If you are successful at creating a studio-style atmosphere in your classroom, students will follow or not follow the professional excerpts you have read with them. They will also enjoy the models you write in front of them sharing your own life experience, but they may do this Name Piece their own way. That's a good thing. Remember, we're trying to encourage students to render their life experiences as honestly as possible, choosing the forms and formats that are most comfortable for that rendering. Two teacher friends in Denver have been especially successful at creating classroom environments that engage and excite their student writers. Betsey and Charles Coleman have shared the following name pieces, which their students wrote after exploring the excerpts shown earlier.

Cassandra's piece has a bit of the feel of Sandra Cisneros with surprising and even coded images. In the second paragraph, Cass borrows a bit from Dan's piece relating how others used and misused her name. She does a good job of tracking the history of her names and embedding that history in personal experience: "just a glance at the baby name book."

The Only Me[2]

I am a long, hissing snake as my name rolls off my tongue and out of my mouth, uncurling. The snake is venomous, but doesn't strike because it dances fluidly, mesmerized by a wooden flute. Sitting in a circle on the carpet, other children were "hope", "wished for child", or "Christmas baby", but I was "the Greek temptress of men." (Although later I would learn that my name was really the Greek prophet who no one believed and who was raped during the Trojan War. I wondered if that was what the book actually said.) Those same children with plain, garter snake names would call me "her" because I was too long to remember.

I was "Cass" to my softball coaches because it was easier to call while I was running for the ball. People have always tried to be cute and friendly by calling me "Cassie" as they bent over and talked to me in baby voices, but "Cassie" is a stupid, line-dancing, short jean-skirt wearing Texan, and that wasn't me. I was long, elegant, smart, three syllables. So I always said, "No, it's Cassandra." Even then, it was mispronounced as "Cassaaahyndra" with a scrunched-up, dripping, red nose, long A in the middle.

My middle name was a beautiful tribal girl tracking a deer in some exotically exciting rain forest. I didn't learn how to spell it until second grade when the standardized test asked me for my full name and I didn't know how to spell it. My middle name, like my first, wasn't my great-great-grandmother's name, the name of the person who saved my mother from drowning, or anything of that nature. It was just a chance glance at the baby name book. That was the same place where my parents found the name for my possible male self. Spencer. Frankly, I can't say I'm disappointed that I came out a girl.

The last part of me is German, which is why we bought a German Weimaraner dog and named it "Otto." My last name is short and rude. It is hard, a stone tossed into the flowing water that is me, plopping in and creating ripples, making me close my eyes and flinch as it splashes.

I am unique. I don't have to share me with anyone else. When people talk about me, they know it's me, not, "Now, which Sarah do you mean?" I looked it up on the computer, and I am the only me in the entire world. The only "Cassandra Adair Stroud."

—*Cassandra Stroud*

Lauren Young-Smith, ever the poet, writes a name piece full of crisp images and wonderfully fresh verbs. Like Cass and Cisneros, she *reveals* by sharing biographical data and *conceals* by using graphic and coded images. Her piece is both photographic and impressionistic.

To Grow a Name[2]

My name means equal opportunities. My name is broken beer bottles in a field of poppies. My name is vanilla, never French vanilla but vanilla extract, brown in a stained vial like liquid childhood. The dictionary says I am evolved from the Greek *laurel* plant, as if I had bloomed from in between curling freckled foliage and fluttered into existence on a sweet olive breeze. My name is a note-to-self scribbled onto a crumple post-it note, slipped into the back pocket of my jeans, forgotten until someone else points it out. I am somewhere in between where my mother begins and my father ended, hanging from the wires that string both their names together. I hack off the evidence of my origins and leave two stately initials clinging to each other. My name is yellow apples and bitter dark chocolate. It means pennies in the street and tastelessness. It means nothing until it is teetering off of someone else's tongue; it slides out between clumsy syllables. It is a hush, it is kneeling.

In downtown Denver in December, you can hear my name crystallizing at the edges of the dirty windows of Suburbans. It was given to me almost as if by flippancy, a "why not?" sort of gamble. It tells no stories, channels no shadows of great alabaster princesses. Like it crawled out of a Baby Name Book, attempting weakly to be seen and brandished. My parents were no renegades.

It isn't mine to flaunt or lock away, neither does it define me nearly as well as every other identification I've made for myself. It bounces from lip to lip through the currents of people in hallways, familiar in taste, low in meaning. If I could, I would break it into pieces and slip them into empty palms, curl the fingers of the lonely over it. Those who don't have enough of themselves inside them. I would plant my name in the warm April soil and watch it spread its fingers out over park benches and ponds, a name bereft of fruit and strangely motionless in the wind. I would watch the seasons swallow and vomit my name back up, with each turn of the pinwheel sun. I will never be the only Lauren. But to be the only me is enough as my name quietly climbs the graying walls of my house, as the earth whispers it, I will know that it's mine.

—*Lauren Young-Smith*

Courtney's piece is a fresh-faced explication of her names. She reveals some of her personality and then launches into family connections to her names. Like many teen writers, she uses informal, even conversational, dialect. Notice that the piece is untitled and is collected in her Writer's Notebook only as "the name piece." We encourage students to delay naming pieces until they are sure what they are really about and how they might be used in their memoir.

The Name Piece[2]

My name is an anomaly. Many are associated with important people and places—things that mean something to everyone. I am not a "little," "the fourth," or "the six hundred and twentieth." Simply Courtney Nicole Engle. The one and only.

Courtney: *french* (not hardly): from the court, for whatever that's worth. It's a name for dancers, luckily. Poise. Grace. Dedication. Strength. Endurance. Creativity. Flexibility. Passion. My name is not unique, by any means; there are three in the high school alone. I, personally, would have chosen Katania or Alissa.

Nicole: *french* (again?): victory. At fifteen you can hardly expect me to have ended world hunger, or expelled the infidels, or cured cancer, but I try. I've always known that if Nicole were my first name I would go by Nikk. Something less girly—stronger. Nicole and Courtney both imply that I cannot throw a ball. I can. That I do not lift weights. I do. That I am simply about manicures, boys, and shoes. Okay, the shoes part is true, but everyone has a weakness. Someone with bright pink nails and a spray tan wouldn't be caught dead slide tackling people to get a round piece of plastic. I would.

I have no siblings to compare my name to, but I have parents and grandparents. My mother: Bernice Vee Engle. Yes, "Vee." She does indeed have a letter phonetically spelled for a middle name, as does my uncle: Donald Dee Fossett. My dad: Bruce James Engle. Pretty typical and average. Not like my dad at all (let's just say he was a rebel, though *he* never admits it). My grandmother: Viola Belle Davis. Again, mediocre. My grandfather: Emery Evert Fossett. My papa: Joseph Osmar Engle. Oddly enough, his initials are J.O.E.: Joe—his nickname. My nana: (this is where it gets tricky) Laura Joyce Pokock. She, however, went by Betty Ann for her entire life. No one called her Laura Joyce, not even her parents. Overall, names in my family are pretty normal; nothing exotic; nothing gets twisted around and comes out like peanut butter.

I have only one common nickname: Court. Big surprise there. My best friend calls me Courtie, and golf mates call me Sparkey. Yes, Sparkey. It's a long story. We have a motto in my house which will summarize the end of this paper: "I don't care what you call me, as long as you're sure to call me for dinner."

—*Courtney Engle*

What we like about all of these student pieces is the uniquely personal voice in each. We encourage students to develop and tune that voice as they write additional exploratory pieces. Don't be discouraged if the first name pieces you get from students are perfunctory, routine, or uninteresting. This is the beginning of the journey toward memoir and many student writers don't find a really powerful memory, metaphor, or anchor piece until they have written several pieces. Remind them that the spider persists in throwing out filaments, and many of them fail to make a connection. If your class becomes really rowdy during writing time, remind them that the spider is also "noiseless and patient."

The Name Piece should launch memoir study with enthusiastic student participation. Use that momentum to keep them writing new pieces each week. In the following chapter, we will offer two more detailed examples of our approach to teaching memoir that have worked well for us. As you read these examples and think about your own classroom, return to Chapter 2 to examine the Studio Values we offered. We find that we need to remind ourselves often of what we are trying to do with our instruction and to remind ourselves of what student behaviors we really value in our classroom.

Notes

1. Walt Whitman's poem, "The Noiseless Patient Spider," is often anthologized. It can be found in numerous collections of Whitman's work and in many literature anthologies.

2. The student authors featured in this chapter were all students at Colorado Academy with Betsey Coleman as their English teacher. We print all students' papers as they were written, without correction.

Works Cited

BAKER, RUSSELL. 1982. *Growing Up*. New York: Plume Books.

CISNEROS, SANDRA. 1989. *The House on Mango Street*. New York: Vintage Books.

DILLARD, ANNIE. 1998. "To Fashion a Text." In *Inventing the Truth: The Art and Craft of Memoir*, edited by William Zinsser, 141–61. Boston: Houghton Mifflin.

MOMADAY, N. SCOTT. 1976. *The Names*. Tucson: University of Arizona Press.

WELTY, EUDORA. 1983. *One Writer's Beginnings*. Cambridge, MA: Harvard University Press.

WOLFF, TOBIAS. 1989. *This Boy's Life*. New York: The Atlantic Monthly Press.

ZINSSER, WILLIAM, ED. 1998. *Inventing the Truth: The Art and Craft of Memoir*. Boston: Houghton Mifflin.

4

Further Explorations in Memoir Writing

In this chapter we share the process for engaging your student writers in two new exploratory pieces. The Snapshot Piece asks students to remember a particularly vivid childhood incident and then render that memory in the present tense. The Boundaries, or Map, Piece engages students in using their visual memory to write about a special place or neighborhood, beginning by drawing maps or sketches of that remembered place.

The Snapshot Piece

The Snapshot Piece is used for intense, photographic memories—memories that the writer can recall as if they were real pictures in a real photograph album or scrapbook, and sometimes they are. For this Exploration, Dawn usually tells a version of the following story. This story about Dawn's mother will resonate with one of the memoir excerpts that students will read and discuss for this Exploration.

> My mother doesn't complete family photograph albums or scrapbooks. Instead, all of our older family pictures are tossed into a large shoebox and stored in a bookcase. One day when I was about sixteen, I was going through the shoebox, looking at pictures I'd seen a thousand times of my parents as a young dating couple and then as a young just-married couple. If I hadn't already been told that they were my parents, I wouldn't have recognized those people in the photographs.
>
> On this particular day, I see a picture I've never really noticed before. I know the girl in it is my mom because I've learned by now what she looked like then. But the guy in the picture is definitely not my dad. He has on a uniform, for one thing, and he's just not my dad.
>
> "Who's this, Mom?"
>
> "Oh, that's Billy Morrison." She grins. She looks sheepish.

Who the heck is Billy Morrison, I think. I ask.

"I dated him before I dated your father. He had to go off to war, and he told me *not* to date that Charles Latta while he was gone." But of course she did. In fact, she married that Charles Latta.

So that picture creates a story memory for my mother and a story memory for me of the time that I learned a tidbit about my mother before she was a married woman.

Once we have told that story or related a similar specific and vivid memory, we ask students to jot down memories that are so vivid, so clear that they *could* be a photograph in a family picture album, even if they don't really exist as an actual picture. Sometimes, we even ask students to bring in such a photograph, one that prompts an intense memory for them. After they have thought through some initial ideas, they are ready to read.

Readings

One of the key writer's craft techniques that we want students to try as part of the Snapshot Piece is that of telling a memory from the past in the present tense (*is, am, are, runs, stops, write*) and in the present progressive tense (*is running, am stopping, are writing*). This is a tricky technique since the propensity in writing about an event that occurred in the past is to write it in the past tense (*was, were, ran, stopped, wrote*). But writing about an event in the present and present progressive tenses can draw the reader into the event and make it seem as though it were happening in the here and now. Doing so—combined with dialogue, vivid detail, strong verbs, and the many other techniques that empower memoir—gives the event immediacy and audience appeal.

To reinforce the power of this technique, we use readings with students that are memoir excerpts written in the present or present progressive tense. (See Figure 4–1.)

The discussions that surround these readings focus on the power and effect of these tenses, their ability to help the reader see the scene. As we read each excerpt, we ask students what the snapshot—the photograph—of each piece would be if one existed. We consider what other writer's craft techniques are exemplified in the excerpts, too, and how they resemble other pieces listed in our framework (see Figure 3–3). For example, the excerpt by Huggan is also a Parent Piece since it reveals insights about the narrator's parents; the piece uses the first-person voice of the child telling the event, a technique used to achieve intimacy and immediacy; dialogue is present, though its lack of traditional paragraphing makes the piece seem more like a stream-of-consciousness piece, again creating a here-and-now feeling in the piece; and the power of the piece relies on the reader's ability to make inferences, illustrating the author's skill and light touch in her writing. We usually bring in a recording of "Who's Sorry Now?" by Connie Francis so that students can hear this 1950s song—one that will seem as if it comes from ancient history to our students—and then we discuss what it is in these characters' lives for which they may be sorry. We discuss similar relevant writer's craft techniques for additional Snapshot excerpts that we read.

Snapshot Excerpts

Excerpt #1: From *Elizabeth Stories* by Isabel Huggan

My mother is teaching me how to dance. It is a rainy Saturday afternoon and I am listening to the radio in the kitchen as I stand by the sink polishing silver. . . . I turn up Connie Francis singing "Who's Sorry Now?" just as Mavis comes into the room. "Heavens, is that back?" she says. "That was popular when I used to go dancing with Tim, goodness, 25 years ago." She comes over and slips her arm around my waist, humming. I am startled and pull away, not used to this kind of impromptu embrace, but she is determined, and begins to turn me around the floor. "Come now, Elizabeth; this is a good song. No wonder it's come back." "Who's Tim?" I ask. "Was he your boyfriend before Daddy?" "Oh, I suppose you could say so," she says. "He was a brother of a girl in our office and he used to take me dancing out on the Pier. Oh my, he could dance!" Her voice is reflective and I can tell she is seeing things I am not. The song ends and I want to ask her more but I can't think how to start. As if she reads my mind, she volunteers some information. "We saw each other for a few years, Elizabeth, but all we had in common, really, was the dancing. And when you decide to settle down with someone, you have to have more in common than that!" She smiles and leaves me here at the sink. I am thinking about how she and Frank never dance, how he says it's a waste of time to walk around to music. I wonder what it is that they found in common.

Excerpt #2: From *Cherry: A Memoir* by Mary Karr

The next morning, you leave the house for Meredith's wearing the monk's robe and what you call Lecia's slave-girl-of-Caesar sandals, with leather thongs that wrap around your calves. But unless they're tied so tightly that your circulation's cut off, they tend to slop down around your ankles. Halfway to Meredith's, you untie them and sling them over your shoulder like a string of fish.

    Thus monastically clad and unshod, you walk the tar-sticky roads holding your mother's orange-and-black yoga book. About halfway there, a roaring truck draws up on the rough shoulder holding a whole crowd of bikini-clad girls and boys in cutoffs in back, including the luminous John Cleary sitting high on the side, a blue towel around his neck. Some girl asks real loud, where's the Halloween party, while everybody else breaks in half laughing. Somebody (you want to think it's John) says, C'mon you guys, and the truck roars off, leaving a wake of titters that you halfway believe visible—little clicking black birds swarming from the silver truck to where you stand, eyes welling up.

    At the threshold of Meredith's icily air-conditioned house afterward, she says, Well, hey. Don't you look all Buddha'd up.

    You shove past her, saying, Lemme in fast. I'm baking alive in this thing. You dive the length of the sofa, letting your hair shield your face since crying ruined this morning's Egyptian eye makeup.

Figure 4–1. *Snapshot Excerpts*

Writings

Once we have read and discussed several Snapshot Pieces, students are ready to write their own Snapshot Piece. Students generally begin by adding to their initial brainstorm list of their most vivid memories, the list that they started before engaging in any readings. As they are refining their brainstorm list, we caution them to select remembered events that are short in duration, ones that cover only a few minutes, not several hours or days. In order to use this technique most effectively, writers need to capture a quick, precise, well-defined moment in time for the Snapshot Piece. Sometimes, students bring a photograph to class and write the story of that picture. Sometimes, they write from a memory that is so clear it *could* be a photograph but isn't.

The most difficult task for student writers in this piece is to stay in the present and present progressive tenses rather than drifting into the past tense. Later, in their Writer's Groups, students circle any past tense verb that appears in their Snapshot Pieces and convert it to the present or present progressive tense. Sure, the occasional past tense verb may be necessary in the piece, but generally not. Here is a student draft of a Snapshot Piece from Lee.

Car Crash[1]

I couldn't even feel the tears. The burn of breathing in the talcum powder was like acid being forced down my throat; the throbbing pain on my neck, and the sting on my cheek, and the sharp pain on my chest weren't apparent until five minutes had past. The vivid tearing noise, and the sound of folding metal on metal was accompanied by my quiet intake of air, and inability to exhale. The screaming from the other car beat up against my chest as all of my joints cramped, and my vision blurred. The shattered glass reflected all of my shame. Tracy Chapman's lyrics of, "Baby can I hold you" were drowned out by my desperate cries; the pure fear and disappointment in myself surpassed all other feelings. Sitting, listening from my car's inverted atmosphere, I gathered my traumatized thoughts. The Panera bagel sat untouched beneath my trembling feet.

Driving down Wadsworth alone for the first time, I was calm about finding my way to CA from my earlier dentist appointment. I turned from Wadsworth into the broad concrete lot of Southwest Plaza for lunch before my soccer practice. Leaving Panera in my car, I was unaware that I had turned onto Bowles instead of Wadsworth. Glaring up towards the sun at the unfamiliar green signs reflecting off of my windshield, I panicked. Assuming I was merely going in the wrong direction, I turned around and continued to hunt for a familiar road. I began to ceaselessly swear, my eyes began to tear up, and I became extremely agitated because I did not know where to go. Feeling flustered, I continued to pay close attention to the street signs; Cody, Brittany, Flower . . .

There were no cars in front of or behind me. I stared blindly up at the street sign "Flower". With the sudden revelation that I had not checked the light as I drove through the intersection at approximately 30 m.p.h., I frantically looked up to find myself feet from the car crossing perpendicular to me.

Too panicked to react, my black Audi crashed head first into the economy car in front of me. My heartbeat doubled, knowing I could not take it back I tried not to respond to the foul shrieks of the young mother through the shattered glass, "My f-ing baby, my f-ing baby is in the back!" She was only feet away from me, I dialed my mom, my fingers trembling; "Mom I crashed. Mom I crashed into another car. Mom it is my fault. Mom, she's mad. Mom she's yelling. It's bad Mom and It's my fault . . . No I'm not hurt." The adrenaline pushed itself through my body and my sentences blurred together; luckily my mom remained composed and was able to derive my location from my distorted cries; "Lee I'm coming, are you sure you're not hurt?"

"Yeah, but she's so mad . . . the ambulance is here now . . . Mom, I have to go."

As I stepped from my broken car, with exploded air bags and a mangled front end, the mother's hate radiated from her and seemed to pull me deep into the damage I caused. Sobbing, I was escorted to the ambulance where the mother, her daughter and I were evaluated for injury. Still waiting for my mom to come, the young paramedic decided I needed to be transported to the hospital. Still struggling to get a full breath, I sat, my entire body trembling; I told the paramedic, "I don't need to go to the hospital, it doesn't hurt." However, he was quick to tell me, "You have minor whiplash, minor burns from your airbag, and an inflamed and irritated mark from your seatbelt across your chest. Unless your mom arrives soon, because you are a minor, we will have to take you to the hospital. Sitting across from the now much calmer woman, and her unharmed daughter, the pressure between my eyes intensified from the guilt. My stomach caved and my back slouched, I was ashamed to have been the cause of such a terrible event.

Clambering down from the elevated ambulance, the sun's brilliance was initially too bright for me to see. The police officer talked with me and asked me various questions, none of which I can remember. Walking to my mom's air-conditioned car, all I can remember wanting from my car was my cell phone and my bagel. I decided to let my mom discuss the crash with the now, seemingly kind woman. Sitting in the cool car, the burns on my neck, chest and cheek became more apparent. My mom approached the car and I grudgingly rolled down my window and let some of the cool air escape from the sheltered area. "She's not mad, Lee." I sat and observed, regularly sighing from the restlessness of guilt, as the turmoil of my wreck was sorted out for me.

—*Lee Burkett*

Notice how Lee uses very specific details—Wadsworth Boulevard, Tracy Chapman lyrics, Panera Bread Company—and notice also uses of quite detailed dialog. These features work together to create a sense of immediacy and of photographic replay.

Jennifer tries a different approach to the Snapshot. Using strong sensory images in list form, she takes her readers to the Stock Show. We smell the smells and hear the sounds of the chaotic arena and grounds.

Country Comfort[1]

National Western Stock Show. Buzzes with children's shrieks, a bellow of cows, a crinkle of leather, a rustle of chaps. Multitudes of shows, events and displays. The applause is politely quiet as a football game. The buzzer of a bull rider's victory; the longest eight seconds in sports.

Scorching, tough turkey legs sizzle on the tongue. Humidity forms in beads of perspiration on the hearty meat. Grease and juice on smiling faces. Mint chocolate

Dippin' Dots for the used but precious bookstore. The yellowing pages have a musty mint smell. Dark chocolate words form rich rustic settings and captivating plots.

Smells of pelts. The wild hanging on racks for my touch of desire. Sheared beaver soft and fine as velvet cattails. Grey wolf's thick guard hairs protecting fine insulating fluff. A linger of musk clinging still.

I remember shopping for trailers proving my authenticity. Asking viable questions to curled mustached faces. Straw cowboy hat with drawstrings on hair golden as straw. Sky blue eyes shining at engraved leather belts and work gloves. Sauntering along concrete aisles at pace fast as molasses. Moving along like a grazing herd of cattle.

There were cows in the pen and cows between my burger buns and cowboys galore. Men with tightly close-cut jeans and button up shirts with collars. Horses like assorted shoes. Large and bulky, grand and round, light and strappy. All polished and groomed like burnished coins. Sheep smart as sea slugs. Sheepdogs lazy as a mother cheetah.

The Grand Prix. Well dressed riders on impeccably groomed horses. Giants that ripple muscles under shining coats of chestnut, bay and gray. Luscious tails that flow behind beating hindquarters and hard hooves. A course of wooden jumps of immense difficulty. Courtesy circle to survey surroundings. Cross the line and a buzzer sounds the rest is a whirlwind. Towering vertical after foreboding Liverpool then follow the roar of the crowd to the final jump. No faults and it's a job well done and on to the next horse. The English side of a western stock show.

A friendly feeling spreads from horse lover to dog owner, swine shower to boot polisher. It's the country comfort and swagger settling into Wrangler jeans and Stetsons. A simple people with hearts big as the barns we own. My people and here I belong. Here we flow to the pulse of living in today with of knowledge of nature.

—Jennifer Kelley

As teachers we're sure you notice that both Jennifer and Lee have difficulty staying in present tense and in narrowing their pieces to cover only a few intense minutes of time. Your writers will find that the Snapshot Piece is more challenging to write than it first appears, but we have found that our students enjoy playing the "tense game," as they call it.

The Boundaries (or Map) Piece

The purpose of the Boundaries Piece is to explore the literal and figurative boundaries of childhood. Delving into maps and boundaries works the writer's visual memory and calls to mind special places. We find that drawing floor plans of favorite homes and/or maps of important places and their proximity to each other helps student writers to work their memories in this area.

Readings

As we read the memoir excerpts associated with this Exploration, we find some key questions that aid our discussion include the following:

- In what home (if you've lived in more than one) or in what part of your home did you feel most secure and comfortable?
- How far could you go from home?
- Where were the places that you definitely were not supposed to go? Did you go anyhow? Why? What happened?
- When did you have to be home in the evening?
- Try drawing a map of the place that the author discusses in this excerpt. What new insights do you find by doing so?
- What can you discover about your memories of home and/or of your neighborhood by drawing a map of them?

These memories will also spark connections to people and to setting. In fact, in some published memoirs, the locale of the memoir is so powerfully described and figures so prominently in the story that the place of the memoir becomes as important and relevant to the story as are the characters. Student writers may find that they want to devote much of their final memoir to explorations of place, boundaries, and the limitations of childhood.

Writings

Once students have read and discussed excerpts like those shown in Figure 4–2, it is time for them to write about their own boundaries and/or to draw their own maps. Students may want to go on the Internet and print a map of their town, their neighborhood, or of either one in relation to other nearby locations that were significant to them. They may also draw a map or a floor plan, but the map isn't the end of this Exploration. A piece about the map still needs to be attempted. The map alone may appear in the final memoir, the written piece alone may appear in the final memoir, both may appear, or neither may appear. The key, however, is to trigger visual memories and then to write about them accurately so that the reader also envisions the place being described.

Cassie Gallegos tries the Map Piece by using her room as her spiritual and literal base. As she drew the floor plan of her bedroom, she discovered how frequently she peered out her windows through the blinds. She cleverly "pulls open the blinds" on the windows of that room to tell a more detailed story of childhood.

Room of Dreams[2]
This is where I dream. It's the place that knows me. It's the place that understands me. It's where I can do whatever I want.

My room is the place in this house that is completely mine. When I need to be alone, or listen to whatever music I want, I come to this room. Music fills this room from corner to corner and I am inspired to write. The words on the page reflect how I feel, and somehow they fit with the sounds filling my space.

I pull open the blinds and I stare out into the backyard. My childhood is there. Two swings, a rope, a slide, the little turquoise playhouse, and the grimy sandbox. I spent long summer hours and days playing there. My mom made me go outside instead of sitting on the couch and reading. So I'd take my book with me to the swings. On the warmest summer days the slide was too hot so I'd put the hose at the top and turn it on. It cooled the slide, but the water made it so slippery that I would end up halfway across the yard laughing. I loved skidding down that slide in my slippery Hello Kitty bathing suit.

In the winter blizzard of several years ago, I opened the blinds to see my summer fun gone replaced by snow drifts hanging over the gutters. I bundled up and went out. As I stand here now looking through the blinds of my room, I can still see that crazy kid standing waist deep in a hole she had dug in the snow.

This room is my place of dreams and memories.

—Cassie Gallegos

Not a bad first draft, Cassie; lots to like. As her teacher coach, what questions and suggestions would you have for her if she wants to take this piece further?

Some students may want to explore figurative, not just literal, boundaries as do several of the authors in the previous excerpts. Such pieces are ripe with metaphor and interconnections. One of Dan's former students wrote several pieces about events that occurred in a field not too far from his home. The field was behind a white fence. He had strict instructions from his mother not to venture beyond the white fence, but he did anyhow. All of his friends did, too. In that field he played baseball, looked at his first girly magazine, tried his first smoke, and learned some of the hard lessons of life. He used the metaphor of the white fence to represent the off-limits parts of his life, both literally and figuratively. The white fence was a metaphor that resonated strongly with his readers and added depth to his final memoir.

Another way in which we get students to think metaphorically about mapping is to engage in the Map of My Heart Activity that Dawn created. Dawn hands each student a piece of pink paper with these instructions:

1. Below, draw a large heart. Divide the heart into sections in whatever manner you wish. Label each section with something you care about, something that is close to your heart.
2. Jot some notes in response to these questions: Why are these things important to you? What do they reveal about your values, concerns, culture, family, and so on?
3. After you have labeled your entire drawing, circle the ones that are most important to you. Why are they most important? Jot some notes.
4. Share some aspects of your heart map with your Writer's Group.
5. Select one or more aspects of your heart map and write a piece about it/them.

Some of our students are quite creative as they section off the areas of their drawings, while others—like Dawn—just draw lines to create random sections. Favorite sections of the drawings often carry labels such as family, pets, travel, cooking and eating, leisure time, humor, caring for younger siblings, my room, and the like. Once

Excerpts for Boundary (or Map) Piece

Excerpt #1: From *An American Childhood* by Annie Dillard

I walked. My mother had given me the freedom of the streets as soon as I could say our telephone number. I walked and memorized the neighborhood. I made a mental map and located myself upon it. At night in bed I rehearsed the small world's scheme and set challenges: Find the store using backyards only. Imagine a route from the school to my friend's house. I mastered chunks of town in one direction only; I ignored the other direction, toward the Catholic church.

On a bicycle I traveled the known world's edge, and the ground held. I was seven. I had fallen in love with a red-haired fourth-grade boy named Walter Milligan. He was tough, Catholic, from an iffy neighborhood. Two blocks beyond our school was a field—Miss Frick's field, behind Henry Clay Frick's mansion—where boys played football. I parked my bike on the sidelines and watched Walter Milligan play. As he ran up and down the length of the field, following the football, I ran up and down the sidelines, following him. After the game, I rode my bike home, delirious. It was the closest we had been, and the farthest I had traveled from home. . . .

My father forbade me to go to Frick Park. He said bums lived there under bridges; they had been hanging around unnoticed since the Depression. My father was away all day; my mother said I could go to Frick Park if I never mentioned it.

I roamed Frick Park for many years. Our family moved from house to house, but we never moved so far I couldn't walk to Frick Park.

Excerpt #2: From *Falling Through Space* by Ellen Gilchrist

This is my house. This is where I was born. This is the bayou that runs in my dreams, this is the bayou bank that taught me to love water, where I spent endless summer hours alone or with my cousins. This is where I learned to swim, where mud first oozed up between my toes. This is where I saw embryos inside the abdomens of minnows. This is where I believed that if I was vain and looked too long into the water I would turn into a flower.

This is where I learned the legend of the greedy dog. There was an old dog on a raft and he had a bone in his teeth and he looked down into the water and saw a dog carrying a bone and he dropped the one he was holding to snatch the other dog's bone away and so lost both bones, the real and the imaginary.

That's a new bridge. The one that was here when I was small had a beautiful elaborate scaffolding on top. I thought I must be a princess, of royal blood, to have such a bridge with such a magnificent top. To have such land with so many bugs and a bayou with so many fish and mussels and gars and maybe even alligators.

This is the porch that at one time ran all the way around the house. My grandfather built this house and my mother came here when she was four years old. My brother was born in that front bedroom. I was born forty miles away in a hospital and only came here three days later.

Figure 4–2. *Excerpts for the Boundary (or Map) Piece*

Excerpt #3: From *Clear Springs: A Memoir* by Bobbie Ann Mason

There aren't any big cities around, unless you count Paducah (pop. 26,853), twenty-six miles to the north. The farm is typical of this agricultural region. A lane cuts through the middle, from front to back, and two creeks divide it crosswise. The ground is rich, but it washes down the creeks. The creeks are clogged with trash, dumped there to prevent hard rains—gully-washers—from carrying the place away. At one time this was a thriving dairy farm that sustained our growing family. It was home to my paternal grandparents, my parents, my two sisters, my brother, and me. There were at least eleven buildings along the front part of the farm, near the road: two houses, a barn, a stable, a corncrib, a smokehouse, two hen houses, a wash-house, a milk house, an outhouse. I even had a playhouse.

The gravel-and-mud country road ran in front. Sometimes the school bus couldn't get through the mud. Before the road was paved and fast cars started killing our dogs and cats, we would sit on my grandparents' porch and say "Who's that?" whenever anybody passed. . . .

I am product of this ground. . . .

The farm now lies entirely within the Mayfield city limits. To the east, the subdivisions are headed our way. Behind the farm, to the south, we can glimpse an air-compressor factory. Just across the railroad, to the west, the four-lane bypass leads around town and to the parkway and to everywhere on the continent. Across the road, in a thirty-acre cornfield, which is like an extension of our front yard, is the landmark of the town.

Excerpt #4: From *Virgin Time* by Patricia Hampl

I must be four. I don't go to school yet. I can't read. People are always telling me to go outside and play. I can walk to the end of the block. That far. I must not cross Oxford Street. But there she is, standing across Oxford. I have seen her many times. And now again. Her hands are clasped behind her back, and she is swinging back and forth in a self-contained motion. She is answering the question that I have finally emboldened myself to ask her. "Grace," she calls across the great neighborhood divide. "My name is Grace."

"I'm Patricia," I holler back. The next thing seems inevitable, easy: "Will you be my friend, Grace?" My brother has friends, but there are no girls on our block. She is the nearest one, as far as I know. Her hair glows in the sun. I don't understand I am not looking in a mirror of desire, wish meeting wish. Isn't what's in my heart in every heart? Doesn't Grace need Patricia?

She shakes her head, her hands still behind her back, still rocking to her own rhythm. "No," she says. "No, no, no." It doesn't occur to me that, after all, she lives by remote control, too, and cannot cross the street. I only see her now as she turns from me, her honey hair swinging back and forth as she runs away, calling out *No, no, no* forever, escaping down the block where I don't dare to follow.

Figure 4–2. *Continued*

again, students are thinking analogically about what's important to them as a means of prompting memory and entering into writing.

Adding to the Pieces on Your Own

What we have highlighted here so far are several examples of how we use the Memoir Framework to combine reading, writing, thinking, and discussing. We have also set forth a template of Spider Pieces that you might want to develop further as you delve into reading the genre of memoir. Next, we want to underscore several more of the Explorations that we often use within our classes in order to fire students' imaginations and help them to produce a wealth of writings from which they will cull pieces for the final memoir. Space limitations here simply prevent us from detailing all thirty or more of the Explorations, including companion reading excerpts and written Spider Pieces, that we have developed for memoir, but we can direct your reading a bit. We also encourage you to seek out exemplars for the Explorations that you want to use with your student writers as you read further in the genre of memoir.

The following chart in Figure 4–3 will help you to connect the Exploration, the purpose of the Exploration, the professional exemplars, and the Spider Pieces that students might produce.

As you discover new Spider Pieces for your students to try and as you locate new exemplars from your readings of memoir, we'd love for you to test them out, make notes about them, and then share your findings with us at conferences. We're interested in hearing how you're expanding the Memoir Framework to suit your teaching situation.

Principles for Reading like a Writer

As students work constructively with the excerpts and with their own writings in order to discover connections among the readings and their own personal experiences, they benefit from knowing how to *read like a writer* and *write like a reader*. Basically, the principles for these activities are derived from the idea that both reading and writing are active processes that can be learned well, and that readers and writers look for different features in text.

Readers look for the meanings submerged in the text, put there most likely by the writer. They are trying to connect their experiences with those of the writer. They are trying to envision what the writer is describing or explaining. They are attempting to understand the vocabulary of the writer and to follow the writer's logic. They want to ascertain that they understand the writer's theme and purpose for writing. When texts are fuzzy in logic, have vocabulary that is too specialized or advanced, or describe experiences that are too idiosyncratic, readers may fail to comprehend the text and *get lost*. They put down the text in frustration, missing the point, the purpose, and the joy of the reading experience.

ADDITIONAL EXPLORATIONS IN MEMOIR WRITING: LINKING EXPLORATIONS, PURPOSE, AND PROFESSIONAL EXAMPLES

Spider Piece; Exploration	Purpose; Territory to Explore	Professional Examples*
Artifacts	Treasured things. Collections, a talisman. Hold the artifact and recall a special time, place, person, event.	Green, London, Nekola, Shulman
Family	Stories, characters, relationships, special occasions, rituals, birth order, roles and responsibilities.	Baker, Campbell, McBride, Delaney, Kübler-Ross
Ethnicity, Race, Culture	Immigrant stories, racism, overcoming barriers of culture, strangers in a strange land.	hooks, O'Hearn, Liu, Gates, Jr., Lee, Kuusisto
Family Mysteries	Family secrets, unsolved puzzles and riddles, unsolved crimes.	Kehoe, McBride, Scully, Williams, Wiesel
Parents	Relationships, individual quirks, tensions, joys, intense times, old news, before-and-after stories, habits, sayings, appearance.	Min, Raines, Dodson, Lee, London, Welty, Lyden, Bragg
Conscious Artist	Addressing the audience directly to talk about the work of writing and/or of writing memoir. Talking about the form, the challenges, and the problems of writing memoir.	Dillard, Gates, Jr., Hampl, Wiesel, Karr, Baker
Difficult Times	Life in crisis, family problems, failing health, uncertainty and doubt.	Williams, Jamison, Conway, Davis, Shulman
Uses of Language	Dialect, unique speech, bilingualism.	Min, Cisneros, McBride, Wiesel, Karr, Ashworth, Healy, Fuller

* See our complete bibliography in Chapter 12 for the bibliographic information for these authors' works.

May be copied for classroom use. © 2007 by Dawn Latta Kirby and Dan Kirby, from *New Directions in Teaching Memoir* (Heinemann: Portsmouth, NH).

Figure 4–3. *Additional Explorations in Memoir Writing*

Writers try to imbue the text with meaning by telling the reader enough information to capture the reader's understanding and imagination. Writers try to use techniques to draw the reader into the text, to create interest in the text and in the writer's point and purpose. They want to experience the joy of having readers nod their heads: *Yes, yes, I get it; I agree.*

When students learn to *read like writers*, they learn to see how the writer organized the text; to study the images and vocabulary the writer used, working to understand the nuances; to figure out the writer's point and message in order to connect the reading to their own lives. Similarly, when students learn to *write like readers*, they learn to anticipate what and how much information readers will need in order to comprehend the text, which logical forms of organization and emotional appeals will assist the reader to follow the points of the text, and which details will capture the reader's imagination. Ideally, students *write like readers* and then *read their own* (and others') *text like writers*. When they do, they are more likely to communicate well with their readers, to produce a well-crafted piece of writing, and to complete their writing work with a sense of achievement and accomplishment. These again are some of the goals for which we strive as our students engage in the Memoir Framework.

Now that we have clarified the Memoir Framework and given some examples of paired readings and writings for various Explorations, let's examine in the next chapter techniques for drafting, revising, and sharing pieces within the memoir studio classroom.

Notes

1. These student authors attended Colorado Academy. Student excerpts are printed as the authors wrote them, without change or correction.

2. This student author attended Skyview Academy in Thornton, Colorado, and had Marne Gulley as her English teacher. Student excerpts are printed as the authors wrote them, without change or correction.

Works Cited

Dillard, Annie. 1987. *An American Childhood*. New York: Harper and Row.

Gilchrist, Ellen. 1987. *Falling Through Space*. Boston: Little Brown.

Hampl, Patricia. 1992. *Virgin Time*. New York: Ballantine.

Huggan, Isabel. 1997. *Elizabeth Stories*. New York: Penguin.

Karr, Mary. 2000. *Cherry*. New York: Viking Books.

Mason, Bobbie Ann. 1999. *Clear Springs: A Memoir*. New York: Random House.

5

Writing Memoir Pieces

Within the studio classroom, the work of writing is a cyclical process that involves reading and thinking as well as drafting, revising, elaborating, crafting, trying the piece out on one or more audiences, compiling a Writer's Notebook, and maintaining a portfolio. Each of these processes is integral to the entire Memoir Framework and to enacting the philosophies underlying both the framework and the studio classroom. Recall that the key here is that writers are working constructively and epistemically as memoirists to build authentic, meaning-rich texts for themselves and others. Recall also that the key value in the studio writing class is work—work that is meaningful and authentic—that is, work that is producing real texts for real audiences.

Notice that we frequently use the word *authentic*. Assuredly, working to create authentic texts for authentic audiences is paramount to the goals and outcomes of the studio writing classroom. Memoir is a real genre; it exists in the world, and people read it. Even though our students may not be writing the next *New York Times* best seller, we want them to work *as if* they were, *as if* they might be writing now the kernel of what will one day be a published text. Of course, many venues exist for *publishing* a work, many beyond the famous and the best-seller lists; and that is how most of our students will indeed become published. But who knows when the next Henry Louis Gates, Jr., Annie Dillard, Stephen Kuusisto, or Chanrithy Him (please, oh *please*, let it be so!) may be sitting and writing in our classes? We don't know, and our students probably don't know, either, if such is to be their outcome in life; so we work now to instill the working processes and habits of mind that will serve our student writers for a lifetime, regardless of what their eventual writing and publishing venues will be.

To that end, we work with our students to engage them in the full range of writing processes, from idea finding and drafting to taking their written pieces public. Our student writers often display not only their finished memoir pieces but also representations of their work—their writing processes—that surrounded and supported the final texts. In this way, fellow students and parents, administrators, and our teacher-colleagues begin to understand a bit more about the Memoir Framework, its grounding theories, and its value for writing instruction and for learning.

In this chapter we will share with you some of the routines, rituals, and processes that we think are important for developing memoirists in our classes and the ways in which those processes promote quality instruction and learning in the studio writing classroom.

First Steps: Establishing Routines and Rituals in the Studio Classroom

Billy Collins hints at a writer's ritual when he writes tongue-in-cheek in his poem, "Advice to Writers," that you may scrub your house all night and even go outside to scrub nature, but that when you return home, you'll select a sharp pencil and write sentences "like long rows of devoted ants. . ."

Similarly, Donald Hall offers his daily ritual in his book *Life's Work:* "The best day begins with waking early—I check the clock: damn! It's only 3:00 AM—because I want so much to get out of bed and start working. Usually something particular beckons so joyously—like a poem that I have good hope for, that seems to go so well. . . . I feel the work-excitement building, joy-pressure mounting—until I need to resist it no more but sit at the desk and open the folder that holds the day's beginning, its desire and its hope."

These authors approach their writing work with anticipation and hope. They are comfortable in their habits and confidant in their work rituals. Just as professional writers generally establish a working routine (write every day from 9:00 a.m. to noon, for example) and have rituals that they follow for writing (sharpen every pencil available before sitting down to the computer to write, for example, as our friend Tom Liner used to do), so too do students working in the studio classroom need to establish some familiar work patterns. These familiar patterns—what we call routines and rituals—help students to know what to expect in your classroom and help them to work epistemically, to work as do real writers and to develop the habits of mind that assist published writers.

As the teacher, you will want to establish the initial routines and rituals for writing in your classroom. You have a vision of how you want students to work in your classroom. You have some values in mind and a working design for how the class ought to proceed. Develop a framework of ritual activities and familiar routines for approaching the writing work: We always share our writings in groups on Thursday, or we always read and discuss excerpts from professional writers on Mondays. Spend time teaching those rituals to students. They will appreciate your predictable structures and quickly adjust to the routines and rituals that you put into place in your classroom. We offer the following guidelines to help you design an appropriate instructional infrastructure that will not only represent what you value in your classroom but also signal to students the practices you believe to be essential to their success in the studio classroom:

1. *Consider your values for the studio writing classroom.* Return to our discussion of the values of the studio classroom in Chapter 2 to see which of our values

fit well with your thinking about how to orchestrate instruction. List your values in priority order.

2. *Consider the writing activities that you want to instantiate into the daily occurrence of your classroom.* Think about the use of journals, Writer's Notebooks, literature selections, reading processes, writing processes, genre studies, minilessons, response groups, publishing students' written products, partner work, conferences, celebration of success in writing and learning, and other activities that come to mind. Then, select activities that match well with your values. For example, if you value highly student practice with writing, you may want to use journals and plan for some type of daily writing to ensure that students receive sufficient practice with their composing. Make a comprehensive list, pairing the activity with its value to writers.

3. *Consider how much time each activity will take.* For example, will you devote an entire instructional period to response groups, half of a period, or divide the class so that one-half of the students are in response groups while the other half of the students are in conferences with you?

4. *Consider how often you will engage in each activity.* For example, will every Monday be devoted to publishing and celebrating the gems and nuggets from the previous week's drafts? Will every Friday be devoted to Writer's Groups? Will you begin every day with a minilesson based on difficulties that students are exhibiting in their drafts? Will students read and write every day? Will students submit a draft to you weekly for your response?

5. *Draft a chart on which you plan out several days' or weeks' worth of the rituals and routines that you want to instantiate in your class.* Don't worry right now about the specific content of the lessons. You know that, for now, we're focusing on memoir and that the specifics of the content will come as you continue to read this book and develop your own ideas. What matters at this point is to establish routines and rituals that will suit almost any literacy content that you are teaching, with only minor adjustments. What appear to be the flaws in your design? What seems to be working in your design? Be as specific as possible.

6. *Consider standards.* Which standards will you be able to meet as you institute the writing studio as a vehicle for your students' learning? Consider district goals and objectives, state standards, and national standards. You may be surprised at how many standards the studio-classroom methodology will assist you in meeting within the context of authentic instruction. No longer will you have to labor to contort your content to fit standards because authentic literacy activities naturally adhere to most published standards.

7. *Consider evaluation.* We discuss our ideas for evaluation of writing in the studio extensively in Chapters 10 and 11, but do some thinking on your own now about grades and grading. How often will you grade writing? How can you use tools like the portfolio and the Writer's Notebook to assist you in the sometimes monumental task of evaluation?

8. *Consider state- and/or district-mandated testing.* What types of writing are required on your district and/or state test? How will the writing activities that you have planned for use in your studio classroom help to foster students' authentic understanding of literacy and of written forms of expression? We are *not* advocates of teaching to the test. We are, however, realists who understand that such tests are often the tail wagging the instructional dog. What we have found is that students who are engaged in authentic composing and reading activities that focus on meaning, as we do in the studio classroom, improve their ability to write and to make meaning in genuine ways, which, in turn, helps them to perform well on mandated tests.[1]

As you read this book, you will discover the routines and rituals that we typically incorporate into our writing classrooms, all of which are influenced by our experience of what works for our students and for us, and by our values as writers and as teachers ourselves. Once you write down your ideas about routines and rituals in a format—such as a chart or a list—that you can easily use as a reference, then you are ready to situate into your daily instruction in the studio classroom the activities associated with the vital writers' tasks of drafting, revising, and going public with writing.

Drafting the Memoir Pieces

First draft, rough draft, zero draft, freewriting, getting started—drafting goes by many names in the professional literature about writing processes. We're betting that you're already familiar with writing processes, that you have the posters hanging on your classroom's walls, that you took the pledge and gave your heart to writing-process pedagogy long ago. (If not, check out some of the many books on promoting writing processes in your classroom, including *Inside Out, Third Edition* by Kirby, Latta Kirby, and Liner, which contains information as well as a resources chapter.) So, how is drafting unique in the studio writing classroom?

1. *Drafting happens several times a week in the studio writing classroom.* Too often, in conventional English classes, students write one draft for a piece every two weeks or so. Worse yet, they write a draft one day and turn it in the next as though it were the finished product, thus diminishing the role of the draft in writing and blurring the distinctions between *draft* and *finished product*. In the studio, practice is one of our highest values. Writing needs to occur often and students need to try out new drafts, however sketchy, each week.

2. *Students need to write to see what they think and what they have to say.* How do I know what I think until I see it in writing? Even now, as we write this chapter, we are finding the just-right words and expressing our ideas in unique ways that we've not used before to write about the importance of drafting as a process of writing. The draft lets student writers get ideas down onto the page, look at them, and see if they still agree with what they said they thought.

3. *Writing needs time to gel, to rest, to simmer in the writer's mind.* Most students' drafts need to be composed and then set aside without much attention for a while. (Unless of course the draft has so engaged writers that they just can't quit working on it.) But writers can't afford to be idle; just ask any professional writer. Most professionals talk about their established routines and times for writing. That is part of the *work* and *habit* and *discipline* of the writer. If we are to write every day, then that means that some days we compose new pieces, and some days we return to previous drafts, choosing one or two to rework.

4. *Students write in class often, working with an idea to which they've just been introduced.* The written pieces are thus fresh. But they also read like drafts, not like finished products. That's fine for now, but later we'll need to revise the ones that matter to us, the ones about which we care enough to get just right.

5. *As writers accumulate multiple drafts, they are creating a body of work, an artist's repertoire, from which they can draw pieces for further work.* Remember that part of the essential work of drafting multiple Spider Pieces is to look for the *hook* or *anchor piece* around which to weave the entire final memoir. In order to weave together the entire memoir, with all of its attendant Spider Pieces, the writer continually and actively searches for the thread, the touchstone, the motif, the commonalities, the metaphor that will hold those pieces together as a unified literary work. We suggest encouraging your students to use a Writer's Notebook to hold all of their drafts. In the Writer's Notebook they have all of their writing in one easily accessible location. Student writers can readily search through all of their drafts, even the ones that they didn't think held much promise, looking for the metaphors, threads, motifs, and commonalities that will help unify their final memoirs. Those commonalities aren't always immediately apparent, so having a body of work and a Writer's Notebook to hold it will assist in this process of discovering the meaning in the works.

6. *Drafting, in the studio classroom, does not happen in a void.* We pair drafting with our reading of professional exemplars to spark the student writers' imaginations, to give them fresh ideas or a sense of how a piece might sound, how it might be organized, and what types of details and images might resonate with readers.

7. *Drafting, in the writing studio, is part of a social and communal learning process.* After we have produced a draft, we share it with our Writer's Group to see what ideas they have about the piece and if their responses match our intentions as writers. We learn to rely on feedback and suggestions from our group members. We get a sense of whether the piece is worthy of further work, and we gather ideas for a revising and redrafting effort.

Revising the Memoir Pieces

The notion of authentic revising—that is, of seeing a piece of writing with fresh eyes, forming fresh ideas for how to improve and enliven it—hence the word *re-vision*—is important for student writers because the writers in our classes need to understand two important points: (1) Writing takes time, effort, and work; and (2) Final written products do not spring whole and perfect from writers' heads when writers first sit down to write. When inexperienced writers read a published work, many think that the published version was the first and last version of the text. Our developing writers need to experience firsthand the challenges of moving from initial drafts to polished pieces.

In recent years, professional authors have been more willing to be open about their struggles to produce texts. We like to read to students pieces in which published authors discuss their difficulties with writing, the various drafts and revising efforts that a piece underwent before final product, and the ways in which the initial written pieces evolved over time with consistent and determined revising work by the author. One fine source for such excerpts is Zinsser's (1998) *Inventing the Truth* in which he interviews authors of memoir about their processes and ideas for writing that eventually produced their published texts.

Once students have seen that even professional, published writers draft and revise extensively, perhaps they, too, will come to value working with their own writing over time, putting the effort into the pieces that matter so that their revision efforts allow a piece of writing to emerge from draft to finished product.

Over the years of reading and writing about revision as one of the many composing processes and of watching what our students do as they work on their texts, we have delineated several Revision Behaviors associated with the process that most people generally refer to as *revision*. Take a look at Figure 5–1 for an overview of these behaviors.

Too often, students focus on the lower-order Revision Behaviors and claim to have revised their writings. Our job as coaches of writing, however, is to help students focus on the higher-order behaviors, the ones that we see as authentic revision processes. We coach primarily by asking the writer questions: How can you *show* this powerful relationship with your mother? Why is this detail important? What happened before/after this incident? Where do you want to go next with this piece? Revision is not a quick, down-and-dirty process, easily learned and quickly accomplished. Initially, it is probably best done in class under our supervision and coaching. That makes teaching students how to revise well a labor-intensive effort. Revision is integral to successful writing, highly complex in its most sophisticated forms, occurring both during drafting and after achieving a decent draft worthy of more effort. Most important, revision is something that inexperienced writers can be taught to do.

In the studio classroom, Revision Behaviors occur with first drafts, in subsequent versions of those drafts, and later when students are working on their final memoir piece. As we read and discuss published memoir exemplars (see examples in Chapters 3 and 4), we try to help students read with a writer's lens to discover the techniques that these published writers employ. Then, students attempt those specific techniques while drafting their own memoirs. After they have achieved a draft, they review the piece and take it to their Writer's Groups to see if they have been able to utilize the techniques of the published authors in their own writing, revising as needed to heighten their implementation of those techniques.

REVISION BEHAVIORS OF WRITERS

Higher-order Revision Behaviors include the following:

Behavior	When	What
FORMING and FINDING	Ongoing throughout writing processes	· Sorting and resorting · Focusing and narrowing · Changing lenses · Discovering · Inventing
TRANSLATING and TRANSCRIBING	In-process during drafting	· Moving ideas from head to page · Selecting in the head and on the page · Moving from inner speech to written language · Getting ideas down onto the page in order to work with them later
ELABORATING	After writing the first draft	· Telling it all · Adding: details, dialogue, vivid verbs, etc. · Finishing the story · Fleshing it out · More, more, more
REVISING	After writing a rich draft, one that holds promise	· Seeing the writing again with new eyes · Telling my story my way · Cutting unnecessary stuff · Making and clarifying my point · Writer-directed; writing like a reader
Lower-order Revision Behaviors include the following:		
EDITING	After drafting	· Crafting, shaping · Giving the piece of writing an *authored* look · Reader-directed; reading like a writer
PROOFREADING	Last step before pronouncing the written piece as *finished*	· Looking across the surface of the written piece at cosmetics · Conforming to standard conventions for punctuation, mechanics, usage, etc. · The final touch

Figure 5–1. *Revision Behaviors of Writers*

In preparing students to draft the Snapshot Piece, for example (see Chapter 4), we develop a minilesson in which we emphasize several techniques that Huggan employs in her *Elizabeth Stories* excerpt. We look at that piece together as a class and purposefully notice and point to explicit features, including the following:

- Immediacy of the experience: How does the author achieve that?
- Use of precise details: Point to some. (A song playing in the background, for example.)
- Use of the present progressive tense: That tense helps to draw the reader into the experience of the piece. Point to its use in the text.
- Hints at relationship: The narrator, even as a child, calls her parents by their first names, states that she is not used to embraces from her mother, and wonders what her parents have in common. What do those small scenes suggest about her relationship with her parents? How can you give hints in your writing rather than just telling the reader stuff?

As students draft their Snapshot Pieces, they try out these techniques in their writing. When they take this piece to their Writer's Groups, they may focus primarily on the story and the telling of the story, but can also focus on how well these techniques play out in their writing. When they revise the draft, they may return to the Huggan excerpt to study her technique and then try anew to integrate those features into their writing. Clearly, when the work is going well, reading, discussing, thinking, drafting, and revising processes intertwine in a recursive manner, allowing the writer to move forward and backward toward the creation of a "meaning-full" text.

In addition to focusing on Crafting Options (see pages 70–74 and Figure 5–4) during the processes of revision, writers in the studio classroom are also actively searching for the threads, connections, and commonalities among their pieces, crafting their pieces to heighten those *hooks* or *anchor pieces* as they discover them. Thus, the ideas that will resonate in their finished memoirs begin to emerge during students' reading, thinking, drafting, and revising processes.

Strategies for Revising Memoir

Within the studio classroom, revising constitutes much of the work of writing. Once students have an idea and have decided to run with it, their drafts need considerable higher-order work, even if they rather like what they have already produced. The concept of revising even the pieces that are pretty darn good from the outset is one for which many students will need some encouragement to incorporate into their values as writers.

REVISION FEATURES CHECKLIST

The first revision behavior in which we engage our students after they have produced a draft is to consider a checklist of features relevant to that particular Spider Piece. We derive these features by studying the techniques used by the published writers of our exemplar pieces as we demonstrated in the Huggan piece earlier. Students then examine these checklists individually, discussing them with their Writer's Group, looking for revisions with which they might experiment in their drafted Spider Pieces.

For example, let's say that a student has just drafted a Spider Piece about a special or significant place. (See Figure 3–3 in Chapter 3 to review the possible Spider Pieces.) Perhaps among their exemplar readings, students have read the excerpt by Ellen Gilchrist about her home (see Chapter 4 for the excerpt), and they have written about a place that holds significant memories of a specific time, particular people, and precise events that occurred in that place. The student writer likes his first draft and wants to work on it more. That's when your work as writing coach and the Revision Options (see Figure 5–2) come in. If you find that you have not anticipated the precise Revision Options that interest the student and/or that suit his exact piece, don't worry; you don't have to lose this teachable moment. Work with the Revision Options that do fit the piece and then invent a just-in-time minilesson overnight to respond to what that student writer needs at the moment. Chances are, if this just-in-time technique will work for one student writer, it will also meet the needs of another student writer—maybe even *before* another writer anticipates the need. As you continue to develop these just-in-time minilessons, your own repertoire of revision strategies and prepared minilessons will expand, and you will soon have an entire inventory of them from which to draw as you teach.

You might also take to class a first draft of your own writing and use the following Revision Options checklist (see Figure 5–2) to point to places in your draft where such strategies would make the piece more powerful. Teacher's Hint: Write your draft strategically by leaving some places in your draft where these strategies might fit. Let students learn by doing as they *help* you to make your piece better.

When we teach in this manner, we find that our students become actively involved in higher-order revising, learn specific strategies, and learn to apply them to their own and others' writing. To aid this writerly development, we create a Spider Piece–specific guide for revising that incorporates techniques important to that particular type of writing. For the Place Piece, we work with a checklist such as the one in Figure 5–2 to guide students' revisions at this stage of their writing processes.

Revision Through Elaboration

The second Revision Behavior in which we engage students after they have produced a draft that they think may have potential (and not all drafts fit into that category) is that of Elaboration. Elaboration basically involves *adding more*: more detail, more dialogue, more of the interior thoughts of the characters involved in the story being told, and more information about the people and places involved in the story. We find that inexperienced writers often write the first version of a story or event too quickly. They have the *We just want to be done* mentality, so they dash through the writing, hitting only the basics. The draft needs . . . more. Elaboration is a process of returning to the piece in order to tell the *whole* story or event, leaving out nothing significant, drawing the reader into the story, and starting at the beginning and not stopping until the end.

Checklist of Revision Options for the Place Spider Piece

<u>**Directions:**</u> Review your Place Spider Piece to see where you may revise your
piece using some of the options below.

· **INTENSIFIED IMAGES:** Find chunks of description in your piece that
can be sharpened by adding sensory detail. Work with light, temperature,
and sounds. Let us feel it and see it.

· **TELLING STORIES:** Deepen your descriptions by extending the narrative. Tell the history of the place. Connect yourself to it.

· **LENS CHANGING:** Shift between *up close* and *far away* lenses. (1) Once
you have written about the up close details of the place, widen your lens and
look farther away—around the curve in the road, beyond the backyard,
between this place and three blocks in every direction. (2) Return to your
close focus of the place and add in important, specific details: a porch swing
where people sat, a kitchen table, a piano, a dirty window with lace curtains.

· **CHARACTER STUFFING:** Few places remain devoid of people.
Populate your place with some of the people found there. At what times
of day are they there? What do they do there? Focus on specific details
such as their posture, clothing, facial expressions, and skin.

· **EMOTIONAL HOLDS OF THE PLACE:** Why is this place so special
to you? Does it offer emotional calm, spiritual ease, or a transformation of
mind when you're there? Why does this place have such a hold on you?
Be subtle. Help the reader to understand what is special about the place
through your descriptions and details.

Figure 5–2. *Checklist of Revision Options for the Place Spider Piece*

Elaboration can occur for the revision of an individual Spider Piece. It can also
occur more globally once the writer has identified the three or four (more or less)
Spider Pieces that he will weave together for the final memoir.

In order to help students with Elaboration strategies, we consider what precisely it is
that quality memoirs contain, and then we encourage students to add those sorts of
details and information to their writing. Figure 5–3 is a handout that we use with our students to guide their Elaborations. This concept of elaborating writing applies well to any
type of writing. We try to select the specific Elaborations that match the kind of writing
on which the student is working. Consider these Elaborations for memoir writing:

Elaboration Strategies for Memoir

<u>Directions</u>: Begin this process by working alone to mark your own draft; then, read your piece of writing aloud to your Writer's Group and see what they think you can add to your draft.

Write directly on your draft, indicating where and the types of Elaborations that you might add to your draft.

Try at least *two* Elaborations. The idea for now is that more is better.

Label your Elaborations and put a copy of your labeled and expanded draft in your Writer's Notebook.

PEOPLE DETAILS: Have the people in your piece of writing come to life by giving the reader more detail. How is she dressed? How does she smell? Describe her smile and eyes. How does he walk: strolling, swaggering, or loping along? Give the reader additional sentences and phrases that make these people come to life and exist in the reader's mind.

CONVERSATIONS: Let us hear what your characters have to say. Try showing feelings, personality, and emotions by using conversation. Try to capture their personality by choosing the precise words they would say. You can correct punctuation later, if necessary, or consider using some of the avant-garde–style conversation formats as found in several of our professional exemplars.

PLACE DETAILS: Develop several scenes and locations in your piece in greater detail by adding phrases and sentences that help readers to picture the place. When you close your eyes and picture the place, what do you see? Use those pictures to add the details readers need to envision the places in your memory.

INSIDE/OUTSIDE INFORMATION: *Inside* information consists of thoughts, feelings, and emotions—the private stuff that we all keep in our heads but may not say aloud. *Outside* information consists of details that you can see around you, conversations that you can hear, the setting, and all of the stuff in the external world. Work to balance and to shuttle between the *inside* stuff with the *outside* stuff.

TELL IT ALL: What else you know about this memory? Ask yourself, "What happened next?" Tell the whole memory. Fill in the rushed places in the story. Start at the end of your piece and keep writing to tell it all, right to the end.

Figure 5–3. *Elaboration Strategies for Memoir*[2]

Once students have engaged in this type of revision, discuss with them the ways in which they are re-seeing their writing and engaging in higher-order revision strategies well beyond merely fixing the commas.

Revision Through Crafting

The third type of Revision Behavior that we structure for students is that of Crafting. Like the Elaboration Strategies, Crafting Options can be used to revise an individual Spider Piece that seems to be worthy of intensive work and revision. Crafting Options can also be applied more globally to the final memoir piece.

After student writers have worked their options for Elaboration to the maximum, we encourage them to refine their pieces further through *Crafting*. We know that good writing is often *crafted*—worked on extensively without having that *worked on* look. We tell our writers that Crafting consists of working deliberately with the reader in mind. The successful writer spends a good deal of time finding just the right word or image to invoke a particular feeling in the reader. The good writer works and reworks a scene or a critical moment in a piece so that it draws the reader in.

Crafting Options can be developed for all types of writing. We encourage you to analyze carefully professional examples of any piece of writing you ask students to compose. Identify the key features of that writing, and note where inexperienced writers are likely to need revision practice to create successful pieces. Then, construct your own Elaboration Options and Crafting Options handouts for each type of piece. We have delineated these particular strategies specifically for memoir pieces based on our study and reading of professional memoirs.

Some of the most difficult parts of writing well include producing enticing *beginnings* and satisfying *endings*. Students also need to work at this level with pacing, sentence structure, organization, and word choices. In order to help them do so, we begin with minilessons on techniques for writing beginnings and endings. Our objective in these minilessons is to have some fun with our writers and to encourage them to experiment and try out possibilities.

BEGINNINGS MINILESSON

Begin the Beginnings minilesson by asking students to take out drafts of several different Spider Pieces. We generally ask for volunteers to read the opening paragraph to their drafts. We tell our students that listeners' responses will indicate to them how well their beginning is going at this point.

Teacher's Hint: If you are teaching seventh grade and have created a positive studio atmosphere, 90 percent of the kids will raise their hands. If you're teaching tenth grade, no matter how positive your class environment is, only two kids may reluctantly volunteer. We go with what we get and find that the lively discussion and specific revision work generally draw in many of the reluctant students.

Because you prepare for every eventuality—such as reluctant student volunteers—you also have several samples of your own Spider Pieces cleverly written somewhat poorly so that, again, students can *help* you improve them. If necessary, start with your own writing, modeling how this teaching and revising work will go, and showing students that this is a low-threat, helpful activity.

We take students through five or six possible optional beginnings, such as these:

The Hook   This option is a standard newspaper technique. The writer tries to create reader interest immediately, perhaps by offering partial information or by creating a mini-mystery: "I should have known Mrs. Swartz hated kids." The sentences following that opening line add to the mystery: "She had **Keep Out!**, **Beware of Mean Dog**, and **This means YOU!** signs posted everywhere." Of course, when writers use The Hook to get readers interested, they have to deliver a good story.

Scene-Setting   This is your basic narrative technique. The writer creates a picture for the reader, puts the reader there, creates a mood, or sets the atmosphere. The writer must use specific details to pull off this opening. Remember when Snoopy was writing his novel, he never got past the first line: "It was a dark and stormy night."

Telling Detail   Sometimes a single unique detail can draw the reader into a much larger story. We often get the "When I fell off my bike and hurt myself real bad" story from middle school kids. High school writers tell much more graphic and hair-raising car wreck stories. Many of them begin in formulaic and trite ways. We encourage writers to replay the scene and review again what they remember. One seventh grader said, "I remember that they brought my tennis shoe to me in the hospital." "Ah ha!" say we. "Picture this: After they carted you off to the hospital, your tennis shoe lay on the pavement."

Character Throwing   We love this opening. We ask kids to try opening their pieces without exposition of any kind. Just throw a character at the reader. "Teddy Howland was the skinniest, ugliest kid in Eureka. His arms were too long, his legs were too long, and his eyes stuck out like lightbulbs. His Adam's apple looked like someone had glued a tennis ball to his neck. His squeaky, high voice sounded as if it belonged to a third-grade girl more than an eighth-grade guy. Teddy Howland was a freak of nature, but his parents bought him every new toy in the world. Teddy was my best friend."

Walking   This is another no exposition, no speechifying, no telling beginning. Student writers have a proclivity for giving speeches at the beginning of narrative pieces. They love to tell readers what they are going to say with explanations such as, "In a moment I will be telling a terrifying story of how difficult it was for me to get a dog. See, my father was deathly opposed the idea, but my mother was kind of okay with it. Anyway, as you will see in my story, I finally got the dog after a lot of trouble." To remedy such bad habits, we tell our kids just to walk right into the middle of the story in the first line. If possible tell the gist of the whole story in the first line. Don't hem and haw. Don't dawdle around. Just lay it out. Here's an example: "Giving credit where credit is due, if it hadn't been for my mother, I never would have gotten him in the first place mainly because my father didn't like dogs." (That line, by the way, is from an old favorite of ours, *The Temple of Gold*, by William Goldman.) Notice that these Walking openings are often sentences that are informative, yet a bit mysterious, and somewhat gangly. That technique is part of their charm.

Dialogue Few student writers think to begin narratives without exposition by dropping the reader into a conversation that is already underway. This technique essentially invites the reader to eavesdrop, a favorite pastime of Dan and of many writers who are always on the lookout for quality, real-life dialogue. As an example of this technique, we set up the proposition that sometimes first dates are awkward and a bit tense. In writing about such a time, the writer doesn't need to explain that point; instead, the writer can show it with a dialogue that also draws the reader into the piece. The exposition that the writer wants to use to begin the piece occurs, in effect, in the writer's head, allowing the written opening to be immediate and enticing for the reader. We use a dialogue like the following to demonstrate how to begin a piece with conversation *sans* exposition:

"I'm not sure I even like you."

"I'm not particularly crazy about you, either, now that I think about it."

"Fine. So, how in the world did we end up on our first date ever, in the back seat of this stretch limo, on our way to the Prom?"

"I think it's Shannon's fault. She told me in Chemistry class that you secretly liked me and wanted me to ask you out."

"Shannon is an unreliable narrator."

We may continue to work on various beginnings for quite a while as students draft individual Spider Pieces. We engage in the same types of activities for teaching *endings* strategies. Then, when students are working on pulling together their final memoirs (see Chapter 6), we return to these techniques, asking students to view their memoir writings more globally and to craft them carefully. It is at this point that we consolidate the various Crafting Options, such as *beginnings* strategies, into a concise handout as a guide for final revisions. Here in Figure 5–4 is a sample of one such handout of Crafting Options for Memoir that we use with our students to offer ideas for their revising efforts.

Once students have engaged in these revision strategies, perhaps needing to perform several of them, and more than once, to hone their writing, they are well on their way to having more polished papers.

When student writers feel that their memoirs are approaching completion—and only then, for the most part—they will be ready to engage in the lower-order Revision Behaviors shown in Figure 5–1. One way of focusing on the lower-order behavior of proofreading the pieces—to locate common surface errors that students have in their writing—is through the use of minilessons in which you take five to ten minutes daily to review with students ways to correct the mistakes they are making, such as appropriate apostrophe use; the differences among common homonyms such as *its* and *it's* and *there*, *their*, and *they're*; subject-verb agreement; and the like. We firmly ground these minilessons of common errors within the context of the students' writing, teaching minilessons on *only* those errors that students are actually making. Students can remember only so much information at any one time. Offering a smorgasbord of minilessons on all possible surface errors may just addle students who are trying to get control of their specific mistakes. If all students in a class have, for example, flawless subject-verb agreement in their written works (we can always dream . . .), then we don't conduct a minilesson on that skill, focusing our valuable instructional time instead on the errors that *are* occurring in their writing.

Another way to focus communally on the lower-level editing and proofreading concerns of students' pieces is to work in Writer's Groups to seek and destroy the errors. Dawn has had good success with rotating papers around all of the members of a Writer's Group. Each member of the group selects a colored pencil and signs the top of the paper with that colored pencil; then the student writes with that colored pencil directly on the paper when it comes to her. This way, the author knows who made which corrections.

The first time students read a paper, they look for needed corrections in a specific common error such as apostrophes; we select the error for which students should look based on difficulties they have exhibited in their writing. Every group member reads every paper, looking only for apostrophe (or whatever we have selected) errors the first time. The second time, group members read every paper, looking for a more global feature such as sentence variety, paying attention to pacing and balance between short, quick sentences and longer, slower sentences; they may also look for sentences that are too choppy or so long that they are confusing. Again, we select a problem area with which students seem to be having difficulties. We focus on just a few (two to four) errors that students should seek out. Naturally, not all of the suggested "corrections" will be correct, but this activity then provides an opportunity for small-group discussion of the suggestions, with students looking up rules and uses in their grammar handbooks. This method does far more to help students learn such rules than mere lecture or having the teacher mark papers to death in red ink.

After this entire revision process, using both higher- and lower-order strategies, students should be able to see a pronounced difference and improvement in their written products from first draft to finished product.

Teacher's Hint: We understand that you need to give grades—and lots of them—daily and weekly, and for minor and major assignments. This requirement of massive grade-generation in schools does *not* in any way necessitate that you move prematurely to a so-called finished product. Such rushed writing is rarely the student's best work, nor is it reflective of your best teaching abilities. Instead, we find that working deliberately on various Revision Behaviors yields numerous products that can, in turn, yield individual grades. Grading is a stipulation of schooling, not the raison d'être of our teaching. We are teachers who want our students to learn to write well; we are teachers who grade because we must. The two do not have to be contradictory and exclusive behaviors.

Crafting Options for Memoir

<u>Directions</u>: Now it's time to work like an artist to craft your writing by making deliberate changes in your memoir piece. Work to enhance the reader's response to your piece.

This is the tough part. You have to work alone, and you won't always know what you're doing. Begin first with chunks, pieces of text that are several sentences long. Then, you'll do some sentence- and word-level work.

Write directly on your draft, indicating where and the types of Crafting Options that you might add to your draft. Or, use sticky notes. Or, use different colors of ink, or change your font to note your revisions.

Try at least *two* Crafting Options.

Label your Crafting choices and put a copy of your labeled and revised draft in your Writer's Notebook.

Beginnings (try at least two)

1. The Hook: "I should have known Mrs. Swartz hated kids."
2. Scene setting: "It was a dark and stormy night."
3. Telling detail: "There on the pavement was a small child's tennis shoe."
4. Character throwing: "Teddy Howland was the skinniest, ugliest kid in Eureka."
5. Walking: "Giving credit where credit is due, if it hadn't been for my mother, I never would have gotten him in the first place, mainly because my father didn't like dogs" (Goldman 2001).
6. Dialogue: "I'm not even sure I like you."

Endings (try at least two)

1. Circle: End where you began.
2. Ah ha!: Sadder but wiser, or gee, look what I learned.
3. A feeling: Stuck in Mobile with the Memphis blues again.
4. Drawstring: "And that's how it happened."
5. Surprise: The strange twist at the end.

Moving Chunks (no limit; cut and paste)

1. Movement: Pacing readers, making them play your game.
2. Paragraphs: Have some. Keep them short unless they have pictures.
3. Scenes: Shuffling the story.

Figure 5–4. *Crafting Options for Memoir*[2]

Deleting Chunks (no limit; follow rules)

1. Nice but doesn't fit. Save it.
2. Not nice and doesn't fit either. Cut it.
3. Eradicate chaff words: "-ly" words, "being" words.
4. Compact and compress. Cut the "telling."
5. Now that the hard part is done, turn to some relaxing sentence-level revisions. Make at least ten specific changes.

Sentence Level

1. Concrete detail. Add sensory stuff.
2. Specificity. Name stuff.
3. Strong verbs. Get rid of those adverb props.
4. Search and destroy the *is*'s and *was*'s.
5. Cure a serious case of the *would*'s.

Figure 5–4. *Continued*

Using Effective Writer's Groups

In addition to the Drafting and Revision Behaviors discussed previously, we find that having our students work closely in Writer's Groups also hones their composing eyes and ears to what their written products need in order to become more audience aware and therefore less egocentric, helping our student writers to move toward polished, crafted, and finished pieces. Our students meet in Writer's Groups once every week or two, depending on the stage of writing in which we find ourselves. In the studio classroom, the use of Writer's Groups helps to build the social and communal aspects of work that support all artists, including writers. Too often, the general public still retains the notion that writers are rather weird folks who write alone in a dark garret. Some writers might still fit this stereotype, but the writers we know often participate in self-initiated formal or informal Writer's Groups, sharing their drafts, receiving feedback, garnering support for the trials and triumphs of living the writing life. This social aspect of writing is part of what keeps writers grounded in the real world with the ability to write for real audiences. In our classrooms, we value response groups for both literature and writing, and we use them frequently.[3]

As you are thinking about how to incorporate Writer's Groups in your classroom with your students, consider our Principles for Developing Effective Writing Response Groups, shown in Figure 5–5.

Principles for Developing Effective Writing Response Groups[4]

Consider the following principles as you think about using effective Writer's Groups in your classroom with your students:

1. **The teacher's response to students writing establishes the ground rules for the responses of all others.** Your appropriate modeling is the key to effective response groups. Whether orally or in writing, how you handle the words of your students will signal to your students how they are to talk and respond to each other's writings.

2. **Establish a "no hunting" rule for your responses and enforce that rule for students' responses to writing.** The rule basically means no cheap shots at writers as they try to express their ideas. Avoiding judgmental and unkind remarks toward writers must be a value in an effective response group. Similarly, gratuitous and insincere or inaccurate comments about student writing are not helpful.

3. **Appropriate response generally begins by trying to understand what the writer is trying to say.** Summarizing the piece or restating what seems to be the message of the piece of writing lets the writer listen to what the audience has made of the piece. Talk about the piece as a whole. Try specific comments such as, "I like the order of events," or "I like the way you wrap this piece up."

4. **Finding things to like in the piece is important.** Point very specifically to features of the piece that work. Try specific comments such as, "I like this opening," or "I like this verb right here." Point out where you think the piece is going well. Try comments such as, "I like the voice in this passage," or "Nice transition here." Writers need to know what they are doing well in order to keep doing it.

5. **A suggestion for how the writer can elaborate on what is already written is probably one of the most helpful responding postures.** Rather than suggesting that the writer make changes or correct errors, find places in the piece that have potential for more development. Through a series of questions to the writer, draw out elaboration possibilities. Try questions such as, "What happens next?" or "What additional details can you add to the story?" Try comments such as, "I'd like to see and hear more about this character," or "I'd like to hear more about this part here."

6. **As a reader, try musing aloud.** When the writer hears what his audience is wondering about based on a reading of his piece, he begins to see points for elaboration, clarification, and further amplification. Try

Figure 5–5. *Principles for Developing Effective Writing Response Groups*

thinking aloud comments that begin with "I wonder . . . ," "What if . . . ," "If this were my piece of writing, I might . . . ," and "I notice . . . ."

7. **Question the writer about what he or she plans to do next with the piece of writing.** The writer will need to decide if he plans to work more on a draft or just file it in his Writer's Notebook for a while. In order to help clarify such plans and decision-making processes, try questions such as, "What will you work on next?" "Where do you see this piece going from here?" and "How is this piece related to other pieces that you have written?"

8. **Give the writer the chance to ask questions of the response group.** The writer will no doubt want to clarify response comments and to ask advice and counsel about revising the piece when he returns to work on it. The questions that the writer asks can be prepared in advance based on what the writer wants to be sure to find out about the piece. Spontaneous questions will also arise and should be pursued. Model for writers how asking genuine questions is far different, however, from seeking false praise from the response group. That is, "I'm concerned about my opening. What can I do to draw the reader into the piece right from the start?" is far different from "I like my opening. Don't you?"

9. **Always focus on the piece, not on the writer.** It is easy to be sidetracked by the emotional content of the piece of writing, especially with memoir writing, which often delves into personal challenges and moments of revelation as experienced by the writer. Avoid the temptation to be too sympathetic or to become the psychoanalyst, priest, or rabbi. Continue to focus on *how* the experience is rendered rather than on the experience itself. Rather than a comment such as, "Oh, how did you feel when your mother told you she had breast cancer?" try "This is an emotional moment when your mother tells you she has breast cancer. How will you capture that emotion in your writing? Maybe though dialogue?"

Figure 5–5. *Continued*

After you have internalized these principles and others that you may want to have as a feature of response group work with your students, try modeling a Writer's Group in front of your students. We call this technique the *fishbowl* methodology because you and one carefully selected, not too shy, not easily intimidated student will conduct a simulated response session in front of the class. The student will present a piece of writing to you for your response, and you'll model the principles for appropriate responding as you, in fact, respond to the student's piece of writing. As the remainder of the students in class hear the types of questions that you ask and the ways in which you respond to the paper, they will begin to see the principles in action. Be sure to conduct a debriefing discussion with students after the simulated response group session in order to highlight the ways in which the two of you interacted and the ways in which you responded gently but specifically to the writing at hand. This activity not only models behaviors for students but also provides an opportunity to learn inductively.

Just as you will need to think carefully about how to model and enact Writer's Groups in your classes with your students, the student writers themselves will need some guidelines for operating effectively within the community of writers. For the first Writer's Group session in a class, we often give students a set of principles for their interactions as an ongoing group. At the beginning of each Writer's Group session, we display these on an overhead or post them on our classroom wall so that they serve as reminders for appropriate behavior. See Figure 5–6 for a sample of the guidelines we use for students' response groups.

Discussion Guidelines for Writer's Group Responses

1. No apologies and no whining. Forget telling your group about how you had too little time to work on this piece for it to be any good. Suspend the belief that "To love me is to love my writing."

2. Read your piece of writing aloud to your Writer's Group. Group members, take notes as you read along on your copy of the writer's piece. Note what you like in the piece, places in the piece that need clarifying, questions that you have about the piece, and so on.

3. After reading your piece aloud, put your hand over your mouth (if necessary). Don't talk. Take notes about your group's responses to your writing. You may answer any direct questions your group has for you. Don't apologize, whine, or make excuses.

4. Group members: Begin with positive statement such as, "I like the part about . . ." or "I like the way you described . . . ." Give specific responses. Avoid general praise such as, "That's good."

5. Group members: Give a specific suggestion, such as "I think I would be drawn into your piece of writing more if . . . ." All group members should offer a suggestion and a response to the piece of writing.

6. Ask questions of your group to clarify your understanding of their responses and to cover specific questions that you as the writer have about your piece. Make notes about your group members' responses to use as you revise this piece later.

7. Decide what you will do with this piece of writing: Work more on it, finish it, file it in your Writer's Notebook for now. . . .

Figure 5–6. *Discussion Guidelines for Writer's Group Responses*

We have good success with community-building and fostering students' learning through the use of Writer's Groups. Groups take patience to set up and initiate, but with careful modeling and your guidance throughout each working session with individual groups, Writer's Groups are an effective methodological tool.

These stages of drafting, revising, and sharing writing with a constructive audience in the form of Writer's Groups support the development of writing and the emergence of polished products. They embody the philosophies (epistemology, constructivism, and phenomenology) and the values of the studio classroom as discussed in Chapter 2. Once you have effective routines and rituals in place and students are focused on the work of writing, they are ready to move into the next stage of pulling together several of their Spicer Pieces into a final memoir. Techniques for doing so is the subject of the next chapter.

Notes

1. To read more on the subject of instruction and mandated testing, we recommend that you see two sources: Kirby, Dan, Dawn Latta Kirby, and Tom Liner. 2004. *Inside Out: Strategies for Teaching Writing.* 3rd ed. Portsmouth, NH: Heinemann. And, Kohn, Alfie. 2000. *The Schools Our Children Deserve: Moving Beyond Traditional Classrooms and "Tougher Standards."* New York: Mariner Books.

2. For additional information on Elaboration and Crafting Options, please see Kirby, Dan, Dawn Latta Kirby, and Tom Liner. 2004. *Inside Out: Strategies for Teaching Writing.* 3rd ed. Portsmouth, NH: Heinemann.

3. To read more on our specific suggestions for Writer's Groups in the English/language arts classroom, please see Kirby, Dan, Dawn Latta Kirby, and Tom Liner. 2004. *Inside Out: Strategies for Teaching Writing.* 3rd ed. Portsmouth, NH: Heinemann.

4. These principles also appear in Kirby, Dan, Dawn Latta Kirby, and Tom Liner. 2004. *Inside Out: Strategies for Teaching Writing.* 3rd ed. Portsmouth, NH: Heinemann.

Works Cited

Collins, Billy. 2002. "Advice to Writers." *Sailing Around the Room: New and Selected Poems.* New York: Random House.

Goldman, William. 1957; reissued and updated, 1985 and 2001. *The Temple of Gold.* New York: Ballantine.

Hall, Donald. 1993. *Life Work.* Boston: Beacon Press.

Kirby, Dan, Dawn Latta Kirby, and Tom Liner. 2004. *Inside Out: Strategies for Teaching Writing.* 3rd ed. Portsmouth, NH: Heinemann.

Zinsser, William, ed. 1998. *Inventing the Truth: The Art and Craft of Memoir.* Boston: Houghton Mifflin.

6

Finding a Scheme

As your students' portfolios and Writer's Notebooks fatten up with multiple drafts and their short, exploratory pieces, it is time to break the news to them that their writers' problems are about to become more complex. We usually break this news as gently as possible, something like this: "Okay, most of you have a collection of short pieces from your life experience: a name piece, maybe a boundaries piece, a parent piece, a place piece. So you're on your way to becoming a memoirist. But remember that a memoir is not a single story but a collection of stories with which the author somehow creates a coherent and compelling narrative." The class is silent. Not even a groan or a sigh. Just silence. "So your next big task in this journey toward a finished memoir is to begin to select from among the accumulated short pieces those that you may weave together into the final Memoir Piece." The room is still silent, but now it has become an uneasy, noisy quiet and their brains begin to churn.

As a teacher you have already been observing happenings in the studio classroom to assist this process. Your student writers already have some personal favorites and their Writer's Groups have given them a sense of which pieces are connecting with an audience, eliciting emotions and responses that spur the writer on to further drafts and revisions. They are also likely already sensing which people and places in their lives are appearing frequently in their writings, holding power and interest for them. They're also getting some insight from you as coach, and Studio Master, as you have begun to praise some of their pieces as worthy of more concentrated effort. This scheming business is partly writer's intuition at work. We encourage them to rely on their felt sense of what is working in their pieces and the extensive response and feedback they have received from other writers as they develop a *scheme* for melding their short pieces into a completed memoir.

What Is a Scheme?

This concept is one that Dan developed in order to help students make the challenging transition from short writings to a longer, coherent memoir. The idea of a *scheme* is relatively easy to explain to students and much more difficult for writers to orchestrate effectively. As in the classic art studios of Europe, students must assemble a collection of their short works into a coherent and artistically rendered composition. Or as one student said, still trying to figure out what Dan was asking of them, "You mean, stick 'em together with . . . transitions?" Well, something like that, but the problem is more interesting and discovery oriented than that. One of our favorite stories of how students understand the concept of scheme was when we were working with a group of second graders. We had given them our scheme spiel and many of them seemed to get it and began sorting through their portfolios to find favorite pieces that might work together. About ten minutes later a future engineer, no doubt, came over to where Dan was kneeling beside a student desk. The child had taken his three favorite pieces and taped them together in a long continuous piece. "See, I have a very looooong memoir."

We tell our students that a *scheme* is not a simple putting together of multiple pieces but rather the development of a *plan* or a *pattern* for how to connect shorter memory pieces. But a scheme is not just an outline: "I'll use my grandfather piece and then my dad piece, and then I'll close with the piece about my name." That's not a bad beginning, tape or no tape, but to *scheme* a piece is to find a common thread among the shorter pieces, or to find a controlling metaphor that unites the pieces, or to find common ground among multiple pieces and use those common elements to develop a theme or motif to build a coherent memoir.

For example, when we say the words *birthday party* or *Thanksgiving dinner*, and then ask you to think about your experiences related to those phrases, you will no doubt be able to recall a range of memories about each one. Not all of the memories are necessarily vivid or even particularly emotional, but some probably are. As your brain sorts all of the possible data it stores in order to come up with just those precise memories triggered by just those specific phrases, it has followed a *schema*, which is technically an array of electrical impulses traveling along various nodes and nodules in the brain. But for our purposes as writers, what is interesting about this process is that the brain is capable of sorting by *pattern*, by *keyword*, and even by *metaphors* and *images* to find commonalities and threads of related experience.

This ability to sort data by pattern, or by scheme, helps the writer to summon up relevant details and to block out extraneous details of other experiences, at least for now. Because we are already thinking according to a pattern, we are likely to recall similar, related patterns and the details that accompany them. For example, while I'm recalling my most recent birthday celebration, I might also recall my mother's eightieth and my daughter's eighth birthday parties. These parties are still triggered by the pattern phrase of *birthday party*, but I've branched out now to think of significant birthday parties that I've given and attended for family members close to me. I can choose to continue to follow these new patterns of thought, perhaps continuing to branch out even more to additional related memories, or I can pull back to think only of my specific birthday. Such related patterns of thought assist writers as we compose text, support readers as we work to comprehend text and relate it to personal experience, and aid responders to text as we work to help writers see what does or does not work in a text for a particular audience. We use such patterns of thought as we read like writers, write like readers, and respond as constructive reviewers to texts.

In our classrooms, we explain a simplified version of this information to our student writers, depending on their abilities and age level. Our purpose in doing so is twofold:

1. For the student writers also to understand what a scheme is, and
2. For the student writers to comprehend that they will be looking for such patterns—threads and commonalities—in their writing in order to help them weave together their various selected Spider Pieces into a final memoir.

Applying the Concept of Scheme to the Studio Writing Classroom

The concept of a scheme is also relevant in the studio writing classroom. As we explained in Chapter 2, in the traditional art studio, artists are continually trying out patterns and plans, versions of their pieces, and techniques for their artworks. The studio is, primarily, a place where planning and practice occur. Similarly, for writers, the writing studio is a place to plan and practice, moving from smaller pieces of work to larger, more comprehensive and more complete pieces, just as artists do. Recall the work habits and patterns of Sargent that we discussed in Chapter 2. He first collected small drawings and incomplete and preliminary sketches in a notebook. Later, he transformed some of that early exploratory work into more finished drawings and paintings. Eventually, he painted and finished a large picture of the woman who later became the central figure in his massively sized piece titled *El Jaleo*. Just as he finished first smaller pieces and then larger pieces, weaving the smaller pieces into the larger ones, so too will writers in the studio classroom weave together smaller exploratory pieces into the complete final memoir. But before they can select pieces and figure out how to weave them together for a final memoir, they need a scheme—a recognition of patterns in their work and a plan for optimizing them.

Once students understand what a scheme is and how it is relevant to writers, they are ready to begin the work of selecting a scheme for their own writings.

Answering the "So What?" Question

One of the first steps in selecting a scheme for a memoir is to consider the point and purpose for writing the memoir in the first place. To emphasize this principle, we once again turn to the many memoirs that occupy the bookshelves of our classroom during our teaching of this framework. (If you float from classroom to classroom as you teach, we recommend stacking the books on a rolling cart and taking them with you from room to room.) By now, our students have read several of these titles, and we have conducted many booktalks on various memoirs, so that the general idea of many of these volumes is at least familiar to our students. We begin by asking questions such as these:

- What did the author of this memoir want the reader to understand as a result of having read the book?
- What was the author's main message to the reader?
- What was the author's theme or main idea in this book? Try to state it in one sentence.
- What one word encapsulates this book for you? What three- to four-word phrase summarizes this memoir for you?

Once students are able to focus on the main point of the published authors, we then focus students' attention on the fact that knowing this main idea is relevant for writers *before* they get too far into the writing. Recall that Contemporary Memoirs, in contrast to traditional memoirs and biographies, are most often published by individuals about whom we knew nothing until we read their memoirs. In order for their experiences to be relevant to anyone other than their closest friends, they must have a point, a theme, a purpose for writing that they convey clearly to their audiences.

In our classes, we call this purpose and point the "So what?" We phrase the question this way not to be impudent or disrespectful with students but to emphasize that they need to have a point, a purpose, a message that readers are to know and understand as a result of having read their memoir pieces. This phrasing seems to resonate with our students and to give them a more personal way of identifying *theme* in literature.

For example in *The Blessing*, Greg Orr writes about the horror of accidentally shooting his own brother. His "So what?" for this memoir includes coming to terms with his own actions and their impact on his family, certainly; but he also must learn how to find meaning in the face of death, a purpose for writing with which many readers can relate. In *The House on Beartown Road*, Elizabeth Cohen writes about taking into her home her father who has Alzheimer's disease and also raising her young daughter alone after her husband leaves her. Her "So what?" for this memoir is the juxtaposition of her young child's developing and creative mind with her father's deteriorating mind, the poignancy of which anyone who has experienced either process can relate to. She reminds us that even when life spirals out of control, it is possible to find hidden courage within ourselves and messages about life in the experiences of those around us, all of which allows us to triumph instead of merely survive. Finally, in *The Color of Water*, James McBride writes about his Jewish mother who marries an African American man, lives in Harlem, and raises her family of twelve African American–Anglo children. The "So what?" here includes a tribute to McBride's remarkable mother, surely; but he also draws the reader's attention to clashes of race and culture, religion and identity, issues to which any reader who has ever sought a personal identity can relate.

Once students understand the purpose of the "So what?" question, we direct them to their own writing and ask them what their "So what?" will be for their memoir piece. For example, one student indicates that she was raised by two loving parents who are important to her, so she will use her Parent Spider Pieces (see Figure 3–3 in Chapter 3 for sample Spider Piece options) for the main part of her memoir. As writing coaches, our response to her initial expression of her idea is something like, "Okay, you love your parents and think they're great, so you want to write about them. So what? [We smile gently here to remind her that we're using this phrase in a literary, coaching sense, not a snide one.] What is it in the story of your relationship with your parents that your readers will be able to relate to? What is it that you want your readers to understand as a result of having read your memoir?" Such focusing of student writers' preliminary thoughts on the purpose and point of their memoir pieces will help them more deeply direct their thinking about theme and purpose, message and point—and about the power of literary texts to speak to an audience in meaningful ways. It also helps them, as writers, to move from a somewhat staid and trivial idea to a theme of more power and depth, which is the hallmark of all quality literary texts—both those by published authors and students.

With the answer to their personal "So what?" question in the foreground of their thinking, students are then able to revise and craft their writing with those schemes and themes in mind. They work to draw appropriate awareness to their points and clarify their messages for their potential audiences, again making the process of revision more authentic and tied epistemically to the ways in which published writers craft and shape texts.

Once writers understand what the "So what?" question accomplishes for them as writers and revisers, and as readers and responders to texts, then they are ready to investigate further the scheme that they will use for their memoir pieces.

Determining a Personally Relevant Scheme

Establishing the answer to their personal "So what?" question helps writers to know the message and the point that they want to develop and emphasize in their memoir pieces. Now they are ready to find the patterns, threads, connections—in other words, the *scheme*—that will help them weave together their Spider Pieces and highlight their theme for their memoir piece.

In order to hold power for the writer and ultimately for the reader, schemes must be personally relevant. As with all composing based on meaning, not just on format, writing that comes from personal experience and that has personal significance carries with it more power, authenticity, and connectedness than does writing that comes from rote, vague supposition or second-hand experience. Like readers, writers exhibit more strength in their texts when they write from *lived* experiences. When a writer reveals her emotions, depicts the people and places that made up her encounters in life, and otherwise draws readers into the text, readers are able to live through the writer's life happenings along with the writer. It's as though the readers, too, were seeing and hearing the occurrences alongside the writer. This experience of *being there* with the writer creates connections between the writer and the readers, and between the writer's life experiences and those of the readers. In this manner, literary texts are often a reflection of life, perhaps imitating life, perhaps enhancing it.

Step 1: Writer's Insights

Schemes that are personally relevant derive from what the writer senses as powerful within his Spider Pieces, whether that involves primarily people, places, a type of event, or emotions. The Writer's Group has responded to enough of the Spider Pieces by the student writer so that he knows what connects with an audience, and the teacher as Studio Master and writing coach has commented enough on what works in the students writer's pieces so that he has some ideas about what a skilled writer thinks has power in his pieces. These insights, combined with his own intuitions and interests about his memories and writings, will help him to detect possible schemes in his Spider Pieces. Answering the "So what?" question will further direct his focus so that he can select a scheme that will complement his purpose for writing and his message.

We ask writers to jot some notes about what they think at this stage of their processes as writers about their pieces. Which ones have engendered powerful responses from responders? Which pieces and events, people, and places are most interesting to the writer personally? Which writings seem to be connected to his "So what?" for his memoir? We then invite student writers to discuss these jottings briefly with a partner, mainly for the purpose of hearing themselves begin to think aloud, helping them to continue to construct individually relevant meaning.

Step 2: Returning to the Writer's Notebook

As a second step in determining a personally relevant scheme, we ask student writers to return to their Writer's Notebooks in which they have filed all of their writings in the Memoir Framework to date. They will have their Spider Pieces, perhaps several charts and graphs, comment pages from their Writer's Groups, brief notes by the teacher in response to their writings, and other indications of their work in the studio classroom to date. The student writers then carefully select three to five (or so) pieces in the Writer's Notebook, looking for those pieces that resonate with them personally and with audiences who have read and responded to the pieces. We invite students to refresh their Writer's Groups about those pieces, seeking affirmation that those, indeed, are pieces that have potential.

Step 3: Searching for Connections and Commonalities

Once three to five Spider Pieces have been selected from the Writer's Notebook based on their potential for further development, their vividness of the associated memory, the positive responses that audiences have given the pieces, the interest they hold for the writer, and similar factors, we then direct students to look carefully at those pieces for the connecting threads, people, places, type of event, metaphors, or emotions that run through them. Are three of the five pieces about the writer's sister? Did four of the pieces involve various *Firsts*? (See Figure 3–3 in Chapter 3 for sample Spider Piece options.) Is the writer despondent in two of the five pieces? We invite students to look for such patterns, to make notes about the patterns that they notice in their writings, and then to share their observations with their Writer's Group for their responses.

Step 4: Once More to the Writer's Notebook

Next, we return students to their Writer's Notebooks to seek out additional Spider Pieces with the same or similar threads and patterns as are present in the pieces first selected by them. Are there two more pieces in the Writer's Notebook about the writer's sister? Do three more pieces show additional emotional states of the writer? If so, these additional pieces may hold gems and nuggets of good writing that can be used in the final memoir. Sharing these additional options with their Writer's Groups may trigger more connections as the student writers hear themselves categorize and summarize the pieces under consideration.

Step 5: Deciding the Scheme

At last, the writer has reviewed enough text, deliberately searched through enough written pieces, and thought aloud with his Writer's Group enough to be ready to decide on one preeminent scheme that will help to unify the final memoir. The scheme may center on a person, a place, an emotion, an event, a metaphor, a chronological sequence, an artifact, a metaphor, or on any other device, theme, pattern, or commonality that sparks the writer's creativity and imagination, that resonates for readers, and that helps to hold the various Spider Pieces together as literary text.

This process sounds a bit intricate and complex as we have detailed it here. We think that is because these are processes that occur rather intuitively for many skilled writers but that become more complex sounding as we parcel them out into individual steps. We have found that many students are able to grasp the task and move rather quickly to decision making about their scheme. Other students need more guidance. We offer these steps as guidance for those who need it, but we do not enforce these procedures on those writers who have experienced an epiphany about their schemes for their writing from the outset.

Step 6: Going Public with the Scheme

Once schemes have been established by each student, we hold a brief individual conference with each writer to determine the validity of the scheme, including its power and its strength for enhancing the final memoir. At this point, we work as writing coaches to ascertain with students that they have a rich scheme, one that will augment their final memoirs, one that they will be able to handle effectively in their writing, and one that will hold authority for the audience.

Another favorite procedure of ours at this point is what we call the Student Press Conference. For this procedure, we simply call on each student, one after the other, row by row, to tell the class and us what their memoir scheme is and which Spider Pieces they think they will weave together for their final memoir piece. Often, as students hear each others' ideas, they are able to revise and enrich their own ideas for their schemes. It is also a time for interaction among the students, a time to ask questions to help focus the writer's thinking, and a time to respond as an authentic audience to the scheme offered by the writer. By doing so, we continue to build on the constructivist and social natures of the studio writing classroom. We also stress that this is preliminary thinking, that students are not stuck with these Spider Pieces as the only ones they may use in their final memoir piece, nor are they stuck with this scheme if a better or more refined scheme occurs to them later. Sometimes, writers need to start with an idea and then write their way into a better idea. Such is the stuff of real writers.

In order to present these steps for finding a personally relevant scheme to our students, we often create a handout that guides them through the processes described earlier. Figure 6–1 is such a handout.

Once students have made their initial decisions about a scheme and about which Spider Pieces they may use in their final memoirs, they are ready to commit some of their thinking to paper. At this point, we use a handout like the one in Figure 6–2 to help student writers map out their writing procedures and jobs to come.

The prompts on this particular map of the piece (MOP) for Memoir will not surprise students since the prompts harken back to the features of published memoir texts that students examined at the opening of the Memoir Framework as we discussed it in Chapter 3.

We find that such planning documents enable students to think more objectively about the writing tasks to be accomplished rather than getting mired down in a host of undistinguished composing jobs. We recommend devising and using such planning documents for many of the literacy tasks that your students will undertake throughout their learning processes.

The Final Step: Revising and Drafting Anew

Once students have established their scheme for their memoir piece, they will likely find that they now need to engage in considerable revision of their existing Spider Pieces. They will need to shape and craft those pieces to suit the scheme. They may need to write new pieces to fill the gaps between existing pieces. They may need to hack away at existing pieces to filter out the extraneous details that don't fit the established scheme. They may need to reorder the pieces, split them up, or otherwise work with sequencing. They make these decisions and authentic revisions with the scheme and the "So what?" of the piece firmly in mind as they shape the structure of the final memoir.

Scheming the Piece

Directions: The purpose of this handout is to guide you through the process of discovering and establishing a scheme for your final memoir piece. The problem is a challenging one. You must find a way to link together three to five (or so) of the Spider Pieces in your Writer's Notebook. The type of linking and connecting you do is strictly up to you. You must devise some scheme to guide the selecting and weaving together of pieces that may seem, at first, to be quite independent of one another. The scheme is some sort of underlying logic or overarching structure; you figure that out. Then, you'll put the final memoir piece together in such a way that a reader understands your writer's logic.

You may approach this problem in any way that works for you. Some students have had success with the following strategies.

Strategies:

JOB 1: It's you and your Writer's Notebook, one on one. Pull out all of your writings, short and long, pieces and parts. Evaluate the stuff. Which pieces work best? Which pieces do you really like? Don't eliminate any pieces just because they need more work. Do you have a hook or an anchor piece or idea?

JOB 2: Begin to think about ways in which these pieces are related. By time? By geography? By feelings? By characters? By artifacts? What is the common ground in these pieces? Rethink your reasons for writing each piece. Reread from the excerpts by professional writers, looking for and targeting key ideas you see therein that have resonated with you personally.

JOB 3: Mark strong sentences and passages in all of the pieces. Think about moving these bits and chunks into another piece. Think about writing additional pieces to make your scheme work, to fill in the gaps. Or think about modifying and elaborating existing pieces to fit your scheme.

JOB 4: Try piecing it all together. What kinds of transition problems arise? How can you give the collected Spider Pieces a seamless look? How will you begin the collection of pieces? How will you conclude the final memoir? What title will you give the final memoir? What special layout and presentational problems will you need to figure out in order to weave the pieces together effectively?

JOB 5: Talk to your Writer's Group about your scheme and the Spider Pieces that you think you'll use in your final memoir. Read a cut-and-paste version to your Writer's Group. See if they sense your writer's logic. Ask them to respond to your scheme.

Figure 6–1. *Scheming the Piece*

Map of the Piece (MOP) for Memoir

Name: _____

<u>Directions:</u> Respond to the prompts below as a way of thinking about and planning your final memoir. You are not stuck with these ideas just because you write them here, but you do need to begin to make decisions in these areas as you move into the final phase of writing your memoir piece. Discuss your ideas with your Writer's Group to see if they have additional helpful suggestions. File this sheet in your Writer's Notebook so that you can refer to it as you work on your final memoir.

<u>Focus statement:</u> Write two to four sentences about what you want readers to understand and connect with in your paper. _____

_____

_____

_____

_____

<u>Working title:</u> _____

<u>Existing Spider Pieces that I may use:</u> List them and rate the shape they're in. _____

_____

_____

_____

_____

<u>Pieces I may need to write:</u> _____

_____

_____

_____

Figure 6–2. *Map of the Piece (MOP) for Memoir*

Where does the piece begin? Will you use a dedication, preface, significant quote, epigraph, flashback, snapshot, explanations . . . ? _____

_____

_____

_____

Possible order of the pieces: _____

_____

_____

_____

Connective techniques: Will you use subtitles (metaphoric or literal), white space, dating the pieces, one integrated piece . . . ? _____

_____

_____

_____

Conclusion: Will you use an epilogue, author's note, the "So what?" question explained . . . ? _____

_____

_____

Other goodies that I may use: What else might you include in your final memoir?

      Picture ideas: _____

_____

_____

      Layout ideas: _____

_____

      Cover design ideas: _____

_____

_____

Figure 6–2. *Continued*

Sample Schemes

As we have worked with the Memoir Framework and the studio classroom over the last fifteen years or more, we have watched the processes that our student writers have used to develop their schemes, and we have been surprised and delighted by several of the schemes that students have devised to hold together their memoir pieces. Some of our favorite student-devised schemes follow:

·   "Behind the White Fence": All pieces take place in the same location.
·   "Dirt": The writer grew up in a suburban neighborhood where rows of houses were under construction simultaneously. In some cases families divorced while the house was under construction and the piles of dirt in front of the unfinished houses became a child's lonely playground.
·   "Castro Valley Snapshots": All are neighborhood pieces.
·   "Hands": All pieces focus on hand-holding, with a parent, with a boyfriend, with an ailing grandparent.
·   "Ballet Shoes": Three views of ballet shoes over fifteen years: brand-new, wearing out from hours of joyful practice and performances, treasured relics.
·   " '56 Ford," by Dan Kirby: Three experiences in and around the car.
·   "Me, Alone and in the Dark, Waiting": The piece opens with a teenage writer standing on a dark, foggy road, waiting for the school bus in the early morning. She uses that image as a metaphor for her own uncertainty about her life and who she is.

Once students have established their memoir scheme and planned their final document, they are ready to draft in earnest their final memoir pieces. Much of the writing has already been accomplished in the Spider Pieces, but more writing and revising will need to occur in order to produce polished, authored, authentic pieces.

When a final draft for the memoir that is in rather good working order is complete, students are ready to consider formats, audience-friendly features, and presentational aspects for use in their finished memoir pieces. Those items are the subjects of the next two chapters.

Works Cited

COHEN, ELIZABETH. 2003. *The House on Beartown Road: A Memoir of Learning and Forgetting.* New York: Random House.

MCBRIDE, JAMES. 1996. *The Color of Water: A Black Man's Tribute to His White Mother.* New York: Riverhead Books.

ORR, GREGORY. 2002. *The Blessing.* San Francisco: Council Oak Books.

7

Exploring Forms and Formats

In the typical artist's studio, you will see many drafts and drawings, numerous finished but unframed pieces, some leaning against the wall, some on easels. The artist can no doubt show you the preliminary drawings in a sketchbook that ultimately contributed to the creation of a finished piece of art. The finished piece may not, at first glance, resemble the preliminary sketches in many ways, but the artist can trace for you the evolution, creative energy, and thoughtful inspirations that combined to create the final artwork as you would see it framed in a gallery.

Much of the same process is true for written texts. If you have ever viewed the original manuscript pages of a book prior to its publication, you know that the appearance of the manuscript pages as prepared by the author and the appearance of the published book as prepared by the publishing company differ vastly. For example, we are preparing the manuscript pages for this book on our computer. We are incorporating no fancy layout features, no cover, no special font. But all of those features, and more, are now in your hands as the published book derived from our original, simply typed pages.

The same principle applies to student writers as they work on polishing their final memoir pieces. The drafts and even the finished manuscript pages that they have produced up to this point in their writing processes look far different from the appearance that we hope the finished, polished final memoir pieces will have.

The difference between the manuscript pages and the finished, polished pages will be comprised of two main types of features: (1) stylistic elements, and (2) presentational aspects of the piece. In this chapter, we discuss the stylistic elements that enhance readers' understandings of the written pieces and that will augment the depth and polished effect of the writer's work. In Chapter 8 we address the presentational aspects of published memoirs that student writers can adapt for use in their own final products.

The Role and Message of Format in Writing

Just as Contemporary Memoir (CM) is inventing itself as a literary genre through innovative uses of narrative technique, intimacy with the reader, voice, and the specific detailing of experience, so, too, are the authors of CM experimenting with a wide variety of forms and formats to enhance their life stories. Because memoir is personal and revealing as a literary work, connecting with an audience in intimate ways that most other literary genres do not, authors find that including family photos, maps of towns and homesteads, genealogies, and other personal features enhances not only the appearance of the published book but also the manner and the depth to which an audience feels that they come to know the author, almost personally as a close friend or colleague or member of a support group. In short, memoir has become a genre that opens doors and insights into real lives in ways that have not previously been attempted in traditional nonfiction genres. Authors, of whom we knew virtually nothing prior to reading their published memoirs, are inviting us into their experiences, giving us the pictures and the road maps to get there alongside them.

When we read like writers, we experience the ways in which these extra stylistic elements affect us, and we then determine to have a similar effect on the audiences of our own works. For that reason, we introduce and discuss with our students the power and the lessening of distance between author and audience that these techniques achieve, and we encourage our student writers to experiment with alternative stylistic elements as they are moving toward the polished, final versions of their memoirs.

Considering Stylistic Elements

One of the more enjoyable aspects of completing a finished memoir for our students is the consideration of which stylistic elements they will incorporate into their final memoir pieces. Since we have already examined a variety of published memoirs using our reading guide titled Examining Contemporary Memoir Texts (see Figure 1–1 in Chapter 1), through our readings of various memoirs, and in the course of our book-talks of numerous books, our students are aware of many of the stylistic elements used by published authors and are eager to make use of some of these in their own writings. When our student writers see how the addition of these elements can transform their memoirs from simply typed pages to more professional and polished-looking pieces, they sometimes want to include one of everything in their memoirs. Instead, we encourage them to act as more discriminating authors, choosing only those techniques that most specifically suit their writing style, their theme, and their intuitions about what will help an audience relate most directly with their written works without being overwhelming.

Following are some of the elements that our students have enjoyed using and with which they have had success in enhancing their own writings.

Opening Remarks

Authors use a variety of opening remarks in order to acknowledge and thank those who have been instrumental in inspiring or otherwise bringing to fruition the published memoir. These opening remarks usually appear directly after the title page of a book and come in several forms. Students may select any one type—or in some cases, more than one of these—with which to open their final memoir pieces.

DEDICATIONS indicate the person or persons whom the author wants to credit or recognize as being instrumental with the memories associated with the book. In some cases, the dedication is as simple as "For Nene," as in Ken Wiwa's *In the Shadow of a Saint*. Others, such as Tony Hillerman in *Seldom Disappointed*, use more elaborate and detailed dedications: "To Marie, who wanted me to do this and to all you other writers, wannabes, shouldbes, willbes, and hadbeens included, I dedicate this effort. You're the ones who know it ain't easy. May you get as lucky as I have been."

ACKNOWLEDGMENTS give credit to people who played a role in the book's completion. Chet Raymo in *The Path* writes, "I thank family members, friends, and students who have shared the path with me over the years," and then he goes on to list a number of people by name. Chanrithy Him in *When Broken Glass Floats* writes, "I remember a little girl's wish for the world to learn the bitter chill of her grief, and of the tragic death of her family. Her wish is mine and it is realized. I must thank those individuals who have helped the dream come true," and then she goes on to name those individuals.

Annie Dillard begins *For the Time Being* with a page-long **AUTHOR'S NOTE** in which she addresses the reader about the contents and form of the book. In part, she says, "This is a nonfiction first-person narrative, but it is not intimate and its narratives keep breaking. Its form is unusual, its scenes are remote, its focus wide, and its tone austere. Its pleasures are almost purely mental." Steve Fiffer also begins *Three Quarters, Two Dimes, and a Nickel: A Memoir of Becoming Whole* with an Author's Note. He writes, "This is a true story. That said, I wish to inform the reader of the following: Many of the events described in this book took place over thirty years ago. I have tried my best to accurately re-create all scenes and conversations and to portray all individuals as I remember them. In some instances, I have changed the name of characters or the details of their lives and, in a few instances, I have created composite characters. . . . None of these changes are material to or alter the ultimate truth of the story." This technique is a means the author may use to tell the readers information he or she wants them to carry into their interactions with the published text.

QUOTATIONS that begin books clearly have personal meaning for the author and accomplish a range of purposes. Sometimes they may relate to the title of the book or contain the title. For example, Jane Jeong Trenka in *The Language of Blood* uses a Joyce Carol Oates quotation, " . . . Because we are linked by blood, and blood is memory without language." Sometimes the quotations may reflect emotional tones or images in the book. For example, Judy Blunt in *Breaking Clean*, a book about her beloved childhood ranch home, begins her book with a Joan Didion quotation, "A place belongs forever to whoever claims it hardest, remembers it most obsessively, wrenches it from itself, shapes it, renders it, loves it so radically that he remakes it in his image."

Authors who are poets or lovers of poetry sometimes begin their books with a **POEM**. Janisse Ray in *Wild Card Quilt* opens with Rainer Maria Rilke's poem, "God Speaks to Each of Us." Neely Tucker in *Love in the Driest Season* opens with song lyrics from Cassandra Wilson's "Solomon Song."

More typical openings include **PRELUDES**, **PREFACES**, and **PROLOGUES**. They are somewhat similar, distinguished mainly by what the author chooses to call them and what use he or she chooses to make of them. Jill Ker Conway in *A Woman's Education* begins with a prelude in which she recounts an autobiographical incident that leads to the memoir content. She begins, "If we're lucky, the places and people that can give our lives an aura of magical potential enter our experience at the right moment to sustain our dreams." Henry Louis Gates, Jr., in *Colored People* uses his preface to write a letter to his two daughters who were the original audience of his memoir. He writes, "Dear Maggie and Liza: I have written to you because a world into which I was born, a world that nurtured and sustained me, has mysteriously disappeared." Pat Conroy in *My Losing Season* begins with a rather lengthy prologue that is essentially an extended essay on sport and competition. His opening line, with typical Conroy self-deprecation and honesty, is, "I was born to be a point guard, but not a very good one."

And, of course, the inimitable Tom McGuane in *The Longest Silence* merely begins with what he calls "Opening Remarks."

Dividing the Text

Authors divide the totality of the text into sections, chapters, individual books within a book, and in other ways. These divisions help to order and organize the chronology of events, mark individual stories that make up the memoir, or otherwise offer boundaries to readers about the story being told. Sometimes these divisions have titles, as in chapter titles, and the author will include a table of contents detailing the titles and beginning page numbers of each. Sometimes, the table of contents is missing because the sections are denoted merely with extra white space, asterisks, or a dividing line. Whatever method the author chooses, most employ some technique for separating long expanses of text into more easily read chunks of text.

Pascal Khoo Thwe in *From the Land of Green Ghosts* divides his book into three chronologically sequential parts (Part I, Part II, Part III) with separate titles. Dermot Healy in *The Bend for Home* divides his memoir into five books (Books I through V), each with a separate title. Alma Guillermoprieto in *Dancing with Cuba* has nine chapters, numbered (one through nine) and titled, listed in her table of contents. Kathryn Harrison in *The Kiss* uses only extra white space, a new page, and dividing lines to denote the sections of the story. Jamaica Kincaid in *My Brother* doesn't divide the

book in any way so that it reads like a single story. Clearly, text divisions are idiosyncratic to the author and to the author's intuitions about how divisions enhance or
hinder the readers' experiences with the text.

Photographs and Graphics

Authors include photographs, pictures, maps, family trees, and other graphics as elements of their books in order to give readers visual representations of people and places
detailed in their memoirs. *Reading* about how Rick Bragg's grandparents look in *Ava's
Man* is one thing; *seeing* them in a picture, however, brings the descriptions to life. The
trend in memoir is to include more and more graphics, so students will benefit from
experiencing firsthand this addition to their own writing as they work like memoirists.

MAPS are often included in multigenerational memoirs and in memoirs that are
situated in a particular locale. For example, Bobbie Ann Mason in *Clear Springs*, a
one-hundred-year history of the four families who constitute her ancestry, includes a
copy of a county section map to locate her relatives' farms and homes within the
Panther Creek, western Kentucky area.

FAMILY TREES and **GENEOLOGY CHARTS** indicate the relationships bio-
logically and historically among various family members, helping readers to recall who
is related to whom and how. Again, Bobbie Ann Mason in *Clear Springs* includes a
two-page genealogical chart of the Mason–Lee family members to help readers place
numerous people that she discusses in the one–hundred-year accounting of her family.
N. Scott Momaday in *The Names: A Memoir* features a genealogical chart of family
members, including names and pictures.

The great majority of **PHOTOGRAPHS** included in memoirs are black-and-
white photos plucked from family albums. Some are grouped in the center of the
book, while others are sprinkled throughout the text, and even others are collaged.
Some authors use pictures to begin chapters or sections of the text. Elie Wiesel in *And
the Sea Is Never Full* groups in the center of the book black-and-white, captioned pictures that show him with world leaders. Cynthia Kaplan in *Why I'm Like This: True
Stories* uses black-and-white collages of family pictures as the inside front and back
covers of her book. Janisse Ray in *Wild Card Quilt* uses the technique of photographs
that are made to look like family slides.

Covers and Titles

Covers and titles help to grab the reader's immediate attention and to single out one
book from another. The trend in covers seems to favor family photographs over graphics or other designs. Covers tend to be in color and artfully designed. Titles often
include the subtitle *A Memoir* or *A Family Memoir* in order to assist the reader in knowing the genre of the book. Covers and titles indicate something about the content of
the story, its location, or the people involved.

COVERS that feature graphics include Stephen Kuusisto's *Planet of the Blind*. On
that cover, the title and the author's name are written in blurry letters as they appear

to one of limited sight such as Kuusisto. Eric Liu's *The Accidental Asian: Notes of a Native Speaker* features a cover with a picture of an Asian rice bowl filled with rice, in the front of which is a chopstick holder, holding a fork, thus indicating the two cultures of his heritage. Lauren F. Winner's *Girl Meets God* has a color cover that shows her reclining on a wood floor with two books under her head. Alexandra Fuller's *Don't Let's Go to the Dogs Tonight* shows a black-and-white photograph of her as a young child in Africa on the cover.

Epilogues and Closing Remarks

Just as authors begin their books with a variety of opening remarks, so, too, do they close them in a range of ways. Some authors place their acknowledgments at the end of the book. Some authors include book references for further reading on a particular subject. And some authors conclude with an epilogue.

For example, Homer Hickam in *Sky of Stone* concludes his memoir with an **EPILOGUE** that tells the reader what has happened since the end of the storyline in the memoir. Alexandra Fuller in *Scribbling the Cat: Travels with an African Soldier* closes with a recent email from the soldier who is the main character of this memoir. Kien Nguyen in *The Unwanted: A Memoir of Childhood* ends with an epilogue that informs the reader that the act of writing his memoir has made his nightmares cease.

Again, the purpose of these closing remarks, regardless of form, is to bring closure to the story told in the memoir, to help the author communicate to the reader final emotions or information, or to anticipate yet another memoir forthcoming from the same author.

Final Thoughts

These stylistic features, then, enhance texts and help them to acquire a polished appearance. Students who are particularly artistic or technically skilled with computer clip art and graphics have the benefit of bringing those talents into the English writing classroom. Skilled writers enjoy the added enhancements that graphics, cover design, maps, and the like bring to their solid writing efforts, and they may find a modicum of pleasure in the somewhat self-indulgent fancy that can be expressed in prologues and epilogues, author's notes and original poetry that accompany memoirs. Whatever the reasons or forms, these features give texts a finished, polished, and published look.

8

Assembling the Memoir

Just as stylistic elements affect the reader's interaction with and the aesthetic appreciation of the finished memoir, so, too, do presentational aspects of the finished piece. Artists are no strangers to the value of the presentation and appearance of artwork as an impact on potential critics and buyers. Artists have long attended to framing and to medium in their art; but in recent years, they have begun to expand the traditional parameters in these areas. Artists now sometimes treat the frame as part of the canvas, painting on it an extension of the framed piece; or they add elements to the frame that will compliment the artwork, such as inlaid turquoise to enhance a piece with a Southwestern theme or twigs to enhance a piece with a Western theme. Artists may frame their works in gold gilt, wrought iron, tooled leather, or glass. Presentation is definitely part of the overall impact of a piece of art.

Publishers have also long attended to the presentational aspects of books and monographs, knowing that a sloppily prepared and presented publication will potentially invite an audience to view the contents and the reputation of the publisher as being similarly shoddy. The quality of the paper, the design of the cover, the font in which the work is presented, and even how much white space is used on each page all impact the appearance of the published work and give subtle hints to readers about the content and emotional force of the work offered up as a finished product.

Just as artists and publishers have worked over the years to improve and augment the presentational aspects of their finished works, so, too, do we attend to this aspect of finished memoirs as we teach in the studio writing classroom, watching this creative aspect of our students' work emerge. In this chapter, we'll indicate some of the presentational aspects of the finished memoir piece that may serve to highlight and enhance the quality writing in the final memoirs of student writers.

Presentational Aspects of Finished Memoirs

When we are working with our student writers in the studio writing classroom, we discuss with them the finishing touches that they may add to their final memoirs in order to highlight the appearance and power of their writing. Using features that correlate with their themes, the emotional state in the writing, the time period (the 1950s, for example) covered in the writing, or the place (the beachfront, for example) indicated in the writing will give the reader visual signals that they will consequently be able to draw into their understandings of the text. While we are careful to emphasize with our students that a merely flashy appearance of their finished pieces and no quality in their writing will not suffice, we also want them to appreciate and work metaphorically to enhance the connections between the appearance of their final product and the quality writing contained therein.

The concerns about presentational aspects of the memoir come *after* students have attended thoroughly to polishing and crafting their writing in their memoirs. Certainly, students may have gleaned ideas about presentation of the finished product as they drafted, schemed, and wrote the final memoir, but we don't direct their full attention to presentation until they are finished or nearly finished writing the memoir itself. In this way, we hope that students are not distracted from quality writing by glitz and glam.

As a first step in this part of completing the memoir, we again turn to our bookshelves and the memoirs that reside thereon in our classrooms. Or, if needed, we again haul boxes and carts of memoirs into the classroom. We renew our invitation to students to examine the published memoirs, but this time we focus their attention on how the memoir *looks*. We offer questions such as those shown in Figure 8–1 to guide their examination of the published memoirs for presentational aspects of the texts.

Once students have examined how the professionals work with presentational aspects of finished works, and once they have discussed their findings with their Writer's Groups, they are ready to pursue their ideas on their own for their final memoir pieces.

Versions and Options for Presenting the Final Memoir Product

After the careful and constructive examination of published memoirs, we ask students to make a list of some of their presentational options, to share those within their Writer's Groups, and then to narrow their choices to a handful that they will use within their final products. We do discuss with student writers the notion of overkill: The idea here is to make *effective* choices about presentational aspects of finished works, not merely to use one of everything for the sake of inclusiveness. Once students have some solid indications of the devices that they plan to use, we again use individual conferences to hone their thinking and the method of the Class Press Conference (see our discussion of this technique in Chapter 6) to construct and critique ideas further within a social and supportive environment.

The creativity and insights of our students continue to amaze and inspire us and their peers.

Examining Presentational Aspects of Published Memoirs

Directions: Now that you have practically finished writing your memoir piece, you are in the process of considering how to enhance the appearance of your completed memoir through the use of presentational aspects of the final piece. You are continuing to work epistemically as artists and writers to devise a presentation of your memoir that will enhance your writing and make visual connections for readers. As a first step in this process, examine a range of the published memoirs that are available to you in class and respond to the prompts below. After you have examined and made notes about these prompts on your own, get together with your Writer's Group to discuss your findings, insights, and ideas for your own memoir's presentation.

· Presentational Aspect for Consideration: **FONT**. What is noteworthy about the *font* of the literary work? Is the same font used throughout the text, or does it vary? If it varies, when and why? What is the impact of the font on the reader?

· Presentational Aspect for Consideration: **WHITE SPACE**. What is noteworthy about the use of *white space* in the work? What size are the margins on each page? Is white space used as sectional or chapter divisions? If so, what is your reaction to that technique?

Figure 8–1. *Examining Presentational Aspects of Published Memoirs*

· <u>Presentational Aspect for Consideration</u>: **COLOR**. Publishing in color is expensive, so it is rarely used in most books. Are there any uses of *color* in the memoir text you are examining? If so, where is the color, how is it used, and what is its impact?

· <u>Presentational Aspect for Consideration</u>: **COVER**. Because the *cover* helps to form the reader's first impression of the book, publishers often work on creating a cover that is connotative of the overall published piece. What is noteworthy about the cover of the memoir text you are examining? How does it convey meaning that is related to the theme, locale, people, or import of the finished work? Does the cover consist of a picture, graphics, or a photograph? How does the cover work to catch your eye?

· <u>Presentational Aspect for Consideration</u>: **BINDING**. Today, most *bindings* used by publishers are rather straightforward. Is there anything unique about the binding of the memoir text that you are examining? For example, does the book employ unevenly cut (ruffled-looking) pages, a hard or a paper cover, or a spiral binding? Is the book an unusual size, either larger or smaller than what you would consider typical? What is the impact of the binding and the outer appearance of the book on your reader's eye?

Figure 8–1. *Continued*

Layout Options for the Final Memoir

Clearly, we get much of our inspiration for the presentational aspects of finished memoirs that we discuss with our student writers by examining what published authors of memoir do—again emphasizing the epistemological and phenomenological theories grounding our teaching of memoir. The following are some of the layout options that we have observed in our reading and study of published memoir texts, all of which we have found translate well for use by our student writers.

Using Fonts Effectively

Using fonts effectively includes typical, emphatic uses of **bold** and *italic*, as well as using font styles effectively. For example, if a letter is part of the final memoir, we invite student writers to consider using actual handwriting or a font style on the computer that simulates handwriting, such as *Fine Hand*, *Gigi*, *Bradley Hand ITC*, or any of the so-called *script* fonts, such as *Freestyle Script*. Because most books are published in one rather standard font throughout, published examples of various fonts within a text are not as easy to find as are some published examples of other presentational features. Look to see what examples you and your students can discover.

Some of the examples of effective uses of font in published memoirs that we have found include those of Michael Heller in *Living Root: A Memoir* in which he uses all capital letters for titles of poems; single-spaced, smaller fonts for letters from one person to another; and unusual chapter openers that include all capital letters, double spacing of the first five or so lines and a more curlicue initial capital letter than in the remainder of the text. In *The Color of Water: A Black Man's Tribute to His White Mother*, James McBride uses italic for chapters that originated as audiotaped transcripts of his mother talking about an event and a more standard font for the very next chapter about the same scene or event as told from his point of view. In *Love in the Driest Season*, Neely Tucker uses all capital letters in *MATISSE IT*—or something very similar—to begin each chapter. The purpose of this font, we think, is to convey the rather rustic and tumultuous qualities of Zimbabwe during the 1990s. In *Sleepaway School*, Lee Stringer begins each chapter by using bold type of a larger-than-normal point size for the first four or five words of each chapter. In *The Language of Blood: A Memoir*, Jane Jeong Tenka uses Asian calligraphy symbols as sectional dividers within the book. Each of these fonts adds to the impact of the memoir.

Using Color Effectively

As we have already stated, color is an expensive item in publishing, so color is a rare commodity in most published texts, memoirs or otherwise. When color is present in published memoirs, it is most often used for photographs, as in *Reason for Hope: A Spiritual Journey* by Jane Goodall with Phillip Berman. Here, the authors include a color inside front cover bleed—meaning that there are no white space margins—of a photograph of a chimpanzee in the rain. One notable exception to the sparse use of color is *Little Things in a Big Country: An Artist & Her Dog on the Rocky Mountain Front* by Hannah Hinchman. This book, which is a hybrid memoir and nature book, features full-color artwork by the author, pages of varying background colors, and a font that resembles handwriting from her journal. It is a remarkable example of how color and font can enhance presentational effect.

Using White Space Effectively

White space opens up a page and rests the reader's eye. It can also be used to offset and thereby call attention to printed elements of text. For example, Ellen Gilchrist in *Falling Through Space* uses extra white space and an Asian-style symbol to denote chapter beginnings. The outer margins on each page are also a bit larger than are the inner margins, giving the page a more spacious feel than the typical printed page carries. Roya Hakakian in *Journey from the Land of No: A Childhood Caught in Revolutionary Iran* uses a combination of symbols to separate sections of text, almost a full half-page of white space to denote new chapters, and more white space to denote sections with chapters. In Hakakian's book, the white space generally denotes the passage of time. We encourage our students to experiment with these and other effective uses of white space in their memoirs.

Creating an Effective Cover

Perhaps it's the growing commercialization of the genre, but recently covers have become more highly designed and graphically engineered than in the past in order to, we think, capture the reader's and potential buyer's eye as he scans the range of possible purchases on the bookstore shelf. Examples of early, perhaps more simplistic but still effective covers, are *Growing Up* by Russell Baker and *Having Our Say: The Delany Sisters' First 100 Years* by Sarah and A. Elizabeth Delany with Amy Hill Hearty, which both contain a picture of the authors. Some best-selling memoirs such as Mitch Albom's *Tuesdays with Morrie* use a splash of color and primarily lowercase type for the title as the entire cover.

The most recent memoirs feature more elaborate covers with increased shelf-appeal for potential buyers. A collage on the cover that combines pictures, graphics, drawings, iconic symbols, strategic use of color, and the printed title and author's name in various fonts seem quite the vogue as we are working on this book. These covers offer graphic representations of the stories inside, much as the opening material of a film always has. For examples of these more recently styled covers, see covers on books like Roya Hakakian's *Journey from the Land of No*, David M. Caroll's *Self-Portrait with Turtles*, Lawrence LaRose's *Gutted: Down to the Studs in My House, My Marriage, and My Entire Life*, and Monique Maddy's *Learning to Love Africa: My Journey from Africa to Harvard Business School and Back*. And you really must *see* them; our descriptions cannot do them true justice.

Creating an Effective Binding

In publishing, most bindings, we confess, seem rather standard to the uninitiated observer and reader such as we are. There are, no doubt, subtle differences among the various binding techniques, but expense and practicality for shelf life and handling by shippers, shelf stockers, and potential buyers prevent most publishers from tampering with bindings that stretch the norm. Book size, however, is a factor, with some finished products being tall and rather narrow, others looking more like conventional books and paperbacks, and still others being short and elongated. Reproducing bindings and covers devised by our students is difficult here. Our students have enhanced their final Memoir Pieces with an array of inventive covers, bindings, and other devices: tooled leather, tartan plaid, family pictures, raffia, glitter, computer art, netting, twigs, dried flowers, and singed pages. We have definitely found that this is one area in which student writers will be able to experiment and create more elaborate and metaphorically relevant bindings than publishers are typically capable of doing.

When students attend to these presentational features as part of the import of their finished memoir pieces, they are combining aspects of visual literacy with print literacy, a combination that might assist you in meeting several of the standards specified for instruction in the English/language arts in your school, district, and state. Further, students who excel at art and possess an artistic flair, and those who are technologically adept, but perhaps are only moderately skilled writers, will have a chance to enhance their finished memoir products, creating a final version that is pleasing to the eye and of which they can be proud. Most important, attending to such features allows writers to consider the symbolic nature of their writing as well as its literal meaning, and then to connect the two with visual devices, working epistemically as graphic designers, artists, photographers, and writers.

9

Alternate Forms of Memoir and How to Write Them

Watch an artist at work in her studio, and you'll notice that a finished piece of art may take on numerous versions before it finds its way to a frame. Dan has spent time in the studio of an artist friend of ours who works in landscapes, and we have watched him frequently paint a second or even a third rendering of a scene that is closely related to the first piece of art because he thought of another way that he could represent the same scene. Maybe the light is different in one, maybe the perspective, or the coloring. In our experience as aesthetic and literal consumers of art, we have found that just as stylistic and presentational elements affect our responses to works of art, so, too, does the experience of watching the working artist create various versions of the same artistic subject. Alternate forms of the same artistic subject, when viewed in proximity, enhance our understandings of how the artistic eye functions, and of the nuances and differences that can be emphasized through multiple representations of the same subject.

Similarly, writers can represent the same storyline in various forms. For example, James McBride in *The Color of Water: A Black Man's Tribute to His White Mother* writes parallel chapters throughout his memoir. One chapter is the transcription of audio recordings of his mother narrating a particular life event in her own words based on her memory. The next chapter is the telling of the same event from the author's memory and perceptions. The stories are parallel; they recall the same event, but their final forms differ. Each enhances the other. Each features differing details and nuances. Each is stylistically individualistic. Together, they form a more complex, subtle, and interpretive view of the storyline of McBride's life and of particular events.

This use of parallel but differing forms of the same subject or story is a technique frequently employed by English teachers. We have often worked with history teachers to develop a themed unit in which students study the facts of events and their impact on world politics, economics, and related events during history class, and then read fictionalized accounts of the same events in our literature classes. Or, we encourage students to read several titles—both fiction and nonfiction—about the same person or historical occurrence to discover what new information and insights each text yields and to discuss the emotional impact of genre, the literary techniques found in fiction and in nonfiction, and the license with facts that authors of both genres take.

Just as artists and teachers have attended over the years to the impact of alternate forms of the same subject, so, too, have we attended to this aspect of memoir writing as we teach it in the studio writing classroom. In this chapter, we'll indicate some of the alternate forms of the finished memoir piece that may serve to highlight and enhance the nuances, perspectives, and quality of writing in the final memoirs of student writers.

Triptych

One of our favorite forms of memoir is that of the triptych. Those of you familiar with art history will recognize triptych as a form of early religious paintings. *Triptych* literally means *three panels*. In early Greece, a triptych was a hinged or folded three-leaved writing tablet. During the sixteenth and seventeenth centuries, artists composed triptychs for religious and sacred audiences by creating three hinged panels or a box with three compartments. These pieces were referred to as *altar pieces*; they were opened for worship and closed at the conclusion of the liturgy. Although the composition of the altar pieces varied, typical subject matter placed the nativity scene in the center, with Joseph and other Biblical personages appearing on the side panels.

In contemporary times, carvers, sculptors, painters, graphic artists, designers, and even musicians and writers have used a variety of approaches to create connections and relationships among three panels. The connections may still be primarily in subject matter, but they may be extended to included relationships of motif, color, design, chronology, theme, melody, or metaphor, for example. Although this art form was most widely used during the Middle Ages, triptych is also quite postmodern in its contemporary renderings because its success relies on consumers of the art form to do some of the mental work required to connect the meaning of the panels and thereby help ascribe meaning to the finished work.

For writers, the implications and metaphors for using triptych as a vehicle for memoir are vast; our students grasp these immediately once they know the artistic history and meaning of triptych. Triptych allows student writers to create three pieces of memoir writing that are literarily related in a manner that students don't need to state explicitly. In fact, stating the explicit relationship among the three pieces is rather like having someone explain a joke to you: If it must be explained, it isn't very effective. In an artistically rendered triptych, readers of the pieces bring their own rich experiences and interpretive backgrounds and skills to the pieces, enriching them and interacting with them in order to bring depth and insight to the student writer's artistic renderings.

106

Getting Started with Triptych

As a way of presenting the triptych form graphically to our students, we give each writer a large sheet of unlined white paper and ask her to fold it into three panels: a large center panel and two smaller panels that fold inward to meet at the center. As we write some drafts of various memoir pieces (see Chapters 3 and 4 for suggestions on various memoir pieces) or as we review the drafts on hand in each student's Writer's Notebook, we ask student writers to sketch a layout or design for which of their pieces might fit the triptych form well. We encourage students to write directly on the panels of folded paper, even to draft and experiment on the panels, so that they get a feel for how the form might work for them as writers and for their specific memoir pieces. If students like this alternate form of the memoir, they will then use the metaphor of the triptych to enhance the presentation of their final memoir pieces, either typing their pieces and pasting them onto folded panels, creating three compartments in a decorated box for the writings, or otherwise using the form and medium of triptych to enhance their finished memoirs. See Figure 9–1 for a graphic representation and a handout on an introduction to the triptych form for memoir writing that we often use with our students.

Triptych Possibilities: Ideas for Pieces

Once students understand the triptych form and its possibilities for memoir writing, they are ready to explore more fully the possibilities of the form and its use in their writing of memoir. Although we are still experimenting with various subject matter ideas in an attempt to find those topics that will fit most readily into a three-part format, here are a few ideas that have worked well for us and for our student memoirists. Remember, the key features here for the writer are using the triptych form as a structure for pulling together three memory-based writings, writings that the author juxtaposes to make a statement about his or her life.

TRIPTYCH IDEA #1: ANCHOR PIECE AND TWO SMALLER, SUPPORTING PIECES

This format works well for family pieces, that is, for writings about the student author accompanied by pieces about the student author's parents, siblings, or extended family. The first task associated with this Triptych Idea is to decide who in the family is the central focus. The piece about that person will be the central, longer, more elaborate piece of writing. Then, the student writer will decide who else in the family should show up in the supporting pieces.

It may be helpful to direct students to Figure 9–1 to remind them of this structure of a central piece with supporting pieces. Also remind student writers to focus on one "So what?" (see Chapter 6 for discussion of the "So what?" aspect of memoir writing), one theme, or one central idea that the three pieces will illustrate to the reader.

Introduction to the Triptych Form for Memoir Writing

<u>Directions</u>: Fold this paper along the lines below so that you have a creased page that can stand up on its own. On each panel, make notes about which pieces of writing you have in your Writer's Notebook that might fit the triptych form, or choose one strong central piece that you have in your collection of pieces and then draft ideas for a new piece or two directly onto the panels.

Place the strongest, most powerful piece or idea for the triptych in the middle. Place the two ancillary pieces or ideas on either side. Remembering that people generally read from left to right may help you decide which supporting piece to place on the left and right sides.

Try jotting an opening line for each piece. Also try jotting a title for each piece, something that hints at but does not explicitly state the nature of the relationship among the pieces. Refer to your "So what?" ideas as you work on titles, selection, details, and opening lines.

After you have worked alone on these ideas, you'll join your Writer's Group for sharing and discussion of the form and your ideas for using it.

SUPPORTING STORY (PANEL PIECE)	CENTRAL STORY (ANCHOR PIECE)	SUPPORTING STORY (PANEL PIECE)

May be copied for classroom use. © 2007 by Dawn Latta Kirby and Dan Kirby, from *New Directions in Teaching Memoir* (Heinemann: Portsmouth, NH).

Figure 9–1. *Introduction to the Triptych Form for Memoir Writing*

TRIPTYCH IDEA #2: MULTIPLE SCENES FROM A PLACE

In this Triptych Idea, student writers aim to reveal the magic of a special or important place through three descriptive views of the place. Maybe one piece is purely descriptive, while the other two pieces show the student author and perhaps others in action in the place. Or, the views may be chronological—the ski slope in the pristine early-morning rising sun, at midday filled with skiers, and at the end of the day when littered and pocked with digs and ruts made by thousands of downhill skis. Or, the views may be seasonal. Other possibilities about how to represent place will occur to you and your students as you continue to explore together this Triptych Idea.

As we are discussing the demands of writing for this Triptych Idea, we remind students of the importance of showing the people in action in the place—not telling or merely stating what happens—as they write these pieces. We also remind them that the various elements of the place itself may also be in action: the river flows, the leaves rustle, the snow glistens. We coach the student writers on the use of vivid verbs and captivating descriptors (which works well with teaching vocabulary, adjectives, adverbs, and the like). Focusing on the central "So what?" idea should help student writers to unite the three views of the place that is special to them.

TRIPTYCH IDEA #3: MULTIPLE STORIES IN WHICH AN ARTIFACT REOCCURS

For this Triptych Idea, student writers select one artifact that is important to them or has been significant in their lives over time. Then they build three pieces around that artifact. The key here is to focus on showing how and why the artifact is important, how it changes over time, or how the student author and others interact with it. Artifacts about which students in our classes have written include ballet shoes, a stuffed teddy bear, a cedar hope chest, a guitar, a desk, and a car. Here, the "So what?" of the pieces should depict the value of the artifact and the student writer's interactions with it.

TRIPTYCH IDEA #4: MULTIPLE VIEWS OF A WRITER'S LIFE

These pieces may show a chronological view of important events in the student writer's life. The student authors may focus on three times they learned a valuable lesson, three moments of emotional or psychological growth and increased self-understanding, three episodes that helped to form or change them, or other similar pieces. For this Triptych Idea, students often write what we call *stepping-stone* pieces, that is, pieces that follow the storyline of *Once Event #1 happened to me, then I was better able to deal with Events #2 and 3 when they occurred,* or *Now that Event #3 has occurred, I can look back and see that Events #1 and 2 yielded essential experiences that allowed me to cope with Event #3.* This last version, of course, is fruitful for teaching about verb tense and flashback writing. Once they get the gist of this version of the piece, your students will devise other forms that will focus on their "So what?" idea and allow them to illustrate their themes to readers.

TRIPTYCH IDEA #5: MULTIPLE PERSONAE OF THE WRITER

We begin this Triptych Idea by reminding students of the literary definition of *persona*, and then extend that definition to encompass one aspect of the student's personality. To illustrate, we tell students that they can be the fun-loving party-goer, the serious student, the ski bum, the devoted child, and many other versions of themselves. They are not schizophrenic nor are they suffering from multiple personalities; they merely have various aspects of their personalities that shine in various contexts, and different people in their lives see them in different ways. We invite students to brainstorm other examples and persona that suit their own lives and personalities. These sessions can get funny or hyperbolic quickly, so we advise students to *keep it clean* and appropriate for a school-based audience.

Once the student author understands this particular extension of persona, then she is ready to create three different views of herself or three different self-portraits. She might write one piece from her own point of view, and two pieces from others' points of view, creating an opportune instructional moment for reviewing points of view. We prompt students to include language and expressions appropriate to the person whose point of view is represented by asking them questions such as the following: What would your mother say about you, and how would it differ from what you have to say about yourself? How about your sibling? Your teacher? Your grandparent? Or, the student author might choose to write in her own voice about three different aspects of her personality. This option also creates an opportune instructional moment for reviewing dialogue, monologue, and voice.

Sample Triptych Piece

This is a form that we have tried multiple times, both as teachers and as writers. Examine this triptych draft by Chelsie. She has chosen to use three memorable occasions when she and her father were together. She uses these scenes both to reveal her relationship with her father and to highlight elements of his character that she admires. Notice also that Chelsie is playing with tense. She is still struggling to use the snapshot technique of present tense and pulls this off best in Part II. As you read this piece, think about how you might coach Chelsie's future drafts to arrive at a consistent present tense.

> **My Father**[1]
> **Part I**
> My dad was the only member of my family who could make it that day. The first cheerleading competition of the year is always the most nerve-wracking for me. I was hot, thirsty, and nervous. I grew more anxious as our team waited for our turn to do our routine.
>
> Just like it always does, the two minutes and thirty seconds we spend on the mats flies by. It's a rush unlike any other, a short thrill that leaves my heart pounding and my adrenaline racing. As we bounced off the mats, a wave of relief washed over me.

Parents and supporters rushed over to offer congratulations on our flawless performance. I searched the crowd for my dad.

I found him. I could tell that he was proud of me, more than ever. My hard work and long hours training for this moment had paid off. I very much want to impress my dad, make him proud. My dad is an athlete; he always has been. My brother and sister have tried to follow in his footsteps, both are very athletic. I am not as coordinated or as competitive as my siblings. I haven't really found a sport I could do well in.

That day, standing among twenty teammates, I am proud of my team and of myself. My dad says, "Good job! You guys looked great!" and he gives me a high five, as he has done many times before with my brother and sister. Although cheerleading is very unlike any sport my siblings ever played, and although my dad knows nothing about it, he is proud of me and he is there for me at this important time in my life.

In some ways I'm glad he was the only one there that day. It made that moment all the more special.

Part II

It's pouring. The ground is covered in muddy puddles and we trample through them on our way to the stadium. From miles away, the roar of thousands of football fans beckons us.

The rain is already chilling my bones through the layers of my clothing. I'm drenched from head to toe. Along side me, my dad silently shivers.

Our seats are soaked but we make no attempt to dry them off before we sit. Our timing is perfect, just before kickoff. No matter how hard the rain comes down, it can't wash off our excitement at being here. Well, it is really my dad's excitement. I enjoy football but mostly I enjoy spending time with my dad. Ever since I was little, he has made an effort to take me to a game each season. It's our tradition that I really look forward to. This game was special even with the rain.

Halfway into the first quarter, my dad makes the hike down to the concession stand. This is out of character for him. It's hard to pry him away from football even for a minute. I sit alone for quite some time. My dad misses a touchdown. Just as I'm starting to get a little concerned, I see him climbing up the steep stairs. The only thing in his hands is a small plastic package.

He settles back into his seat and hands this package to me and I unwrap it curiously. Inside, I am delighted to find a plastic poncho. I can feel my eyes light up and I throw it on without delay. I am immediately warmer and drier.

It wasn't much later in the game when I noticed my dad was still shivering. I was now completely dry. I lean over and ask him why he didn't buy a ponsho for himself. He shrugs, smiles and turns his attention back to the game.

Later that evening, I learned the full story from my mom. Dad was freezing but he bought the last poncho for me.

Part III

Most nights I'm home alone until six or so, but tonight I come home to a note from my mom, telling me that she is at a meeting and I am on my own for dinner. I called a friend to make plans, but she was busy. Looks like I will spend the night all by myself.

I begin making dinner and very shortly I am in a complete mess. The sausage is burning, the water isn't boiling and I can't get the lid off of the sauce. I was in the process of giving up when my dad got home. I had assumed he'd have to close the business, but I am very happy to have his help.

He jumped in and saved the dinner without my even asking. As I watched him clean the sauce off the stove, I noticed how tired he looked. His shoulders are slightly slumped over, and I could almost see the soreness in his back and arms. After a long day lifting tires, tools and parts, and enduring the stress of customers and coworkers, the soreness shows through somehow. Now he has come home to encounter more stress, but as I watch him save me from disaster, I notice how he is smiling and joking with me.

It's moments like these when it becomes clear to me how hard my dad works for us and how much he cares. He's helped teach me the meaning of family, and example of true caring and love.

—*Chelsie May*

Here's another student triptych piece based on Triptych Idea #3: Multiple Stories in Which an Artifact Reoccurs. Rather than one specific artifact, Lauren selects three life stories about candy. Notice that these pieces are quite postmodern in their format. There are no traditional transitions between the pieces, leaving the reader to discover the meaning of the pieces and their "So what?" Notice also that Lauren's artifact piece uses the Snapshot technique discussed in Chapter 4, that these pieces fall into roughly chronological order, and that they feature insights about family. That's another feature of triptych that we especially like: Because it is a *form* of memoir writing, any of the pieces that we suggested in Chapter 4 have the potential to work well as triptych.

Confectionery[2]
I.
Utah. The air tastes like thick red dust, the sun a stain of caramel in an undecidedly blush canvas. My knuckles are turning white around the thick, stubby stick in my hand, tadpoles struggling to avoid its menacing touch. They wriggle with an awkward sluggishness, heads mottled and bulging. The warm rust-colored rock sighs under my calloused knees. Everything around me is earth-toned; I'd never imagined so many shades of brown. After a while you begin to feel the overwhelming unity of your surroundings; you become organic, browning and dust-caked, ready to blend into the backdrop like melting licorice on the asphalt.

I've cornered a tadpole, the base of my stick pressed lightly to the apex of its abdomen so as to keep it pinned but alive. I watch it struggle weakly for a while, and then in one quick motion of impatience, I pop its head. A garbled mess of intestines and miscellaneous anatomy issues out, like pus from a pimple, and after I get over the momentary adrenaline of morbid satisfaction, I notice the color.

The tadpole's entrails are a strikingly garish shade of purple, floating silently to the surface of the puddle. Its empty body remains mangled and grey at the bottom, like a punctured balloon. My stomach heaves at such a gaudy hue, like nature's guilty secret which should've been kept coiled safely in the belly of the tadpole as it sprouted legs and expanded . . . It was sickening, what I'd loosed into such a content landscape. I tossed the stick away and leapt to my feet, leaving the puddle behind to cover up the mess.

That evening I found a box of nerds in my backpack, and guiltily anticipating the manufactured buzz of artificial flavoring, I ripped open the flaps. I'd been living off of saltines and mixed nuts for the past several days. I shook a handful of them into my palm and then, oh! A sickly beat. I toss the nerds—grape—into the brush. The moment I'd seen that fetid bright purple, my brain started crawling with rotting intestines and writhing amphibians.

I swallow down half of my water-bottle, warm and stale with iodine, and finish it off with a handful of walnuts.

II.

"I want one."

I am hunched over the table in front of me, a pile of skittles strewn in a mass of technicolor hardness at my fingertips. The girl points to a stray lime-green skittle, her arm swathed in a baggy red-and-white striped fabric. I scan the area around me surreptitiously, silently pleading for help, and simultaneously I feel this twist of shame that I'm actually *afraid*. We'd been told about how to interact with these kids, but I was submitting to a hard-wired instinct to react negatively towards anything out of the ordinary. I thought about my tendency to aver my gaze from beggars sprawling on urine-stained sidewalks, humbly ignoring the forlorn stump where a leg should've been hanging next to me on the bus. Was it really courtesy or a blemish in my *own* character? Was *I* the problem?

"I want one."

If I were the bearer of some perverse abnormality, would I find comfort in the wave of down-turned heads as I moved through the crowd? Or would I search desperately for the accepting nod or the shift in their eyes as they realize that perhaps we are *all* mistakes, the difference is in the way we wear it.

Feeling her stare burn into the back of my neck, I am pushing the skittles around into lines of an un-premeditated color scheme: Green, purple, yellow, red, orange, and again. I think about planting skittles in the warm earth, watching the candies sprout and uncurl in bright explosions of jewel-tones, like pinwheel blossoms, reaching towards the sun. Green, purple, yellow, red, orange.

"I *want* one."

I reach for the last skittle, the green one, and my hand brushes momentarily against the girl's outstretched index finger. I snatch away the skittle, and in a spasm of embarrassed fervor I wrench my head in her direction. She is a rosy-cheeked young girl, her shoulders hunched up impossibly around her face, which seems to be arranged as if by a severe claustrophobic. There was an uncanny frankness about her stare, as if knew every thought tumbling tumultuously about my skull like she'd seen it hundred times before, and that she *pitied* me.

"Take your pick," I smile, gesturing towards the lines of repeating skittles, hard-shelled rainbow centipedes. She redirects her finger towards my clenched fist, and I remember the lime skittle. As I hand it to her, I notice a small dent in the candy. She looks at it pensively and then back at me, smiling inanely. She places the skittle back into my hand which is resting palm-up on the table, and folds my fingers over it. "Never mind," she says steadily, and lumbers off. I pop the skittle into my mouth.

III.

My grandmother is always saying that she carries everything in her purse but the kitchen sink, and most of the time it's not completely unbelievable. She is forever unearthing precious trinkets and treats wrapped in rice-paper from that immense tapestry cornucopia; tiny teddy bears and Ziplocs of Li Hing Mui. Today we've come to the local Chinese restaurant for Dim Sum. The familiar odor like soy and ceramic dust greets us, along with a cacophony of foreign chatter. My grandmother sits, like a tiny spindled frog, her ebony hair piled wispily on top of her head. She smiles as if she's got the most *delicious* of secrets to indulge us in; her hands laced deeply with veins reach into the recesses of the purse. She pulls out a plastic package of sour patch kids.

"You kids like these things?" she grins, eyes crinkling at the edges, a toothy goofiness both endearing and infantile. I nod (I happened to think sour patch kids were one of the greater things in life) and hold out my hands. She puckers her mouth and shivers exaggeratedly, squawking that they are "Too! Sour! For me!" She watches me intently while I chew unfazed on one of the sugar-crusted candies, as if I was completing some incredible feat. "I don't know how you kids do it," she cackles, head shaking incredulously.

I imagine the sour sugar seeping through weathered layers of muscle, staining her stomach tissue and burning acrid holes in fragile slabs of flesh. I chew, slowly, and swallow.

After we've eaten, I take her arm as we walk down the sidewalk past bright boutiques and tea-shops. My fingers brush along the influx of loose flesh hanging from her arm, as if finally gravity had had its way. The skin is soft and terribly thin, just like the bellies of the geckos that cling onto the walls of my grandparent's garage, you can see the blue traces of their complete anatomy through the skin. I feel her small frame stumbling alongside me, almost ready to be rattled into a hundred intricate pieces that would blow away as soon as they met the air, leaving a crouched china skeleton hanging off my elbow. My best friend's grandmother had just died a week ago. She'd told me, throat thick with tears, that in her last days she was "just like an empty paper sack, the smallest thing could damage her. She just *wasted away.*"

Several weeks from then, I found the half-eaten baggie of sour patch kids all conglomerated into a big melted hunk in my jacket's pocket. I lay in bed, chewing at the misshapen gummies, letting the sour sugar curdle my saliva and burn the edges of my tongue. There was something bruised about the way they slid down my throat, and then clung at the walls of my stomach like rainbow-colored residue. My body protested finally, and I spent the rest of the night vomiting up sickly shades of green and orange. Falling asleep, my hands shook from the sugar that had managed to soak into my bloodstream before I could purge it from me. It was unnerving, the frailty I'd exposed inherent in my system. I dreamt of corpses grinning inanely with empty sockets and blue teeth. Their rotting flesh crawled with gummy worms.

—*Lauren Young-Smith*

114

To give you an idea of how adaptable the triptych form is, consider this piece by Kelly. She is obviously a sophisticated and creative writer who enjoys the challenge of new forms and new frameworks. We like this piece not only because Kelly takes some big risks and mostly succeeds at it but also because she teaches us some new possibilities for the form.

Bodily Fluids

A (future) Vegetarian, Drawn to Corpses

In preschool, we had a bed of dirt outside that no one ever used as a garden. On damp days the worms would come out and I liked to squat over them in the mud while the other kids yelled on the playground. The worms slipped oh so slowly out of their holes next to my velcro shoes. Sometimes I would grow impatient and try to pull one out, the rubbery sack of skin like spaghetti between my fingers. I always expected the worm to slip out easily, but it would stretch instead, the little creases like sock ribbing growing more and more strained until—

It would break. A frantic digging in the soil to find the other half of the creature, as if by reuniting its halves the worm would magically reassemble and inch away, perhaps grumbling at the inconvenience but quite alive. Fear that the teacher had seen me. An ashamed promise to myself that I would never do it again. And yet, on the next wet day, I would find myself in the mud once again, with a scrap of flesh between my chilly little fingers.

It fascinated me that a moving creature could have nothing inside of it except blood; and how the blood did not gush out immediately but instead paused, trembling in the open air, still wrapped in the dirty bandaged-colored tube, before sighing out; and that the blood looked identical to mine, was as red and fresh and good as mine; and that the death was *silent*.

I could not fathom it—how could something so small breathe, burrow, worm about and then, how could I, with the slightest tug, sever the taut lifeline and have a dead thing in my hands?

One Mile

I planned to take a run for the first time that morning. When I came downstairs in my t-shirt and soccer shorts, Mom was on the phone. She hung up while I poured myself a glass of orange juice and told me that Aunt Julie had died. I said "ok," then realized how stupid that sounded.

I jogged towards the park. I had never been terribly close to Julie. We would only go out to lunch together once or twice a year when I was at my grandparent's house. The chemo usually left her tired after an hour or so of talking. She had a way of speaking that made it feel as though you were a confidante in a great secret, even if the secret was nothing except that she was splurging by having sour cream on her baked potato.

I ran perhaps a mile before I realized that I would have to backtrack that mile to get home. Years later, when running impassioned me, a mile would be nothing— but that day, too out of breath and sweating to run anymore, I walked back to my house. As I did so, I thought about my uncle, who ran ultra-marathons. It struck me that he was perhaps running as well right now, only in such a different way, with such a different intensity and reason, that that you could barely call it the same activity.

As I reached my backyard, I spied a burrow of rabbits. There were three kits wriggling out of their hole for the first time. Their eyes were still filmy, like flat buttons, and their face bones looked large beneath their skin, not yet filled out by fat.

I felt a bit dizzy watching them, as if some scientist mixing test tubes had poured Julie's life out before me and into this burrow, and that I had caught a whiff of the noxious elixir with my mortal senses. As if life had physical properties, had weight and mass, could be measured and moved.

Being Strong

The strongest girl I ever knew wore socks to her mother's wake. All of the guests had arrived and were milling about in their starched cottons and polished leather when she came in. She looked composed, wearing a denim skirt, a simple blouse, socks, and no shoes. The socks were light blue with a pattern of big ripe strawberries on them. She had pulled them up to her lower shin, but the tops were sagging and the strawberries distorted under the wrinkles. She slid flatfooted across the hardwood floor, very slowly, from group to group, like a robin gliding about finding its bearings. Before she entered, I had expected to look at this girl and feel sorry for her; instead I felt humbled.

At the end of the memorial service, we filed outside to a large, grassy field. Her father and his friends were handing out white balloons on slender ribbons to each of the guests. We were encouraged to write a message on them in permanent marker. I did not know what to write; I seemed too distant an acquaintance to be worthy of writing to the deceased. I was just her daughter's friend.

When we gathered in the center of the field with our balloons, I saw the girl standing a few paces away on a slight slope. She had found a pair of shoes and was holding the balloon down next to her chest instead of letting it loose at the end of the string. The balloon was covered in careful writing that trekked around and around the white globe like quivering footprints. There were long sentences as well as smaller, disconnected thoughts, all written in different directions. On one of the faces she had written in large, capital letters "I Love You, Mom!" She punctuated it with a bubble exclamation point.

Everyone let go of their balloons at the same time. I cannot remember what mine said—perhaps I left it blank. They bobbed against each other in search for a bubble of space as they rose, and remained cohesive in a pocket of wind as they faded into specks. One of my classmate's aunts, who we called Suzanne, noted wryly that the mass looked like sperm: white bulbous heads and wriggling ribbon tails swimming through an ethereal soup. Not something you expect to hear at a wake. But really—what *can* you expect?—she was right.

—*Kelly Wherle*[2]

We invite you to explore the central notion of triptych—that of three related pieces—with your students, and to share your ideas and those of your students with us and with your colleagues to enhance further your teaching of memoir.

116

"So What?" Stories to Illustrate a Personal Theme

Sometimes, students are able to recount several events in their lives that are particularly significant and that they see as definite influences on the people they have become, on their character, on their values, and on their attitudes. We call these "So what?" pieces because students have, indeed, learned a lesson or been altered by these events.

Some such events are tragic. For example, among recent news stories was an account of the difficulties faced by the Green Bay Packers' quarterback Brett Favre in an eleven-month period of time: His father died, his brother-in-law died, and his wife was diagnosed with breast cancer; yet, he was able to separate the agony of his personal life from the events on the football field and continued to show his strength of character by playing football well as a form of emotional release. Similarly, on the very day that Democratic candidate for vice president John Edwards gave a concession speech to the country indicating that he and presidential running mate John Kerry had lost their bid for national office, Edwards had also learned that his wife Elizabeth had breast cancer. These events indicate strength of character that most can admire.

Our students' stories are often equally poignant. Many have written about the lessons they've learned and the ways in which they have been strengthened by experiences such as the suicide of a sibling, a divorce between their parents, the death of a beloved grandparent, or the experience of being an orphan raised in foster homes. Other experiences are more upbeat, with students recounting lessons learned and strengths gained from fruitful sports-related activities, the struggle and survival of a mother with breast cancer, or awards won after hard work and intense effort.

The key here is that students carefully select events especially significant to them, ones that will resonate with readers, and then focus on the qualities of their character, values, or perspectives that have been enriched and enhanced by those experiences. The focus of the pieces for this form of memoir is on highlighting the "So what?" theme connecting the pieces and on sharing those life lessons and learned character strengths with readers so that both the writer and the reader are inspired or empathetic.

Several published memoirs could certainly fall into this category because they stress, as a part of the memoir, experiences that enhanced strength of character or personal values. See, for example, *Sweet Summer* by Bebe Moore Campbell, *When Broken Glass Floats* by Chanrithy Him, or *Colored People* by Henry Louis Gates, Jr.

Multigenre Memoirs

The concept of the multigenre paper as presented by Tom Romano in books such as *Writing with Passion* (1995) and *Blending Genre, Altering Style* (2000) has become widely accepted and used in English classrooms across the country.[3] We have adapted this popular form to memoir, in part because of requests by our students to do so and in part because it is a form that lends itself well to focusing on the writing and artistic strengths of our students.

For multigenre memoirs, students present their memories in a variety of genre all within the same one final memoir product. For example, they may select poetry, essay, persuasion, or futuristic writings (What will I be like in twenty years?) to use in their final memoirs. They may mix and match poetry and prose writings, and/or art such as drawings, photographs, graphics, music, and realia (real objects attached to the pages or cover of the memoir product) as they compose their memoirs. Expanding the concept of the finished product to include multimedia and multigenre options gives students with varying abilities an opportunity to be successful in the writing classroom, allows them to work epistemically as various artists, and enhances the presentation of the final memoir.

For example, a student may include in her memoir a poem about her name, a first-person account of an important artifact and her interactions with it, a captioned drawing about a place important to her, photographs of her parents that accompany a descriptive piece about them, and a persuasive Snapshot Piece of the time she convinced her parents to help her buy her first car. Or, she might write pieces such as those we suggest in Chapters 3 and 4, unifying them with her "So what?" idea, and then including realia, photographs, and additional art—drawings or ideas drawn from scrapbooking—to enhance the finished product.

This form of memoir is especially popular with many of our students, and we are seeing more of them incorporate some aspect of multimedia and multigenre concepts into their finished memoirs.

We can't resist sharing Cassandra's poem from her multigenre memoir:

Home[2]
home (hom), n., 1. a house, apartment or other shelter that is the
usual residence of a person, family or household.

My room with roses,
Natalie's with clouds,
the basement with spiders.
The kitchen where we eat dinner
and the dining room where we don't.
The family room,
master bedroom,
guest room,
laundry room,
coat closet,
and garage.
Home is all these things,
but these things don't make it home.
What makes home is
the door half green, half tan
because I broke my arm before daddy finished.
Dandelions in Mama's best crystal vase

in the kitchen that smells of curry
and French vanilla candles.
Doorbells that ring through the downpour,
asking if I want to catch
green gutterwater
in the giant plastic bear
that formerly held animal cookies.
The not-so-secret passageway
where I sometimes cried myself to sleep.
The leather couch, all scratched up
from two teeny kittens
with claws like compass points.
Narrow stairs that we slid down in sleeping bags.
Smiling cheeks that smell clean like dirt.
The taboo basement bathtub
with hundreds of spiders
that crawled up through the drain.
Report cards,
chocolate pudding finger paintings,
clay magnets,
on a fridge with sticky handles.
My bedroom window
that I opened every night after tuck-ins,
left to curl under the blankets,
sleeping like a cat with my cat.
Bedtime stories,
and the sorority song,
revised to be the "Umpair" lullaby.
Mud pie hugs and marshmallow kisses.
Home is where you can admit
you put your finger in the rhubarb cobbler
and broke the perfectly browned crust,
without fear of being beaten,
even though you may not want to admit it.
Home is wherever you are
when you don't ever want to
be somewhere else.
Some people never find these things
in the game of life,
and they spend their whole life
trying to find home.

home (hom), n., 9. (IN GAMES) the destination or goal

—*Cassandra Stroud*

Memoir Blends

In our reading of published memoir, we are discovering numerous books that are both memoir and something else. For example, Patricia Hampl writes books that are at once memoir and spiritual journeys; Terry Tempest Williams writes books that are both memoir and nature books; and Kay Redfield Jamison writes books that blend memoir and medical treatises. These *blended memoirs* or *memoir blends*—memoirs that combine the genre of memoir with at least one other genre—as we have come to call them, also offer concepts useful in our studio classroom teaching of memoir with our students. The following are some of the memoir blends that have been successful for our students.

For blends of ***memoir and nature***, students write about their personal experiences and life lessons learned in the midst of the natural world. See our bibliography in Chapter 12 for several professional memoirs that blend with stories of natural world experiences. Student examples of this blend often include stories of camping, biking, hiking, fishing, and even of hunting—often father-and-son relationship stories—and of the lessons learned from observing and living in the natural world.

Blends of ***memoir and spiritual journey*** may be more controversial in the middle and high school classroom than they are in the college classroom, but if your students, their parents, and the school districts' administrators are willing to allow such explorations, these blends require students to reflect on their meaningful spiritual experiences and insights as they occur within the usual fabric of their lives. See Chapter 12 for several professional memoirs that use this type of blend. Student examples of this blend often focus on spiritual insights that have resulted for students who have faced significant family or personal challenges.

History and memoir blends are difficult for younger students to write since they often have not lived through or have no memories of significant historical events, but in recent years our students have successfully blended family stories with events such as the shootings at Columbine High School in Littleton, Colorado, in 1999, or the terrorist attacks on September 11, 2001. Several of our students also know enough of their own family history to be able to write personal histories of events associated with their own lives and with those of past generations of their family members.

The idea for a ***cooking and memoir*** blend was inspired by professional examples such as Frances Mayes' *Under the Tuscan Sun*. Similarly, the ubiquitous Pat Conroy has proved once again that he can turn anything into a winning book. His latest book is a collection of personal tales and favorite recipes titled *The Pat Conroy Cookbook*. Consequently, some of our students write pieces about how food-related festivities, holidays, and celebrations ground and unite their families. Sometimes such memoirs also have cultural or ethnic ties since our students who have chosen this option have also written pieces about their experiences of being Southern, Italian, Greek, Indian, or Jewish, for example. One of our students came from a family who had owned and run a Chinese restaurant for generations, so he wrote about his experiences growing up, playing, working, and observing patrons in the restaurant, adding some luscious recipes as part of his memoir.

The concept for the **music** (or other art form, such as theater) **and memoir** blend is found in published memoirs such as Winton Marsalis and Carl Vigeland's jointly written memoir of life on the road with jazzman trumpeter Winton Marsalis, *Jazz in the Bittersweet Blues of Life.* Several of our students have devoted themselves at an early age to music, theater, dance, sculpting, or other art forms, and they write pieces about how their lives and their artistic persistence and devotion intertwine, one influencing the other. Students who write such pieces often include representations of their art in their memoir, such as the printed music and lyrics for original songs and an audiotape of their playing of the song, original drawings, or videotapes of their theatrical performances.

Similar to the music and memoir blend is the **sports and memoir** blend, but we caution students that just any commonplace participation in team or individual sports with the usual *Sports is like life* theme won't suffice. Professional examples of these blends can be found in Pat Conroy's largely autobiographical novels and in his memoir titled *My Losing Season,* in which he writes of his experiences at The Citadel, this time on a college basketball team that triumphs and comes of age in the midst of an agonizing losing season. As a student example of this blend, Dawn had a female gymnast[4] in one of her college writing classes who qualified for the female U.S. Olympic Team, but who couldn't participate because of unavoidable knee surgery. Nonetheless, she went on to excel and to win top honors as a college gymnast and as a gymnast who even has a move named after her—a rare honor in the world of gymnastics. Her memoir of training, competing, being bitterly disappointed not to be in the Olympics, and yet of triumph in her sport and in her life made for fine and inspiring reading.

Final Thoughts

What we have tried to indicate here is that memoir is a vibrant and versatile genre that can take on several different forms to great advantage for the reader, for the writer, and for the enhancement of the literary experiences of both readers and writers. As we continue to read, write, and teach memoir, we discover and experiment with alternate forms of the genre, and we invite you and your students to do the same. By offering these options in form, in content, and in approach to a literary subject to our students, we help them to develop as skilled writers capable of making stylistic choices, building on *their* personal strengths and interests, and expanding their notions of *art* and *genre.* When we do so, we rather easily meet numerous state and national standards for instruction in the English/language arts, we are working in authentic rather than contrived ways to prepare our students to write well on state-mandated tests of writing performance, and we are building the habits of mind of lifelong readers and writers. We think that is meaningful and useful work well done.

Notes

1. This student author attended Ranum High School in Westminster, Colorado, in Ms. Keyes' English class. Student excerpts are printed as the authors wrote them, without change or correction.

2. These student authors attended Colorado Academy. Student excerpts are printed as the authors wrote them, without change or correction.

3. Because this format is commonly used, we have not elaborated its features and format here. For basic information on the style and format of the multigenre paper, please see either of Tom Romano's books listed below.

4. This student from Dawn's class preferred to remain anonymous.

Works Cited

Romano, Tom. 1995. *Writing with Passion*. Portsmouth, NH: Heinemann.

———. 2000. *Blending Genre, Altering Style*. Portsmouth, NH: Heinemann.

10

Tracking Memoir-writing Processes

When writing process methodology first became ubiquitous in classrooms, teachers and researchers alike heralded this new method as the panacea for solving all of our students' past writing woes. Panaceas, however, are hard to come by. It wasn't long before teachers who faithfully used writing process methods for instruction were talking about how some students' writings still weren't as thoughtful, original, or detailed as they needed to be. The *Steps in the Writing Process* posters hung on the walls of the classrooms (and still do in many of the classrooms we visit), the teachers followed the steps, and the writing still fell short. What had happened? Had the writing process failed?

Yes and no. Moving from thinking about writing as a parts-to-whole production—students must first learn to write good sentences and then good paragraphs before they can be allowed or trusted to write good whole papers—to seeing writing as process was a significant step in getting student writers to approximate more closely what real writers do when they write. The tendency of instruction, however, is to boil down complexities to manageable steps, and that was one of the problems. *The writing process*—singular—just doesn't exist. Processes are as different as the student writers who use them. With all of those processes going on in the classroom, teachers found it difficult to track what was happening with individual students. They realized, however, that forcing every student to create a jot list before writing wasn't much different from forcing them to create outlines first, and the results weren't much better, either.

What we now know is that the complex process of tracking and assessing student progress in writing can become too chaotic or just plain nonexistent unless we have specific tools and techniques, as well as routines and rituals in place as components of our instruction. We have worked over several years and hundreds of students to create tracking techniques that mirror the writing processes we are emphasizing in our classes and that students are using. We have put in place aids to help us track students' progress along their journey from idea to finished piece. As we are better able to monitor this journey, we are also better able to coach writing as it is emerging and developing.

In this chapter, we offer tracking strategies to help you be fully aware of students' progress from start to finish. Most of us have students who are still challenged in their abilities to organize almost anything. Therefore, we offer suggestions for adequately presenting planning structures to students and for encouraging students to develop blueprints or more detailed plans for completing a well-conceived and organized final memoir.

We also focus here on tracking and monitoring writing processes. In the next chapter, we include instruments for assessing and evaluating written products. We have divided these tracking and assessment techniques into two chapters because we know—and want to highlight—that ways of tracking processes and instruments for evaluation of final products are not synonymous, but both are important in obtaining a complete picture of progress and assessment for our students.

Collecting the Invisible Information: Writers' Reflections

Writers are often somewhat insecure. They worry that others might not like what they write. They wonder if they have captured the precise word for a sentence. They verify facts, figures, and terms so as not to make a mistake in their writing. They study what they do as writers, what they like as writers, and the ways in which they are successful as writers, on their own terms and in public terms. Thoughtful writers are highly reflective, and some track these reflections directly in their written pieces while others do so unconsciously. As we studied writers and their products, we began to categorize products and processes that could adapt well to our goals for assessment. Our conclusions about the importance of reflecting before, during, and after writing, and of self-assessments follow.

Reflections Before Writing

Before most writers take pen to paper, they plan and assess their knowledge, set a timeline and due date, gather needed resources, and otherwise prepare to write. Students benefit from the same type of self-assessments and reflections on their knowledge and abilities prior to writing. Therefore, within the studio writing classroom, we build opportunities and provide products that enhance planning, meeting the due date, and otherwise being ready to write. These assessments can be graded, or they can be used for informal goal-setting conferences, or both. They occur not just prior to writing a first draft, but throughout students' writing processes—before writing the third draft, before deciding on a scheme for the memoir, before writing the final version of the memoir, before taking a written piece public, or before participating in a Writers' Response Group. We have found that many *befores* accompany our students' writing journeys.

Following are some of the assessments that we have found useful in helping our students to assess adequately their preparations to write at several stages of writing explorations. We pick and choose from among these tools, depending on the students' needs, the contexts for writing, and the mood of the class as a working whole. Sometimes, we may use one instrument with only one student. Other times, we use an instrument with the whole class and then discuss students' findings and insights. We rarely, if ever, use all of these instruments with a particular group of students since such would likely overkill our goal of illustrating the need and usefulness of planning prior to writing.

Histories

Students assess their prior experience with a particular task, type of writing, or content information. Knowing how one performed in the past in a particular context can help one to avoid past pitfalls and build on past successes. We ask students to freewrite about whether they have previously written about their past or read authors who have done so.

Angstomometer

Students assess their level of fear, concern, and uncertainty. Dealing with fears and worries straight on is often the best way to overcome them. Such an instrument, in our opinion and as our name for it implies, can be treated a bit humorously in order to help alleviate students' fears that arise in connection to the topic being gauged, and it might consist of a simple Likert scale, such as, Circle the one number that indicates your concern about writing a personal memoir:

1	2	3	4	5	6	7	8	9	10
Panic attack at the mere thought of it				Not my favorite type of writing			"Yippee! When do we begin?"		

Naturally, discussion of the students' responses, of their reasons for their responses, and of coping strategies follows the completion of the Angstomometer.

Planning Documents

We have found that planning documents are a tremendous aid to our students. We believe in helping students plan early and plan often. Too frequently, students want to jump into a project before establishing a working plan of action, understanding the features of a project, or properly assessing what they already have and will need for successful completion of the project. We encourage our students to compose to-do lists and timelines. For some types of writing, we find that asking students to write a proposal or a prospectus is helpful. See Figure 10–1 for a prototype of a Memoir Blueprint that we use with our students soon after they have read and examined several published memoirs and have begun writing their own memoir pieces. Later in their writing processes for memoir when they have a better grasp of how their memoir will fit together, we also especially like to use a Map of the Piece (MOP) in order to help students juggle the various pieces of a complex product. See Figure 6–2 in Chapter 6 for a sample MOP for Memoir.

Memoir Blueprint

Planning Blueprint Prototype

<u>Directions</u>: Just as architects need a blueprint of a building in order to check out its design and supervise its construction, so, too, do writers need blueprints of written products that they plan to compose. Take a few minutes to respond to the following prompts. You are not stuck with these ideas in your final memoir. These are simply initial plans and ideas to set your creative mind to work.

<u>Working title</u>: _____

<u>Rationale for your working title:</u> _____

_____

<u>Pieces you may use:</u>   <u>Current status of the piece:</u>

_____   _____

_____   _____

_____   _____

_____

<u>Scheme for the memoir?</u> What is your anchor piece? In what tense will you write? In what order might the pieces appear?

_____

<u>Presentational features:</u> Which, if any, of the following features will you use in your memoir? Make check marks, jot notes, or otherwise plan how these features may enhance your final memoir.

Graphics: _____

Photographs: _____

Maps: _____

Acknowledgments: _____

Figure 10–1. *Memoir Blueprint: Planning Blueprint Prototype*

Dedications: _____

Prologue: _____

Table of contents: _____

Chapters or other divisions: _____

Epilogue: _____

Publication features: Which, if any, of the following features will you use in your memoir? Make check marks, jot notes, or otherwise plan how these features may enhance your final memoir.

Color: _____

Fonts: _____

White space: _____

Cover: _____

Binding: _____

The due date for the final memoir piece is _____.

What is your timeline for completing this piece by the due date?

Due date   Task

_____   _____

_____   _____

_____   _____

_____   _____

_____   _____

Figure 10–1. *Continued*

Although the Memoir Blueprint (Figure 10–1) and the Map of the Piece (Figure 6–2) are similar, they are used at different stages in our students' writing processes; therefore, each serves as an organized way for our students to track their emerging thinking and planning for their final memoir products.

Goals for the Journey

In our efforts to encourage students to see writing as a learning process, we often ask them to set individual learning goals for particular writing frameworks. For memoir, we ask students to establish what they might be able to learn or what they want to learn about themselves personally and as writers as they work on this framework. Often, establishing such goals helps students to determine the "So what?" aspect of their finished memoir.

Inventory

Most writers are picky about when and where they write, their writing routines, and even the materials and instruments they use for writing. Some writers can't sit down to write, for instance, until a row of pencils is sharpened and standing at the ready— even though the writer will compose on a computer. Similarly, we ask students to take inventory of what they will need for a particular writing framework. Will they need tools such as a dictionary and a thesaurus? Will they need information from Grandma and so need to plan a long-distance call to her? Will they need the family photograph albums and scrapbooks? Whatever writers will need, they save time and use their energies efficiently if they take inventory of needed supplies, materials, and equipment and gather the majority of it *prior* to beginning their composing processes.

Personal Assessment

In addition to needing equipment and supplies, writers will need certain personal abilities and skills in order to be successful with a particular writing framework. Taking stock of their abilities and liabilities can help students determine how successful they may reasonably expect to be, how hard they may have to work on a particular product or process, how much time a project may take, and a range of other factors. Such personal assessments can serve as motivators and reality checks for student writers. Our favorite method for accomplishing such a personal assessment is an informal journal entry to which we respond; however, we do not grade such honest, and perhaps vulnerable, offerings from our student writers.

Working Plan

We invite our student writers to establish the *what, when, where, how,* and *why* of completing writing frameworks. To do so, they may use any of the Planning Documents discussed earlier, timelines, to-do lists, journal entries, electronic calendar reminders, or any means that will motivate them to determine the steps and tasks necessary for successful completion of a project. Like writing itself, these Working Plans are often revised and revisited, but their existence and the process of updating them help students to target what they need to do in order to be successful with specific written projects.

Critical Responses

Because we believe that learning is, in part, a communal activity, we create time in our classes for sharing plans with Critical Friends Groups, Response Groups, or other types of groups of supportive student writers who are facing the same composing-process challenges and product demands. We find that peer groups will offer honest, caring critiques of another student's planning and thought processes; after all, they are all facing the same requirements in the same class, and they develop an interest in helping each other to be successful. Often, as a particular student hears himself respond to a partner's ideas and plans, he gains insights about his own working plan. The give and take of such exchanges in a supportive and humane environment helps students to take realistic stock of where they are in their processes and of what they want to achieve.

Reflections During Writing

After students have engaged in planning and reflections prior to writing, they will continue to avail themselves of such instruments as they seriously draft and revise their memoir pieces, working toward their final memoir product. Planning, reflection, self-assessment, and taking stock are processes that we find useful for our student writers *throughout* their composing processes.

Again, we tailor our use of these devices to individuals and to learning contexts, and, again, we rarely grade these assessments other than, perhaps, to give completion points to students who engage in the effective and mindful use of these tools.

Dispatches

The term *dispatch* has a clear military connotation. Soldiers send dispatches from the field to the command post, or they send dispatches to loved ones at home. Soldiers often feel solitary and possess information or feelings about which others need to know. Similarly, writers may send Dispatches to their Writer's Groups, to themselves, or to us as their teachers in order to air feelings or share information about their progress. On occasion, Dispatches are simply cries of distress: "I'm adrift in this writing process, and I don't know what to do next," or "This piece is a mess, and I am clueless about how to fix it." Sometimes, just acknowledging and facing the mess helps to clear a writer's head and enables him to move forward. At other times, Dispatches are affirmations from the writer to himself or to others about where he is now within his writing processes; Dispatches are his stories and recountings of what's going well and what needs work. Such information is valuable for the writer to confront and for the teacher to know in order to provide help, guidance, and coaching at the point of the individual student's needs.

As you'll see in the following student's Dispatch, these pieces are usually written for an audience of the teacher and may express the emotion that the student is trying to capture in the piece. The student may also wonder how effective her writing is. We see both of these features here.

> I wrote this memoir because it is significant to me. I feel that this is where all of my feelings are at, in this time of my life, because my grandfather passed away just recently. Starting out writing this paper, I wasn't sure how to get all of my feelings and outrage on paper. I am still not sure if you can feel the pain I am in. Is there anything that I could do to change that? I absolutely loved the advice that you [the student's teacher], Zack, and Sally gave me in our workshop. I think it helped me a lot. I decided to totally take out the dialogue because it didn't feel real to me. I added some more snapshots of my grandpa but I think there could maybe be more. What do you think? I am not sure this is as good as it could be, but I do think it has potential and that it's a work in progress.
>
> —*Stephanie Cline*[1]

At the end of this Dispatch, the student's teacher, our colleague Shelia Kahney, wrote in green ink "YES! Exactly!" and drew a large smiling face to show that she agreed with the student's assessment that the paper, as it existed at that point, had potential. The teacher also underlined the word *outrage* and wrote, in the same green ink, "WOW" in the margin to show her appreciation of the student's expanding vocabulary and expression of specific emotion. As a result, the student receives encouragement as a writer, and the teacher now knows how to coach this student more effectively as she refines her memoir.

Audits

Think here of an *audit* by a professional bookkeeper or accountant who makes sure that all is in order with the reporting of business-related expenses and income. Writers also have expenses; theirs is an expenditure of time and effort. In an Audit, a student writer reports to us his progress to date; he takes stock of his efforts and of what yet has to be done to complete his writing project, the final memoir.

We use Audits rather routinely in our studio writing classroom and find that they take the place of incessant surprise checks of Writer's Notebooks, a procedure that rather defeats the purpose of the Writer's Notebook as a place for experimentation, anyhow. Dan uses Audits weekly. We usually don't grade these audits per se, but we do use them to make notes to ourselves about who's on track and who needs further encouragement to get busy writing. We also find that students are brutally honest in their Audits, perhaps because we don't grade them, instead using them as conversation and motivation openers with our students. See Figure 10–2 for a sample Audit.

Audit Report for the Memoir Piece

<u>Directions:</u> Take stock of your progress on the final memoir piece, and report your progress to us. Use this opportunity to assess what you have under control and what you still need to do in order to complete your final memoir on time. Respond to the prompts below.

1. To what extent did you use the Map of the Piece (MOP) to plan and organize a working draft of your memoir piece for class today?

2. At this point, what is your working title for your memoir piece?

3. How complete is your working draft of your memoir piece?

4. What are the strongest parts of the draft? What are the weakest points?

5. What is the "So what?" of your memoir at this point?

6. What jobs do you have left to do to whip this draft into shape?

7. What specific help, if any, do you need from us at this point in your writing processes?

8. To what extent are you all caught up in your work for this class? What do you still need to do to be ready for the next workshop?

Figure 10–2. *Audit Report for the Memoir Piece*

Audits consist of one or more paragraphs, not of curt answers such as "Yes," "No," "Maybe," and "Sometimes." It gives the student an opportunity to talk to us on paper, and for us to respond to whatever the student offers forth in the Audit. Here is an Audit written by a student in one of Dan's classes.

> I now have five pieces in my writer's portfolio, the first being our first write starting with "My family is. . . ." and it's in okay shape. It's rough, I did it in a hurry. It'll do, but I can fix it if you want me to. Then I have the summary of my "life parts," and that may as well be in Greek because only I could understand it. I thought we were just going to discuss it and not read it. My third piece is the first of a trilogy of memoirs: I am quite proud of it. In fact, I spent much time and thought on the piece and although none of my group liked it, I still can't wait for your feedback. It's my best piece. The second part (4th piece) is written out & not bad but I'd like to develop it more. The final work I have in my possession is that which I wrote last night; it is weak and I'm getting discouraged. To get something ready for next Thursday, I must really concentrate on my love of writing and the important, positive first impression I want to make. I will probably compile the three for a large synopsis (I'll have to play around with them), I have to purchase some printer cartridges, and you can count on a finished project I will be proud of.
>
> —Anonymous[2]

What is interesting about this Audit to us is the student's honesty. Her in-stock writing for her memoir is not in great shape at this point, but she has a piece that she loves and that her group didn't love. Naturally, she is seeking Dan's opinion of the piece, hoping that he will agree with her that it is a piece of grand potential and promise. She lists small to large tasks to accomplish, and she ends by focusing on writing a product that *she* "will be proud of."

This Audit provides rich material for a pep talk and for a motivational talk about what she needs to do and by when she needs to accomplish her writing goals. It also provides insights about how to respond to a piece of her writing: very cautiously if not totally enthusiastically about it.

We use Audits for a range of purposes; therefore, we'll return to this idea later in the chapter and discuss other uses of Audits for assessment.

Here and Nows

Here and Nows are written *here* and *now*. That is, they are journal entries or freewritings completed in the first ten minutes or so of class to gauge the feelings of students about their work and progress at a precise point in time. Like the weather, these feelings and assessments of progress may change tomorrow or even by the end of the class period, but occasionally taking the barometric pressure of a writer is helpful and provides insights to us about who may need an individual conference, computer lab time, research time, or other assistance and coaching for their writing.

Status Reports

These missives are usually written directly to us as the teachers in the classroom. They are outright progress reports on how well the student is sticking to his timeline and meeting the goals and deadlines on his working plan. If needed, we follow up such Status Reports with individual or small-group conferences in order to nudge students to step up or refine their efforts.

Researcher's Dictionary

Many professional writers maintain a section in their Writer's Notebooks or a file on their computer of specialized terms, unique words, catchy phrases, or interesting quotes that they may use in future written pieces. The Researcher's Dictionary is based on a similar premise. Students, whose knowledge may be imprecise and a bit narrow, benefit from knowing and using precise terminology (Grandpa was a Regional Supervisor, not just a *manager*, and he drove a '57 Chevy Impala, not just an *old car*, for example), the lingo of a particular time and place (the 1960s in San Francisco, for example), or unique, startling words in their writing, all of which help to create an impact on their readers. The Researcher's Dictionary is a place in the Writer's Notebook or a file on the student's computer that affords opportunities to log terms, ideas, and linguistic tidbits for later use in his writing.

Logs

This is one of Dan's favorite devices for checking on students' writing progress. Logs are informal entries in a section of the Writer's Notebook in which students document their ongoing work and effort. We find that students are painfully honest in their Logs, which are written specifically for us in the roles of *writing teacher*, *mentor*, and *coach*. We respond to Logs and encourage more effort and progress from our students, as needed.

Updates

Updates are quickies, usually short and informal, in which students bring us up to date in writing about how they are revising their Working Plans, MOPs (see Figure 6–2), other Planning Documents, or any other part of their written pieces. We find that our student writers often have brain flashes about crafting techniques to try in their writing or of further pieces to write for their memoir. These Updates let us follow their thinking and their emerging plans. We inquire of our students if they have made substantial changes in their plans or pieces; if so, we ask them to give us an Update so that we can stay abreast of their work, ideas, and efforts.

Journals

Like the explorers Lewis and Clark or the naturalist John Muir, some writers just like to keep journals. For our students who fall into this category, we encourage them to use

Journals to maintain a narrative record of their work, efforts, and progress. Such entries may be dated; we, personally, like the orderliness of such a system. Or such entries may be nearly stream-of-consciousness entries by an author at work. Either way, Journals document the writer's journey, provide a visible record of effort and achievement, and allow the student to engage in metacognitive analyses of his processes and progress as he writes and after the written product is completed. We think that such a record and such an occasion for reflection are valuable tools for developing student writers and for us as planners of instruction.

Critical Assessments

Just as groups of supportive, but realistic, peers can provide insights about a student's plans for writing, so, too, can they provide feedback to a student writer about how the written pieces are progressing, how his work effort is measuring up to his personal goals and timeline, and how realistic he is being about his view of his writing and progress to date. Sometimes peers provide a session in tough love; sometimes they offer encouragement and helpful suggestions; but always, we stipulate that such peer assessments and evaluations are fruitful, humane, and generous in spirit.

Reflections After Writing

The learning to be gained from reflection does not cease when the final written piece is finished. Quite the contrary, we find that reflecting on writing *after* the product is done is as valuable as the other types of reflection in which we ask students to engage. It is after the fact, oftentimes, that students produce their best insights about their writing and most honestly assess their progress toward their goals for writing. It is at this time, too, that students can best recount the *should haves* of their writing processes and make resolutions for how to be more successful next time, how to budget their time better, or what to do to the piece if they are allowed to revise it further in the future.

Like the other types of reflections that we structure for students, we rarely grade these assessments, other than to give, perhaps, participation points; but we do respond to these reflections and even ask students to indicate a to-do list for the next writing opportunity, a What I Should Have Done reminder statement to guide their next writing efforts, or any other Note to Self (see the Note to Self section later in this chapter) that will be helpful to them as writers in the future. Also, we do not use all of these devices with all students; rather, we select one or two at a time for use with students, introducing all of these and more across time in our classes, so that our student writers have a repertoire of self-assessment devices to use for reflections on their progress and processes as learners.

Discovery Tales

What continues to please and awe us about writing is that the writer learns so much during the act of composing. Sometimes this learning occurs in a Coleridge-type flash, springing into the student's head as a full-blown insight. At other times, the learning is slow and laborious, emerging only after much effort and reflection. Either way, we think it helpful for students to know what they learned and *that* they learned. Writing accounts of *what* they learned and discovered and of *how* they learned and discovered becomes part of the valuable metacognition processes of writers when they engage in writing Discovery Tales of their learning. Discovery Tales focus primarily on *how* students worked and spent their time and on how their insights emerged. They are mainly reports of processes tried and abandoned, accounts of "What if I tried the technique of _____ in my writing" experiments conducted by the writer, and similar data.

Learning Reports

Similarly, Learning Reports focus primarily on the *what*, not so much on the *how*, of learning. Being able to recount specific pieces of knowledge gained is valuable to students who may try to pass through much of schooling in a bit of a fog. These accounts don't focus so much on actual data (for example, "My grandmother, Vivian Lyons, was born in 1911 in Toledo.") as on new insights about writing, learning, thinking, and reflecting that have been gained by the students during a writing framework.

"What I Think I Did" Reports

As any writer knows, sometimes words just don't cooperate with us. We know what we want to say, we struggle to say it, we choose some words to say it, and we hope those words are successful. "What I Think I Did" Reports provide opportunities for writers to tell us—their peers, teachers, and audience members—what they tried to accomplish in a piece of writing. "I think I captured the agony that I felt when my parents told us kids that they were divorcing," or "I tried to show the joy of holding a squirming puppy in my arms for the first time," or whatever goals the writer had for his expression. Sometimes, knowing the writer's motivation—what the writer *tried* to do in a piece—helps the reader to be more empathetic and understanding of the written words on the page. Knowing that information can also help us as writing coaches to make concrete suggestions about how to express such thoughts in future pieces or in future revisions of the current piece.

Notes to Self

When she was eight years old, our daughter liked to watch an animated show in which the main characters talk into a handheld communicator, muttering expressions like, "Note to self: Don't get beaten up next time." This idea of self-monitoring and of trying to lodge details for future actions into our brains is one that we all perform at some time. When writers jot such Notes to Self in a special section of their Writer's Notebooks or in a file on their computers, they have a valuable record of their learning and insights about writing that they can then apply to future writing contexts. "Note to Self: Writing *anything* takes longer than it takes. Give myself *plenty* of time to write prior to the deadline."

Debriefings

Here, in oral or written form, students try to connect the just-completed learning experience to other learning incidents. Too often, students see learning as nothing more than isolated sound bites in a sea of disconnected utterances. When students strive to build connections and patterns, they are embedding their learning more deeply into the long-term memory areas of their brains. They are seeing the flow of data and of information. They are establishing their own "So what?" for knowing, inquiring, and researching. Finally, they are making their knowing personal and unique, owning it outright in ways that only they can accomplish for themselves as builders of their own knowledge.

Debriefings are not pity parties, gripe sessions, fault-finding missions, or self-aggrandizement festivals. They are genuine self-assessments and opportunities for learning via sharing and reflecting. We usually engage a class in an oral debriefing about a writing framework upon its completion, discussing aspects of the product and processes that the students raise as rewarding or as problematic, and then we reserve ten to fifteen minutes for students to capture their personal insights in writing. This device is a favorite of ours.

Self-Assessments of Product, Plan, or Process

As graders, teachers, coaches, and cheerleaders of our students' writing, we like to know what our students think about their written products, their successes or failures with their plans and goals, and their insights on their writing processes. Therefore, we generally ask students to submit to us a Final Reflection on their products and processes upon their completion of a writing framework.

This Final Reflection is submitted along with the final memoir piece. We read it *before* we read the final memoir itself in order to learn what the student sees as strengths and liabilities in the piece, of what students are especially proud in their writing or what principally concerns them about the writing, and similar information. These Final Reflections guide our responses, but usually not our grades, to the written product, and we respond to the Final Reflections themselves, agreeing with students, encouraging them, and guiding them as writers. Figure 10–3 shows a sample Final Reflection that we use with our students upon their completion of the final memoir piece.

Again, the idea is for students to see the Final Reflection as a communication and reflection opportunity, so we expect paragraph-type responses rather than truncated "Yes," "No, or "Maybe" responses.

Here is Stephanie Cline again, writing her final reflections. We notice that, at the conclusion of the writing, she likes certain aspects of her final memoir and would still

Final Reflection on Memoir

<u>Directions:</u> Take a few moments to reflect in writing about the process that you have just experienced as you schemed your memoir and put together your final product. Answer honestly and thoroughly on a separate sheet of paper. See this as your chance to communicate with me and with yourself about your writing.

· What did you try to do with this piece of writing? What did you want the reader to understand or feel or think after reading your final memoir piece?

· How well does this piece of writing work? What parts of the piece work best? If you were going to continue to work on this piece of writing, what would you do to it? On what parts would you continue to work and to spend more time?

· What were the most difficult parts of this process?

· How helpful was your Writer's Group? What else do you need from them?

· How did you work through the problems with writing that you encountered? What were your work habits?

· What have you learned about yourself as a writer and as a memoirist as you worked on the Memoir Framework?

· Other comments? (No grade whining!)

Figure 10–3. *Final Reflection on Memoir*

work on others if time permitted. We like how she is able to state what she has learned and how she feels about her writing. Like many of our students, Stephanie has also found that memoir writing can be a cathartic experience.

> The main thing I liked throughout this writing piece is that it allowed me to dig deep into memories in my life that I really never had the courage to bring up. This really helped me see my grandfathers death in a totally different perspective, as well as my relationship with my parents. I though this was a great way for me to get these things out in the open.
>
> The thing I liked least about my portfolio is the panel pieces [the two supporting pieces of a triptych-style memoir; see Chapter 9]. After writing my anchor piece I definitely struggled with the panel pieces and how they were going to fit into my writing. I worked hard on them but till this day I don't find them as good as they could be. Another thing I struggled with while working on my portfolio was my anchor piece and being able to put forth my feeling and really make it a memoir. I think I struggled with these things because my grandfather's death just recently happened and it was really hard to write about it so soon.
>
> One part in my story that still eats at me is the part where I talk about my relationship with my mom. I really think I could have dug deeper into those moments and explained more of my feelings toward them.
>
> Things I learned the most as a writer was how to put such a significant moment in my life in a memoir, and make it come alive. It brought me back to that moment and really improved my writing. Some of the reasons why I learned these things is because of the memoir I am reading and the way my teacher helped me see through a writer's eye. As a student this has really benefited me now and in the long run because I know I will be using this form of writing in the future.
>
> —*Stephanie Cline*

Final Thoughts

These are many of the tools and techniques that we find helpful for working with our students to help them become more mindful and skilled writers. We also find these techniques and instruments to be informative for us and for our students, and we are comfortable with the ways in which these techniques and tools match up with our philosophy for writing instruction. These techniques and tools as presented in this and the next chapter are infinitely adaptable to your teaching goals and to your students' needs, and we invite you to adjust them as needed. We, too, continue to work on developing new monitoring, tracking, and assessment techniques and tools and on improving the ones that we offer here for your consideration. In-progress monitoring and final product assessment are, after all, as much of an ongoing process as is writing.

One last caution: Avoid overkill. Students can quickly feel "reflected to death" if they are asked to do too many of these techniques. Pick and choose the ones that best suit your instructional purposes and students. Remember that the goal is not to get students to do one of all of these. Instead, our goals are fostering the habit of reflective thinking and helping students to know how and why they are growing as writers.

Notes

1. Stephanie Cline was a student in Sheila Kahney's English class at Thornton High School in Colorado. Student excerpts are printed as the authors wrote them, without change or correction.

2. This piece was written by a student in one of Dan's classes who preferred to remain anonymous.

11

Evaluating Memoir Writing

If you have been reading the chapters of this book in sequential order and have gotten this far, it is probably clear that what we are proposing here is a shift in how writing is conceptualized and taught. To be reliable and consistent, a shift in conceptualizing assessment and evaluation must accompany the shift in instructional design and delivery. In Chapter 10, we discussed monitoring and tracking writing processes. In this chapter, we offer new tools of assessment and evaluation, which we have developed and are still refining. We share these tools here for you also to consider and adapt so that they work effectively for you and your students, not only as assessment tools but also as learning tools.

The paradigm shift that we are advocating involves a holistic view of literacy, one that views *authentic* reading, writing, thinking, discussing, conferring, mentoring, and coaching as meaningful, interrelated, and absolutely essential for *composing*—for building and constructing knowledge. In this new direction that we are taking toward writing and writing pedagogy, teachers and students assume new roles as co-workers (recall our discussion of *work* in the writing classroom in Chapter 2), co-composers (to us, all authentic knowledge is composed and built by the learner), and co-adventurers in learning (we have vowed that when we stop learning from our students, we'll quit the profession).

Naturally, the teacher remains primarily responsible for the scope and sequence of the curriculum, and for planning and selecting most of the instructional strategies and materials—but not totally. We fully support the notion that has emerged over the last decade or so that instruction, curriculum, learning, and the materials used to support them are negotiated to some extent with students. For us, it makes sense to allow more choice in these areas for our college-aged students than we do for middle school students because we find, generally, the older students to be more self-actualized, more aware of their educational goals, and more capable of handling a bit of ambiguity in the instructional environment. Yet, all students are capable of making choices about their learning.

Words like *accountability* and *high-stakes testing* and *standards* are increasingly part of the vocabulary of teachers—and of the pressure put on teachers to perform according to generalized notions of successful teaching as conceived by those who are usually outside the sphere of education. We understand those pressures and work with teachers and teacher wannabes virtually every day to deal effectively with them. That pressure, however, doesn't change some of the basic facts about assessment and evaluation in the English/language arts classroom, especially for quality writing.

What Testing Is Not

We use large frameworks like memoir, nature writing, and others to teach about genre, writing, and critical issues in our students' lives. We use relevant materials and a variety of texts. We structure opportunities for authentic learning, writing, and interacting with each other and with texts.

Then we give a multiple-choice exam.

Not.

There really is nothing inherently wrong with multiple-choice exams or with almost any other type of test typically given to students—*if* the tests are used in appropriate contexts and for sound pedagogical reasons. We have never seen a multiple-choice exam created by anyone, however, that can adequately inform us about our students' writing abilities. Maybe such a test can inform us about our students' knowledge of vocabulary, comma placement, or sentence completeness, but not of the students' abilities to engage in actual, authentic composing.

Even the state-mandated tests that actually require students to *write* as part of the exam often fail to offer authentic assessments of students' composing abilities. Students do typically write more often and revise more often in the regular English/language arts classroom if the mandated tests in their district require actual writing during one or more days of testing. That's the good news. But such tests are still often isolated, artificial evaluations; they may still foster stylized or even contrived written products; and their existence still consumes precious instructional time spent, not in meaningful activities for learning but in focusing on teaching the test in order to raise the all-mighty scores of the school and district.

We understand the pressures that these tests place on teachers—and even on districts—and we understand that state mandates are prescriptive edicts not to be trifled with. But we have long held the position that such tests are inappropriate and virtually meaningless instruments for informing anyone about students' abilities to write well. We have also long asserted that authentic writing instruction will work to raise test scores in more holistic and wholesome ways than will the current incarnation of teaching to the test typically advocated by school districts and by many instructional leaders in schools. We can teach differently and test differently and still be accountable to the constituents of a school and its community, which is a message that we have tried to illustrate in this book.

We think it is a step in the right direction that some of these state-mandated tests are starting to fade away in a few areas, mainly because they are not cost efficient. Our communities need more firefighters, police, community centers, libraries, and arts programs—not more money spent on artificial testing—and some politicos are beginning to recognize that point.

What Evaluation Can Become

When a paradigm shifts in ways such as the new directions that we are advocating here for writing instruction, methodology, and philosophy, so, too, must a change in assessment take place. The old evaluation tools are no longer appropriate; they no longer suit the new direction and revised context of instruction that have emerged from the new ways of teaching. Instead of the more traditional methods used for evaluation, we advocate the use of product-specific rubrics and evaluation tools, preferably ones cooperatively designed by the content specialist—the teacher—based on sound writing pedagogy and knowledge, but tempered by input and insight from students. We have found that when students help devise evaluation tools, several benefits accrue: They see evaluation as an ongoing process, not as an end-of-the-process activity; students understand the assessment instruments and their fair use more fully; students aren't caught unaware of the criteria for evaluation; and finally, students begin to develop valuable skills that they can apply to their own self-evaluations.

We see evaluation as an informative process for both teacher and student, not as punishment or emotional billy club. The aim is not to be soft-hearted or soft-headed about evaluation and grading. Quite the contrary. Instead, we support the design and use of authentic evaluation tools that will tell a teacher what he needs to know in order to assess his students' learning and progress as well as their abilities and areas for future development. We see evaluation as integral and intertwined with instruction, the one informing and supporting the other to give a clear, holistic picture of students' progress over time.

In short, traditional evaluations and state-mandated tests don't tell us what we need to know about our students' writing abilities, and they aren't very useful in helping students to understand what they already do well and the areas in which they need to improve. For both practical and philosophical reasons, therefore, we began designing our own evaluation tools, products, and instruments so that our students and we could learn as much from these tools as we did from our in-class discussions, writing conferences, and explorations with texts, and so that the evaluations were understood by our students and were a good match for our instruction.

A Word About Grading

Many teachers are under pressure to give daily grades for writing and to offer evidence that they have met district and state standards. Such is currently the reality of teaching for most of us in the classroom. Because our students write frequently, engage in conferences, keep Writer's Logs and Writer's Notebooks, draft, revise, and otherwise perform the work of writers, we find no problem with devising and justifying a daily grade, if needed, for the work that occurs in our classes. For example, students who participate in workshops, who have revised significant portions of their writing, who complete an Audit or a Dispatch (see Chapter 10), or who effectively articulate the Scheme for their memoir piece earn a daily grade (check, A, or 78—whichever format you use) for those products and activities. We also find that authentic instruction of the type we are advocating here rather easily meets the spirit of most district, state, and national standards for literacy learning in the language arts. For example, our students read a wide range of genre, they bring their linguistic awareness to their comprehension of texts, they use technology for various purposes, they read and write for personal purposes, and they view insights formed about texts as a means of understanding human experience. We suggest that you discuss with like-minded colleagues ways in which you might use this new approach to teaching writing and still meet the demands placed on you for achieving standardized benchmarks and for assigning grades.

A Bit of Terminology

Most of the time, terms like *grading*, *evaluation*, and *assessment* are used rather interchangeably as though they were synonyms. Technically, however, each term has a slightly different definition.

Grading

Grading is quite familiar to teachers, students, and parents, and it is the most widely used form of evaluation. Students receive grades of A or of 94. We don't need to belabor the meaning of *grading*.

Evaluation

Similarly, *evaluation* is a prescriptive blueprint of achievement. Just as you might go to a physician for an evaluation of a medical condition and a prescription for medication, school-based evaluations of students' abilities often are accompanied by plans for improvement, individualized instructional strategies, performance goals, behavioral objectives, and the like. Evaluation carries a value judgment. If my evaluation of you as a student in my class is that you rarely turn in homework—I have a count in my grade book of all the times you have failed to turn it in—and that you aren't working very diligently in my class—I also have in my grade book a string of failing grades for assignments that you have submitted—then my accompanying grade for your work will be a failing one. It is the judgmental nature of evaluation and grading that is often responsible for harsh pronouncements that we sometimes hear, such as "Jean is a failing student." Notice that the failure is now the person, not the products or lack thereof.

Assessment

Assessment, in contrast, involves taking stock of a situation. It is a descriptive indication of progress achieved, skills learned, or abilities displayed. Notice that assessments, in and of themselves, carry no judgments. Any judgments made occur by an individual after reviewing the assessment data. Assessments are collections of data, not indications of good or bad. The student is able to dribble the ball 100 times without error. Is 100 a high number? A desirable number? An assessment does not indicate such judgments. Assessments per se are rare in schools, partly because writing such descriptive narratives of achievement and ability is a time-consuming effort, partly because of the open door for litigation by almost anyone that narrative assessments present, and partly because the system that is schooling relies on separating the wheat from the chaff in as many ways as possible. Certainly, colleges examine a range of interview data, references, personal essays, and goal statements from their applicants, but almost all still depend first, if not foremost, on the students' grade point average (GPA) and test scores as prime indicators for determining admission.

Reality Check

In an ideal world, we teachers would *assess* our students and rarely, if ever, *evaluate* and *grade* them. But we are realists, so we have included here instruments that foster assessments, provide for evaluations, and facilitate grading. We also tend to blur the lines between the words *assessment* and *evaluation* as do most school personnel, except when we are emphasizing one over the other, leaving it to your discretion whether an instrument will be used for informative assessment or for graded evaluations. With these caveats in mind, we now move to tools for helping you to plan a comprehensive assessment infrastructure that is compatible with your instructional goals. We also offer several instruments and assessment products themselves.

Mapping the Assessment Territory

Part of the reason that assessment is such a prescriptive, chaotic mess in most of our country's school districts is that few teachers and administrators take the time to realize the benefits and goals of authentic assessment; few want to spend the time and money to develop authentic assessments; most value easily comparable data; and most think that if well-known companies and agencies have developed a test, why not just use that one? That is, they don't want to re-invent the wheel. The problem with that wheel is that it has huge flat spots on it and goes thump and bump in the night. Prescriptive evaluations yield easily counted scores, but they do little to meet the goals of authentic assessment.

To us, assessment is useful when it is a good match with our instructional goals and objectives, with our philosophies for instruction, and with our pedagogical values. Because assessment and evaluation are really about reward systems, we build an infrastructure that aligns with and rewards what we think is important for learning and working in the studio classroom. Although we have covered these points, at least implicitly, so far in this book and in our other publications, let us take a moment to review our values for the studio classroom and for assessment within that context.

Valuing Workers *in the Studio Classroom*

We value workers—the students in our classes. We want to encourage them to learn and we support their efforts to do so. Therefore, we devise and implement assessments that reward the following:

· students' persistence and sustained effort
· their ingenuity and resourcefulness
· their dedication to practice
· their growth and improvement
· their energy for learning
· their willingness to reflect on themselves as workers and learners, and on their work
· their growing sense of themselves as successful workers

Valuing Work *in the Studio Classroom*

We value work and think it the essential value of the studio classroom. If students aren't at work, they aren't learning. Therefore, we devise and implement assessments that reward the following:

· experiments with writing
· individual visions and versions of written pieces
· near misses and partial successes in writing
· commitment to refinement, crafting, revision, and improvement
· willingness to engage in peer response and review
· striving toward quality in writing

Valuing Works *in the Studio Classroom*

We value the written products—the works—that are a result of effort in the studio classroom. Talking about writing, planning to write, and reading various writings are parts of the processes of learning in the studio classroom, but they aren't the final outcome. A written product is. Therefore, we devise and implement assessments that reward the following:

· multiple representations of written work
· prototypes and models of products
· collected written artifacts

- performances of written work, which may occur in a variety of formats
- cooperative and team ventures, including performances, oral readings, edited and compiled written products, acknowledgments of those who contributed to the final written product, and other evidence that writers are not isolated in their work

We don't know of an industrial-strength evaluation instrument or a multiple-choice test that can meet these goals and values. Therefore, we researched the types of products that writers generate in order to devise our plans for authentic assessment and evaluation.

Tracking the Visible Information: Assessing, Evaluating, and Grading Work

Up to this point, we have discussed and offered specific ideas for the ways in which reflection is a valuable assessment tool for student writers and for teachers (see Chapter 10). Such reflections from our students inform us about the invisible work in which all writers engage: planning, creating, thinking, and experimenting. In order to track this work, we ask our student writers to reflect on their learning for an entire semester, grading period, or unit of study. The prompts and format for these Final Class Reflections, or Final Audits, as we also sometimes call them, are similar to those that appear in Chapter 10 for the final Memoir Piece. The difference is that students reflect on the entirety of a unit of study or semester of work. Figure 11–1 shows a sample Final Class Audit that we use with our students.

We have learned much about our students' self-assessments of their own learning and about their assessment of our teaching with such a tool as the Final Class Audit. Below is a student's response to such an audit that was given at the end of a semester-long college freshman composition class.

Believe it or not, the personal narrative essay [Memoir Paper] made the number one spot this semester on my favorites list for essays. The personal narrative was able to surpass the other genres for two reasons: One, I learned a great deal about my personal writing abilities and ways to improve in style and technique and; two, it will definitely be the most useful to me in the future. When one delves into the world of revision, s/he sees that the 'more, more, more' theory [of elaboration] is one which cannot be disputed. I found that even when I was sure a part of the piece had reached its peak (but made some additions here, deletions there, and a few adjective changes), it would take on a new world altogether, and consequently, act as a catalyst for further revision in other sections of the piece. In addition, my past experience with me as the subject was one in which difficulty played a major role. Finding a common theme in a variety of small writing exercises and then merging the pieces together opened my eyes to a way to overcome this difficulty with success.

At the onslaught of this class, the expression of my thoughts through written word always seemed wordy and somewhat choppy, never flowing as smooth as I perceived

Final Class Audit

Directions: Take a few moments to reflect in writing about the process that you have learned and experienced this semester and you worked on your writing. Answer honestly and thoroughly on a separate sheet of paper. See this as your chance to communicate with me and with yourself about your writing.

· What type of writing did you like best this semester? Why?

· How have you progressed as a writer this semester? What specific class activities helped you to progress as a writer?

· How helpful was your Writer's Group?

· How helpful was the textbook?

· What were your work habits for this class this semester?

· What suggestions do you have for my future teaching of this content material?

· Other comments? (No grade whining!)

Figure 11–1. *Final Class Audit*

it should. The largest improvement to my writing has been an evolution from a poetic approach to relaying ideas and information to actually presenting a paper in a clear and concise manner. I have always possessed the ability to write in several voices, but I've never worked on improving any of them. The amount of writing this class requires forces improvement whether one is looking to do that or not. Another improvement has been the time it takes me to compose a first draft. I would say this class has granted me a stronger command of written English, as it now takes me about half the time to compose the same length of an essay than it did at the beginning of this semester.

The progress I've made as a writer can be seen in the improvements explained above. Although faster isn't necessarily better, this demonstrates progression in my ability to relay thoughts and what would otherwise be verbal communication, as written word. I've found strength in writing exactly what I mean to convey, rather than painting a metaphoric picture in which *only* the beholder finds beauty.

Overall, the workshops were helpful, more so at the beginning of the semester than toward the end. The making or breaking factor of workshops is teaming up with others who willingly want to participate in the giving and getting of feedback. I found that, when grouped with students who fit this category, more often than not someone would provide feedback on something that hadn't even crossed my mind. It ultimately added to the fullness of my essays, as well as the incorporation of ideas my readers would want to hear about, but that I failed to introduce. If nothing else, it is always a good thing to read your writing out loud and even better when someone listens and provides you with constructive criticism.

—*Eliot Wong*[1]

Clearly, Eliot knows what he has gained from his work with memoir writing.

In addition to gathering information about students' reflections on their learning, teachers also need to track the nuts and bolts of the work performed by student writers. We have developed a plethora of charts, graphs, and other tools for keeping track of the work that our students submit, of what they are accomplishing, and of where they are falling a bit short in their work efforts. We're betting that you have favorite methods for tracking students' work as well, so we won't belabor this point. Instead, we offer as exemplars just two such tracking devices, Time Sheets and Writer's Group Checklist Evaluation, that we use during the Memoir Framework to stay informed about our students' work and to ease the workload of keeping up with all that students do and produce in our classes.

Time Sheets

The notion of Time Sheets is similar to that of time cards still used by some employers. Time cards allow employers to know when the worker arrives, takes off for lunch and returns, and when the worker leaves for the day. Although they tell employers nothing about how productively work time is spent, they do at least indicate time present in the workplace. Time Sheets are based on the same premise. They give us some information in a self-report format about how much time students are spending on various tasks. Figure 11–2 shows a sample Time Sheet that we use with our students throughout the Memoir Framework.

Writer's Group Evaluation

Although we listen in on our students' Writer's Groups as they are in progress, we find that we still need a method for tracking students' work and preparation for such in-class time. We model and prepare students well on how Writer's Group response sessions are to proceed. Nonetheless, students can drift in their conversations and occasionally fail to prepare fully for group time. In order to encourage on-task behavior and thorough preparation for response groups, we have devised a quick and efficient checklist. With clipboard, pen, and a stack of these checklists in hand, we circulate from group to group, asking each student to show us his work on the spot. We calculate a grade then and there for each student's participation and preparation in the Writer's Group, record the score in our grade books after we have worked with all of the groups, and give the checklist slips to each student as he exits class. We find that this system is easy for us and applies just enough pressure on most students to perform well in their groups.

We create a new checklist each time that Writer's Groups are in session, crafting the checklist according to the requirements and expectations for the work to be accomplished by the group and for the products that each student is to bring to the group. See Figure 11–3 for a sample Writer's Group Checklist Evaluation.

This checklist provides a simple, organized way of grading the student's preparation and participation in the group effort and tracks for the student precisely the areas in which his preparation or participation need improvement. If given to students a class session or two prior to the Writer's Group session, the checklist also serves as an organizational guide for students on what to bring to the group session and on the expectations for the session. This checklist has become a favorite with us and our students.

Grading and Evaluating the Final Memoir Product

Finally, it's time to grade the memoir product itself. We have set the stage for the ways in which assessments inform our instruction and for the ways in which assessments provide students and teachers with useful information. We in no way fool our students, however, into thinking that evaluation and grading will never occur. Just the opposite, in fact. We are very direct with our students in telling them that just as all artists ultimately face a juried evaluation of their work so, too, will they face a grading and evaluation of their final memoir product. As we have taught the Memoir Framework, we have talked routinely with our students about the techniques of published memoirists and the features of published memoirs that we think important for them to attempt in a memoir product. We have enlisted their ideas and viewpoints on the features of memoir that are essential to the genre. We have worked with them

Time Sheet for Writers

Name: _____   Date: _____

Directions: Record the approximate amount of time (hours and minutes) that you have spent so far on each activity. Account for in-class time, homework time, and personal time that you have spent on these activities.

_____ Topic Exploration: listing, talking with a partner, thinking, etc.

_____ Brainstorming: Writing clusters, cubes, mapping, jot lists, etc.

_____ Working with a Writer's Group or peer partner: reading aloud, discussing your writing, etc.

_____ Drafting: individual writing time

_____ Stalling: complaining, moaning, doing nothing, worrying, etc.

I rate my productivity so far as (circle ONE NUMBER):

1	2	3	4	5

I haven't gotten much of anything done yet.

I've gotten some stuff started.

I have done tons of good work and am spending my time well!

Figure 11–2. *Time Sheet for Writers*

Writer's Group Checklist Evaluation

Name: _____   Date: _____

Your preparations for and participation in today's Writer's Group have been evaluated as follows:

I.   Required Pieces (up to 5 points):

_____ Name Piece   _____ Snapshot Piece

_____ Family Piece

II. Completed MOP (up to 5 points):

_____ thorough   _____ partial

_____ sketchy   _____ missing

III. Required Memoir Draft (up to 10 points):

_____ full draft   _____ partial draft

_____ sketchy draft   _____ missing

IV. Readiness of Products for the Group (up to 10 points):

_____ copies of your draft for each group member

_____ at least three specific questions typed in advance for your group members about your writing; copies made for each group member

_____ you enter the group focused and ready to work

V.   Participation in the Writer's Group (up to 10 points):

_____ focused and on track   _____ occasional lapses in your attention

_____ mainly off-track, unfocused, and/or not responsive

This Writer's Group session was worth up to 40 points. Your score is _____ points.

Figure 11–3. *Writer's Group Checklist Evaluation*

to heighten their awareness of factors that will enhance their products and that will ultimately be graded in their written pieces. We conduct a class discussion of features of memoir that students think should be evaluated in their own final products. In short, once students see our evaluation rubric for the memoir piece, they are not surprised at its contents, and they feel confident that they understand the language of the rubric and the expectations behind it.

We have developed more elaborate rubrics from time to time, with specific comments under the **1**, the **3**, and the **5** indicators but students sometimes find such crowded rubrics overwhelming and difficult to read. Therefore, lately, we have gone to a more pared-down version of our earlier rubrics. We find that these new rubric formats are still informative, but that they are somewhat easier to read than the traditional version. As always, we encourage you to use our rubric as a template, adjusting it to your instructional goals and objectives as well as your techniques and procedures, and making it maximally effective and informative for your students' ongoing learning processes. Elsewhere, we have discussed the history and evolution of rubrics, their adaptability, and the time-saving factors of rubrics such as the ones that we use, so we will not dwell on those points here since versions of these rubrics are now rather widely in use among writing teachers.[2] See Figure 11–4 for a sample rubric that we use with our students to grade their final memoir products.

As you examine this rubric, we trust that you find it in alignment with the processes, theories, and viewpoints for teaching and learning that we have discussed throughout this book.

The last point to note is that we talk to students about their grade on the final Memoir Piece as reflected in this rubric as a *working grade* or a *grade in progress*. If students want to take to heart our comments and suggestions about their memoir pieces and extensively revise them, they may do so for a chance at an improved grade. Such an opportunity usually motivates our students to take revision seriously and to work diligently to improve their writing. We have also devised rubrics identical to this one for use as a student's self-assessment tool; after the student grades himself, we grade the final memoir product and then count the student's self-grade as one-third and our grade as two-thirds of the student's final grade on the Memoir Piece. Our point is that even grading can be flexible, negotiated in productive—not whiny—ways, and instructive for students.

We encourage you to continue to find ways to make grading as productive as possible, to lessen the punitive sting of grades, and to use even grades as learning tools.

A Word About Portfolios

In recent years, it has become increasing difficult to say the word *assessment* without also saying the word *portfolio*, and vice versa. We like portfolios and use versions of them frequently in our classes, and we encourage you to do the same when you find portfolios helpful and instructive for you and for your students. We particularly favor them in our studio-style classes because they capture the quality and history of the writer's work and

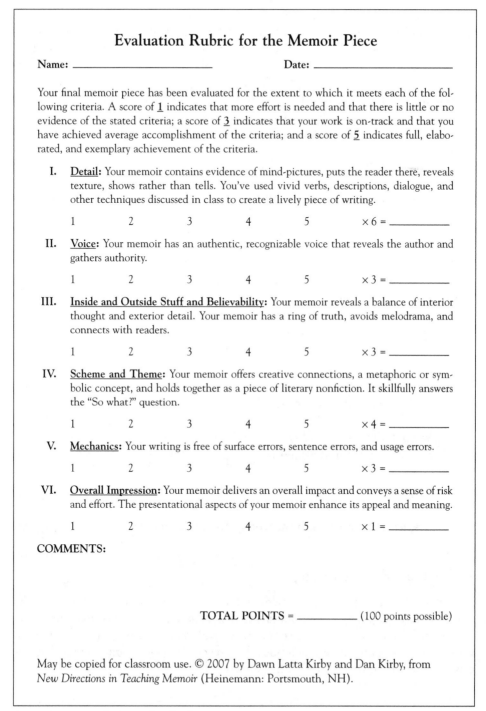

Evaluation Rubric for the Memoir Piece

Name: _____   Date: _____

Your final memoir piece has been evaluated for the extent to which it meets each of the following criteria. A score of **1** indicates that more effort is needed and that there is little or no evidence of the stated criteria; a score of **3** indicates that your work is on-track and that you have achieved average accomplishment of the criteria; and a score of **5** indicates full, elaborated, and exemplary achievement of the criteria.

   I.   **Detail:** Your memoir contains evidence of mind-pictures, puts the reader there, reveals texture, shows rather than tells. You've used vivid verbs, descriptions, dialogue, and other techniques discussed in class to create a lively piece of writing.

        1   2   3   4   5   × 6 = _____

   II.   **Voice:** Your memoir has an authentic, recognizable voice that reveals the author and gathers authority.

        1   2   3   4   5   × 3 = _____

   III.   **Inside and Outside Stuff and Believability:** Your memoir reveals a balance of interior thought and exterior detail. Your memoir has a ring of truth, avoids melodrama, and connects with readers.

        1   2   3   4   5   × 3 = _____

   IV.   **Scheme and Theme:** Your memoir offers creative connections, a metaphoric or symbolic concept, and holds together as a piece of literary nonfiction. It skillfully answers the "So what?" question.

        1   2   3   4   5   × 4 = _____

   V.   **Mechanics:** Your writing is free of surface errors, sentence errors, and usage errors.

        1   2   3   4   5   × 3 = _____

   VI.   **Overall Impression:** Your memoir delivers an overall impact and conveys a sense of risk and effort. The presentational aspects of your memoir enhance its appeal and meaning.

        1   2   3   4   5   × 1 = _____

COMMENTS:

                  TOTAL POINTS = _____ (100 points possible)

May be copied for classroom use. © 2007 by Dawn Latta Kirby and Dan Kirby, from *New Directions in Teaching Memoir* (Heinemann: Portsmouth, NH).

Figure 11–4. *Evaluation Rubric for the Memoir Piece*

effort. When we think of artists' portfolios, we always remember the stories of Juan Quezada, a Casas Grandes Indian potter, as told by Rick Cahill (1991). Quezada's is a marvelous story worth reading, but the point here is to remark on his portfolio: a pile of failed pots in his backyard. He can point to a particular failure and tell you what it taught him and how his pottery craft improved. Quezada celebrates his failures and partial successes because they are the tracks of his growth as an artist. We find that when students collect and catalogue their own work, they begin to develop the same reflective skills.

Much has been written in recent years about portfolios, their uses, and their management. We will simply state here that we think that the difference between a *portfolio* and a *notebook* is the reflective element. In a portfolio, we ask students to reflect in writing on their processes and insights as writers. We use Portfolio Audits just as we use Audits (see Chapter 10) during the writing of the memoir pieces. We use Final Reflections on the Memoir Portfolio just as we do for the final memoir product (see Chapter 10). And, we grade the Memoir Portfolio with a rubric similar to the one we use for the Memoir Piece (see Figure 11–4). See Figure 11–5 for a sample rubric for grading our students' Memoir Portfolios.

As you continue to appraise your own approaches to assessment, evaluation, and grading, we leave you with these final thoughts on portfolios:

· **Portfolios are** teacher-sponsored, teacher-mentored, and teacher-coached,
   but
   they are student-owned and operated.

· **Portfolios are not** a glorified notebook, writing folder, or assignment receptacle,
   but
   they are a collection of tracings, a wealth of artifacts, and the indications of the tracks of a writer's thinking.

· **Portfolios are not** merely another kind of evaluative tool,
   but
   they are a picture of both the worker and his or her work.

A Teacher's Reflective Log

As we have worked on these assessment and teaching concepts and methods over the years, we have received many insightful Audits, Updates, Final Reflections, and other types of reflections and assessments from those with whom we've had the pleasure to work. Here's a response to our techniques by a teacher who went into her tenth-grade classroom and tried them out with her students:

It's Saturday evening, the semester ended yesterday, I collected 55 Memoirs from my sophomores on Thursday, grades are due Monday. I wasn't exactly looking forward to

Evaluation Rubric for the Memoir Writer's Portfolio

Name: _____   Date: _____

Your portfolio has been evaluated for the extent to which it meets the following criteria:

I. Organization and Marketing

| 1 | 2 | 3 | 4 | 5 | × 2 = _____ |

Pieces are difficult to locate. Use a logical system to present your work.

I see some effort in both areas. Put best light on your work. Present it attractively.

Highly organized and professionally presented! Good job!

II. Amount of Writing: Drafts, Experiments, Assigned and Voluntary Pieces

| 1 | 2 | 3 | 4 | 5 | × 6 = _____ |

I see very few pieces of writing here. Are you seriously working on your writing?

Most of the assignments are here, but what about elaboration and voluntary pieces?

Tons of work in evidence here! Lots of pieces and excellent variety!

III. Quality of Work

| 1 | 2 | 3 | 4 | 5 | × 3 = _____ |

I see very little evidence of effort and quality work. How much time are you giving your writing? Use class handouts!

I see evidence of some effort and quality work. Try for more crafting and polishing. Think!

Highest quality work in this portfolio! Excellent effort!

IV. Response Logs: Logs are truthful, thoughtful, and thorough.[2]

| 1 | 2 | 3 | 4 | 5 | × 5 = _____ |

Log entries are skimpy and/or missing. Read, write, and think!

Log entries need further elaboration and brain power behind each response.

Logs are truthful, thoughtful, and thorough. Good connections to your own experiences and writing.

V. Overall Impression of the Memoir Portfolio

| 1 | 2 | 3 | 4 | 5 | × 4 = _____ |

Your portfolio represents your work in this class. Give both of these much more effort!

A good effort, but more time, energy, and thoughtfulness will pay off!

A superior representation of your reading, thinking, and writing in this class!

Comments:

Total Points = _____ (100 points possible)

May be copied for classroom use. © 2007 by Dawn Latta Kirby and Dan Kirby, from *New Directions in Teaching Memoir* (Heinemann: Portsmouth, NH).

Figure 11–5. *Evaluation Rubric for the Memoir Writer's Portfolio*

Teacher's Reflective Log

<u>Directions:</u> Please respond briefly to each of the prompts below. Lists and phrases, jottings and musings are all appropriate.

Reflection Before Teaching: What two or three goals have you set for your teaching and/or internships this year?

1. _____

    _____

2. _____

    _____

3. _____

    _____

Reflection During Teaching:

A. What class or part of your day with students is most enjoyable to teach (or, for internships, to observe or participate in) so far this year?

B. What is going on in that class that makes it enjoyable?

C. What is the chemistry in there that creates joy?

Reflections After Teaching:

A. How can you transfer the chemistry that creates joy in one class to another of your classes?

B. What are some ideas and concepts that you've encountered in this book about which you might continue to think? What specific strategies might you try to adapt to your own teaching now or in the near future?

Figure 11–6. *Teacher's Reflective Log*

an exciting weekend of hasseling to get all the memoirs and logs read and grades averaged, et. al. Until I began reading.

Now I am *so* excited about the wonderful stuff my 15 year olds have been doing that I can't resist sharing some of it with you. Besides having a perfectly fantastic group of kids, I think also the success is partly due to the fact that I have been able to let go of the class more than in the past. I don't read everything—in fact, I've probably read less than half the stuff they've written. And I trained the classes carefully to be response partners. So now they automatically go to one another for feedback and advice and don't hound me at all. That in itself is rare with tenth graders.

Anyway, I'm very proud of their writing. This winter has been one straight from Hell, so I'm especially pleased to have my sophomores to brighten the gloomy days. I love listening to their ideas and reading their stuff. I wanted to share my favorites with you.

—*Anonymous*[3]

Then the teacher had clipped several students' final memoir pieces to her note, and the pieces were a delight to read. We could see how hard she had worked to implement our ideas and to enhance them with some of her own. We could see how hard her students had worked and the care they had taken with writing that they clearly valued. We wish for you the same fate that this teacher and her students experienced.

Because we believe that reflection is an essential part of self-assessment and self-evaluation, we now invite you to take a moment to engage in a few reflections about your teaching. Perhaps you are a teacher of one year or of many years' experience, or perhaps you are just beginning to conduct some internships and observations in other teachers' classrooms. Either way, we think the Teacher's Reflective Log (Figure 11–6) is a valuable goal-setting and reflective tool that will be helpful to you.

We hope that you enjoy the reflecting, learning, and teaching for years to come, as do we.

Notes

1. Eliot Wong was a student in Dawn's composition class. Student excerpts are printed as the authors wrote them, without change or correction.

2. For further information, see Kirby, Dan, Dawn Latta Kirby, and Tom Liner. 2004. *Inside Out: Strategies for Teaching Writing*, 3rd edition. Portsmouth, NH: Heinemann.

3. This English teacher preferred to remain anonymous.

Work Cited

Cahill, Rick. 1991. *The Story of Casas Grandes Pottery*. Tucson, AZ: Boojum Books, a division of Western Imports Publishing and Trading Company.

12

Bibliographies in Memoir

Throughout this book, we have referenced many memoirs and suggested ways in which you and your students might use these memoirs for explorations and frameworks in reading and writing. Following are various bibliographies that you may find useful as at-a-glance tools. The first bibliography is our most recent listing of memoirs. We have found these works to be useful both as a source of good examples to use with our teaching and as our personal reading list to help us understand the nuances and dimensions of the genre. We have also created a second set of bibliographies to illustrate possible groupings around themes, ideas, and topics for reading and writing. Not all of the titles in our bibliographies are suitable for use with all of your students, but many will offer excerpts or exemplars of the genre that you may want to explore with your students. They will also serve to make you more conversant with the genre.

Of course, this bibliography was as current as it could be at the time that we went to press, but it will be out of date as you are reading it because of the explosion of publishing in this genre. We may also have omitted your favorite memoir from our bibliographies because it is virtually impossible to list every memoir ever published. But these bibliographies will provide a starting point for your explorations in the genre.

After perusing our lists, go to your favorite public library or bookstore to look for more memoirs. Memoirs are often shelved among such diverse sections as Biography, History, and Science. Curiously enough, most bookstores have not at this point created specific Memoir sections, suggesting once again that the genre has yet to distinguish itself fully from biography. You may even find memoirs in the young adult and children's sections, as we have. So, broaden your perspectives of the genre and spend some time searching for titles that suit your interests and needs—and those of your students. And, of course, come see us at conferences and workshops where we'll no doubt be adding to these resources.

Bibliography of Suggested Memoirs

ACIMAN, ANDRE. 2000. *False Papers: Essays on Exile and Memory*. New York: Farrar, Straus, and Giroux.

ALBOM, MITCH. 1997. *Tuesdays with Morrie: An Old Man, a Young Man, and Life's Greatest Lessons*. New York: Doubleday.

AL-WINDAWI, THURA. 2004. *Thura's Diary: My Life in Wartime Iraq*. New York: Viking.

ANGELOU, MAYA. 1997. *The Heart of a Woman*. New York: Bantam.

ARANA, MARIE. 2001. *American Chica: Two Worlds, One Childhood*. The New York: Dial Press.

ASHWORTH, ANDREA. 1998. *Once in a House on Fire*. New York: Holt and Company.

ASKINS, RENÉE. 2003. *Shadow Mountain: A Memoir of Wolves, a Woman, and the Wild*. New York: Anchor Books.

BACA, JIMMY SANTIAGO. 2001. *A Place to Stand*. New York: Grove Press.

BAKER, RUSSELL. 1982. *Growing Up*. New York: Plume Books.

BARRIOS, FLOR FERNÁNDEZ. 1999. *Blessed by Thunder: Memoir of a Cuban Girlhood*. Seattle: Seal Press.

BATESON, MARY CATHERINE. 1990. *Composing a Life*. New York: Plume Books.

BATTERSON, ANNE. 2001. *The Black Swan: Memory, Midlife, and Migration*. New York: Scribner.

BAYLEY, JOHN. 2000. *Iris and Her Friends*. New York: W. W. Norton.

BEALS, MELBA PATTILLO. 1994. *Warriors Don't Cry*. New York: Washington Square Press.

———. 2000. *White Is a State of Mind: A Memoir*. New York: Berkley Books.

BEARD, JO ANN. 1998. *The Boys of My Youth*. Boston: Little Brown.

BLUNT, JUDY. 2002. *Breaking Clean*. New York: Alfred Knopf.

BRAGG, RICK. 2001. *Ava's Man*. New York: Vintage Books.

———. 1997. *All Over But the Shoutin'*. New York: Pantheon.

BUCK, RINKER. 1997. *Flight of Passage*. New York: Hyperion.

BUECHNER, FREDERICK. 1999. *The Eyes of the Heart: A Memoir of Lost and Found*. San Francisco: Harper.

CAMPBELL, BEBE MOORE. 1989. *Sweet Summer: Growing Up With and Without My Dad*. New York: Putnam's Sons.

CANTWELL, MARY. 1998. *Speaking with Strangers*. New York: Houghton Mifflin.

CARROLL, DAVID. 2004. *Self-Portrait with Turtles: A Memoir*. Boston: Houghton Mifflin.

CARTER, JIMMY. 2001. *An Hour Before Daylight: Memories of a Rural Boyhood*. New York: Simon and Schuster.

CHANG, JUNG. 1992. *Wild Swans: Three Daughters of China*. New York: Anchor Books.

CHEN, DA. 1999. *Colors of the Mountains*. New York: Random House.

———. 2001. *China's Son*. New York: Dell Laurel-Leaf.

CISNEROS, SANDRA. 1989. *The House on Mango Street*. New York: Vintage Books (autobiographical fiction).

COHEN, ELIZABETH. 2003. *The House on Beartown Road: A Memoir of Learning and Forgetting*. New York: Random House.

CONROY, PAT. 2003. *My Losing Season*. New York: Bantam.

———. 2004. *The Pat Conroy Cookbook*. New York: Doubleday.

CONWAY, JILL KER. 1992. *The Road from Coorain*. New York: Vintage Books.

———. 1995. *True North*. New York: Vintage Books.

———. 2001. *A Woman's Education*. New York: Alfred Knopf.

CRUIKSHANK, JULIE. 1990. *Life Lived Like a Story*. Lincoln, NE: University of Nebraska.

DAHL, ROALD. 1986. *Boy: Tales of Childhood*. New York: Puffin Books.

———. 1988. *Going Solo*. New York: Puffin Books.

DAVIS, HEATHER CHOATE. 1998. *Baptism by Fire*. New York: Bantam Books.

DELANEY, SARAH, AND A. ELIZABETH DELANEY WITH AMY HILL HEARTH. 1993. *Having Our Say: The Delaney Sisters' First 100 Years*. New York: Kodansha International.

DICKERSON, DEBRA J. 2001. *An American Story*. New York: Anchor Books.

DIDION, JOAN. 2005. *The Year of Magical Thinking*. New York: Alfred A. Knopf.

DILLARD, ANNIE. 1987. *An American Childhood*. New York: Harper and Row.

———. 1989. *The Writing Life*. New York: Harper and Row.

———. 1999. *For the Time Being*. New York: Alfred Knopf.

DILLARD, ANNIE, AND CORT CONLEY, EDS. *Modern American Memoirs*. 1995. New York: Harper Collins.

DISKIN, SAUL. 2001. *The End of the Twins: A Memoir of Losing a Brother*. Woodstock and New York: The Overlook Press.

DOBIE, KATHY. 2004. *The Only Girl in the Car*. New York: Delta Trade Books.

DODSON, JAMES. 1996. *Final Rounds: A Father, a Son, the Golf Journey of a Lifetime*. New York: Bantam Books.

DOTY, MARK. 1999. *Firebird: A Memoir*. New York: Perennial.

EDELMAN, MARIAN WRIGHT. 2003. *Dream Me Home Safely: Writers on Growing Up in America*. Boston: Houghton-Mifflin.

ENG, PHOEBE. 1999. *Warrior Lessons: An Asian American Woman's Journey into Power*. New York: Pocket Books.

FIFFER, STEVE. 1999. *Three Quarters, Two Dimes, and a Nickel: A Memoir of Becoming Whole*. New York: The Free Press.

FISHER, ANTWONE. 2001. *Finding Fish*. San Francisco: Harper-Torch.

FOX, MATTHEW. 1996. *Confessions: The Making of a Post-Denominational Priest*. San Francisco: Harper Collins.

FRASER, JOELLE. 2003. *The Territory of Men: A Memoir*. New York: Random House Trade Paperbacks.

FREEMONT, HELEN. 1999. *After Long Silence*. New York: Delta Trade Paperback.

FULLER, ALEXANDRA. 2003. *Don't Let's Go to the Dogs Tonight: An African Childhood*. New York: Random House.

———. 2004. *Scribbling the Cat: Travels with an African Soldier*. New York: The Penguin Press.

GANTOS, JACK. 2002. *Hole in My Life*. New York: Farrar, Straus and Giroux.

GATES, HENRY LOUIS, JR. 1994. *Colored People*. New York: Alfred Knopf.

———. 1997. *Thirteen Ways of Looking at a Black Man*. New York: Random House.

GEERTZ, CLIFFORD. 1995. *After the Fact: Two Countries, Four Decades, One Anthropologist*. Cambridge: Harvard University Press.

GILCHRIST, ELLEN. 1987. *Falling Through Space*. Boston: Little Brown.

GOLDBERG, NATALIE. 1993. *Long Quiet Highway: Waking Up in America*. New York: Bantam.

———. 1996. *Writing Down the Bones: Freeing the Writer Within*. Boston: Shambala Press.

———. 2004. *The Great Failure: A Bartender, a Monk, and My Unlikely Path to the Truth*. New York: HarperCollins Publishers.

GOODALL, JANE. 1999. *Reason for Hope: A Spiritual Journey*. New York: Warner Books.

GOODWIN, DORIS KEARNS. 1997. *Wait Till Next Year*. New York: Simon and Schuster.

GRAY, FRANCINE DU PLESSIX. 2005. *Them: A Memoir of Parents*. New York: The Penguin Press.

GREEN, MELISSA. 1995. *Color Is the Suffering of Light*. New York: W. W. Norton.

GREENLAW, LINDA. 1999. *The Hungry Ocean: A Swordboat Captain's Journey*. New York: Hyperion.

———. 2002. *The Lobster Chronicles: Life on a Very Small Island*. New York: Hyperion.

GUILLERMOPRIETO, ALMA. 2004. *Dancing with Cuba: A Memoir of the Revolution*. New York: Pantheon Books.

HAIZLIP, SHIRLEE TAYLOR. 1995. *The Sweeter the Juice: A Family Memoir in Black and White*. New York: A Touchstone Book.

HAKAKIAN, ROYA. 2004. *Journey from the Land of No: A Girlhood Caught in Revolutionary Iran*. New York: Crown Publishers.

HALL, DONALD. 1993. *Life Work*. Boston: Beacon Press.

HALPIN, BRENDAN. 2003. *Losing my Faculties: A Teacher's Story*. New York: Villard.

HAMPL, PATRICIA. 1983. *A Romantic Education*. Boston: Houghton Mifflin.

———. 1992. *Virgin Time*. New York: Ballantine Books.

———. 1999. *I Could Tell You Stories: Sojourns in the Land of Memory*. New York: Norton.

HANSON, VICTOR DAVIS. 1997. *Fields Without Dreams: Defending the Agrarian Idea*. New York: The Free Press.

HARRIS, ALEX. 1987. *Portraits of Southern Childhood*. Chapel Hill, NC: University of North Carolina Press.

HARRISON, KATHRYN. 1998. *The Kiss: A Memoir*. New York: Bard and Avon Book.

———. 2004. *The Mother Knot: A Memoir*. New York: Random House.

HASSELSTROM, LINDA. 2001. *Feels like Far: A Rancher's Life on the Great Plains*. New York: Mariner Books.

HEALY, DERMOT. 1996. *The Bend for Home*. New York: Harcourt Brace.

HELLER, MICHAEL. 2000. *Living Root: A Memoir*. Albany, NY: SUNY Press.

HICKAM, HOMER. 2001. *Sky of Stone: A Memoir*. New York: Delacorte Press.

Hillerman, Tony. 2001. *Seldom Disappointed: A Memoir*. San Francisco: Harper Collins.

Him, Chanrithy. 2000. *When Broken Glass Floats, Growing Up Under the Khmer Rouge*. New York: W.W. Norton.

hooks, bell. 1996. *Bone Black: Memories of Girlhood*. New York: Holt and Company.

Huggan, Isabel. 1997. *The Elizabeth Stories*. New York: Penguin.

Jamison, Kay Redfield. 1996. *An Unquiet Mind: A Memoir of Moods and Madness*. New York: Vintage Books.

Johnson, Fenton. 1996. *Geography of the Heart*. New York: Scribners.

Johnson, John. 2002. *Only Son*. New York: Warner Books.

Kaplan, Cynthia. 2002. *Why I'm Like This: True Stories*. New York: Harper Perennial.

Karr, Mary. 1995. *Liar's Club*. New York: Viking Books.

———. 2000. *Cherry*. New York: Viking Books.

Kehoe, Louise. 1995. *In This Dark House*. New York: Schocken Books.

Kincaid, Jamaica. 1998. *My Brother*. New York: Farrar, Straus, and Giroux.

King, Stephen. 2000. *On Writing: A Memoir of the Craft of Writing*. New York: Scribners.

Kingston, Maxine Hong. 1989. *The Warrior Woman*. New York: Vintage International.

Kübler-Ross, Elisabeth. 1997. *The Wheel of Life: A Memoir of Living and Dying*. New York: Scribners.

Kuusisto, Stephen. 1998. *Planet of the Blind*. New York: The Dial Press.

Lamott, Anne. 1999. *Traveling Mercies: Some Thoughts on Faith*. New York: Pantheon.

———. 2005. *Plan B: Further Thoughts on Faith*. New York: Riverhead Books.

LaRose, Lawrence. 2004. *Gutted: Down to the Studs in My House, My Marriage, My Entire Life*. New York: Bloomsbury.

Lauck, Jennifer. 2000. *Blackbird: A Childhood Lost and Found*. New York: Pocket Books.

Lee, Li-Young. 1995. *The Winged Seed*. New York: Simon and Schuster.

Liu, Eric. 1998. *The Accidental Asian: Notes of a Native Speaker*. New York: Random House.

London, Joan. 1995. *Jack London and His Daughters*. Berkeley, CA: Heyday Books.

Lopez, Barry. 1998. *About This Life: Journeys on the Threshold of Memory*. New York: Alfred Knopf.

Lopez, Tiffany Ana. 1995. *Growing Up Chicano*. New York: Avon Books.

Lyden, Jacki. 1997. *Daughter of the Queen of Sheba: A Memoir*. New York: Houghton Mifflin.

Mah, Adeline Yen. 1997. *Falling Leaves: The Memoir of an Unwanted Chinese Daughter*. New York: Broadway Books.

Mairs, Nancy. 1994. *Voice Lessons: On Becoming a (Woman) Writer*. Boston: Beacon Press.

Marsalis, Wynton, and Carl Vigeland. 2001. *Jazz in the Bittersweet Blues of Life*. Cambridge: De Capo Books.

Mason, Bobbie Ann. 1999. *Clear Springs: A Memoir*. New York: Random House.

Matousek, Mark. 2000. *The Boy He Left Behind: A Man's Search for His Lost Father*. New York: Riverhead Books.

MAYES, FRANCES. 1996. *Under the Tuscan Sun: At Home in Italy*. New York: Broadway Books.

MCBRIDE, JAMES. 1996. *The Color of Water: A Black Man's Tribute to His White Mother*. New York: Riverhead Books.

MCCALL, CATHERINE. 2006. *Lifeguarding: A Memoir of Secrets, Swimming, and the South*. New York: Harmony Books.

MCCOURT, FRANK. 1996. *Angela's Ashes*. New York: Scribners.

MCCOURT, MALACHY. 1998. *A Monk Swimming*. New York: Hyperion.

MCGAHERN, JOHN. 2006. *All Will Be Well: A Memoir*. New York: Alfred A. Knopf.

MCGUANE, THOMAS. 1999. *The Longest Silence: A Life in Fishing*. New York: Knopf.

MCMURTRY, LARRY. 1999. *Walter Benjamin at the Dairy Queen: Reflections at Sixty and Beyond*. New York: Simon and Schuster.

MELOY, ELLEN. 2002. *The Anthropology of Turquoise: Meditations on Landscape, Art, and Spirit*. New York: Pantheon.

MERRIDALE, CATHERINE. 2000. *Night of Stone: Death and Memory in Twentieth-Century Russia*. New York: Viking.

MILLER, SUSAN J. 1998. *Never Let Me Down*. New York: Owl Books.

MIN, ANCHEE. 1994. *Red Azalea: Life and Love in China*. New York: Pantheon.

MOHR, NICHOLASA. 1986. *El Bronx Remembered*. Houston: Arte Publico Press.

MOMADAY, N. SCOTT. 1976. *The Names*. Tucson, AZ: University of Arizona Press.

MURRAY, DONALD. 2001. *My Twice Lived Life: A Memoir*. New York: Ballantine Books.

NAFISI, AZAR. 2004. *Reading Lolita in Tehran: A Memoir in Books*. New York: Random House.

NASDIJJ. 2000. *The Blood Runs like a River Through My Dreams*. New York: Houghton Mifflin.

———. 2004. *Geronimo's Bones: A Memoir of My Brother and Me*. New York: Ballantine Books.

NEISSER, ULRICH. 1982. *Memory Observed: Remembering in Natural Contexts*. New York: Freeman.

NEKOLA, CHARLOTTE. 1993. *Dream House*. St. Paul, MN: Greywolf Press.

NGUYEN, KIEN. 2001. *The Unwanted: A Memoir of Childhood*. New York: Little, Brown.

NIXON, JOAN LOWERY. 2002. *The Making of a Writer*. New York: Delacorte Press.

NJERI, ITABARI. 1982. *Every Good-Bye Ain't Gone: Family Portraits and Personal Escapades*. New York: Random House.

NORDAN, LEWIS. 2000. *Boy with Loaded Gun: A Memoir*. Chapel Hill, NC: Algonquin Books.

NORRIS, KATHLEEN. 1993. *Dakota: A Spiritual Geography*. Boston: Houghton Mifflin.

———. 1996. *The Cloister Walk*. New York: Riverhead Books.

———. 1999. *Amazing Grace: A Vocabulary of Faith*. New York: Riverhead Books.

———. 2001. *The Virgin of Bennington*. New York: Riverhead Books.

NORTON, LISA DALE. 1996. *Hawk Flies Above*. New York: Picador USA.

O'BRIEN, DAN. 2001. *Buffalo for the Broken Heart: Restoring Life to a Black Hills Ranch*. New York: Random House.

O'BRIEN, TIM. 1991. *The Things They Carried*. New York: Penguin.

O'Faolain, Nuala. 1996. *Are You Somebody? The Accidental Memoir of a Dublin Woman.* New York: Holt and Company.

O'Hearn, Claudine Chiawei. 1998. *Half and Half: Writers on Growing Up Biracial and Bicultural.* New York: Pantheon.

Offult, Chris. 1994. *The Same River Twice.* New York: Penguin.

Ondaatje, Michael. 1993. *Running in the Family.* New York: Vintage Books.

Orr, Gregory. 2002. *The Blessing.* San Francisco: Council Oak Books.

Pamuk, Orhan. 2006. *Istanbul—Memories and the City.* New York: Alfred A. Knopf.

Paulsen, Gary. 1997. *Pilgrimage on a Steel Ride.* New York: Harcourt Brace.

Perry, Michael. 2003. *Population: 485—Meeting Your Neighbors One Siren at a Time.* New York: Perennial.

Pham, Andrew X. 1999. *Catfish and Mandala: A Two-Wheeled Voyage Through the Landscape and Memory of Vietnam.* New York: Picador.

Raines, Howell. 1993. *Fly Fishing Through the Midlife Crisis.* New York: Doubleday.

Ray, Janisse. 1999. *Ecology of a Cracker Childhood.* Minneapolis, MN: Milkweed Editions.

———. 2003. *Wildcard Quilt: Taking a Chance on Home.* Minneapolis, MN: Milkweed Editions.

Rich, Frank. 2000. *Ghost Light.* New York: Random House.

Rose, Phyllis. 1997. *The Year of Reading Proust: A Memoir in Real Time.* Washington D.C.: Counterpoint.

Sacks, Oliver. 2001. *Uncle Tungsten: Memories of a Chemical Boyhood.* New York: Alfred Knopf.

Santiago, Esmeralda. 1998. *When I Was Puerto Rican.* New York: Vintage Books.

Sartor, Margaret. 2006. *Miss American Pie: A Diary of Love, Secrets, and Growing Up in the 1970s.* New York: Bloomsbury.

Sayre, Nora. 2001. *On the Wing: A Young American Abroad.* Washington D.C.: Counterpoint.

Schreiber, Le Anne. 1996. *Light Years.* New York: Anchor Books.

Scully, Julia. 1998. *Outside Passage: A Memoir of an Alaskan Childhood.* New York: Random House.

Sebold, Alice. 2002. *Lucky.* New York: Back Bay Books.

Seth, Vikram. 2005. *Two Lives.* New York: HarperCollins Publishers.

Sewell, Marilyn, Ed. 2001. *Resurrecting Grace: Remembering Catholic Childhoods.* Boston: Beacon Press.

Shah, Saira. 2003. *The Storyteller's Daughter.* New York: Alfred A. Knopf.

Shulman, Alix Kates. 1995. *Drinking the Rain.* New York: Farrar, Straus, Giroux.

———. 1999. *A Good Enough Daughter.* New York: Schocken Books.

Siporin, Ona. 1995. *Stories to Gather.* Logan, UT: Utah State University Press.

Snyder, Don J. 1998. *The Cliff Walk: A Job Lost and a Life Found.* Boston: Little, Brown and Co.

Sobel, Dava. 2000. *Galileo's Daughter: A Historical Memoir of Science, Faith, and Love.* New York: Penguin.

Stringer, Lee. 2004. *Sleepaway School: Stories from a Boy's Life.* New York: Seven Stories Press.

Styron, William. 1992. *Darkness Visible: A Memoir of Madness.* New York: Vintage Books.

Sullivan, James. 2004. *Over the Moat: Love Among the Ruins of Imperial Vietnam.* New York: Picador.

SWANDER, MARY. 2004. *The Desert Pilgrim: In Route to Mysticism and Miracles*. New York: Penguin Compass.

SWEENEY, JENNIFER FOOTE, Ed. 2003. *Life As We Know It: A Collection of Personal Essays from Salon.com*. New York: Washington Square Press.

TAN, AMY. 2003. *The Opposite of Fate: Memories of a Writing Life*. New York: Penguin Books.

THWE, PASCAL KHOO. 2003. *From the Land of Green Ghosts: A Burmese Odyssey*. New York: Perennial.

TRENKA, JANE JEONG. 2003. *The Language of Blood: A Memoir*. St. Paul, MN: Borealis Books.

TUCKER, NEELY. 2004. *Love in the Driest Season: A Family Memoir*. New York: Crown Publishers.

WELTY, EUDORA. 1983. *One Writer's Beginnings*. Cambridge: Harvard University Press.

WIESEL, ELIE. 1995. *Memoirs: All Rivers Run to the Sea*. New York: Schocken Books.

————. 1999. *And the Sea Is Never Full: Memoirs, 1969–*. New York: Alfred Knopf.

WILLIAMS, TERRY TEMPEST. 1991. *Refuge: An Unnatural History of Family and Place*. New York: Pantheon Books.

————. 2000. *Leap*. New York: Pantheon Books.

WINNER, LAUREN F. 2002. *Girl Meets God: On the Path to a Spiritual Life*. Chapel Hill, NC: Algonquin Books of Chapel Hill.

WIWA, KEN. 2001. *In the Shadow of a Saint: A Son's Journey to Understand His Father's Legacy*. South Royalton, VT: Steerforth Press.

WOIWODE, LARRY. 2000. *What I Think I Did: A Season of Survival in Two Acts*. New York: Basic Books.

WOLFF, TOBIAS. 1989. *This Boy's Life*. New York: The Atlantic Monthly Press.

There are also some fine books on how to write memoir. Our favorite features writers discussing their memoir writing ideas, motives, challenges, and techniques, followed by an excerpt from their memoir. It is listed below.

ZINSSER, WILLIAM, ED. 1998. *Inventing the Truth: The Art and Craft of Memoir*. Boston: Houghton Mifflin.

Themed Memoirs and Memoir Pairings

We have found it helpful in our teaching of memoir as genre and as a framework for writing to cluster various memoirs around themes of interest, by culture, and/or by ethnicity in order to compare perspectives of the authors, relate the personal experiences of our students to those of authors with similar or diverse backgrounds, and otherwise promote discussion and writing ideas. The following are some of the themes and clusters that we have found helpful in our teaching.

Again, view these bibliographies with an eye toward groupings that will work for you and your students. These categories are not necessarily mutually exclusive. For example, a category of *African American Women's Lives and Issues* could easily be formed even though we don't itemize such a grouping here. So, rearrange and group titles in ways that enlighten your discussions and thinking about the genre; and, as always, add to our ideas with favorites and new discoveries of your own.

Bibliography of Memoirs Clustered by Culture and Ethnicity

Possible memoir clusters are virtually endless, but here are some that have occurred to us during our study of the genre.

MEMOIRS BY AFRICAN AMERICAN AUTHORS

Cultural studies offer unique views into worlds, experiences, and perspectives that may be both similar to and different from those of the reader. One way to organize cultural studies is by the ethnicity of the author. Here, we feature books by African American authors who speak to the culture, ethnic, and personal experiences that impacted their particular lives. Some of these authors write of experiences unique to African Americans; others write of the experiences of humanity: the appreciation of music, the heartbreak of a divided family, the search for an unknown father. These authors' works will resonate with all readers who appreciate quality writing and well-developed themes.

ANGELOU, MAYA. 1997. *The Heart of a Woman*. New York: Bantam.

ASHWORTH, ANDREA. 1998. *Once in a House on Fire*. New York: Holt and Company.

CAMPBELL, BEBE MOORE. 1989. *Sweet Summer: Growing Up With and Without My Dad*. New York: Putnam's Sons.

DELANEY, SARAH, AND A. ELIZABETH DELANEY WITH AMY HILL HEARTH. 1993. *Having Our Say: The Delaney Sisters' First 100 Years*. New York: Kodansha International.

FISHER, ANTWONE. 2001. *Finding Fish*. San Francisco: Harper-Torch.

GATES, HENRY LOUIS, JR. 1994. *Colored People*. New York: Alfred Knopf.

———. 1997. *Thirteen Ways of Looking at a Black Man*. New York: Random House.

HAIZLIP, SHIRLEE TAYLOR. 1995. *The Sweeter the Juice: A Family Memoir in Black and White*. New York: A Touchstone Book.

HOOKS, BELL. 1996. *Bone Black: Memories of Girlhood*. New York: Holt and Company.

JOHNSON, JOHN. 2002. *Only Son*. New York: Warner Books

KINCAID, JAMAICA. 1998. *My Brother*. New York: Farrar, Straus, and Giroux.

MARSALIS, WYNTON, AND CARL VIGELAND. 2001. *Jazz in the Bittersweet Blues of Life*. Cambridge: De Capo Books.

McBRIDE, JAMES. 1996. *The Color of Water: A Black Man's Tribute to His White Mother*. New York: Riverhead Books.

NJERI, ITABARI. 1982. *Every Good-Bye Ain't Gone: Family Portraits and Personal Escapades*. New York: Random House.

MEMOIRS BY CHINESE AUTHORS AND CENTERING ON CHINESE CULTURAL ISSUES

These titles are written by Chinese and Chinese American authors about their experiences and perspectives associated with being Chinese. Some of these stories are heartwarming; some are heartbreaking. All offer insights for readers of similar and disparate cultures. One of the ways in which we like to use culturally centered titles with our students is to read in search of shared, common experiences. For example, when a Chinese woman writes of feeling unloved by her parents, we question our students about feeling similar emotions and about how they resolved those feelings. These titles are often emotionally challenging to read, but the rewards for the mature reader are those of experiencing quality writing and using that writing to reflect upon our own lives.

CHANG, JUNG. 1992. *Wild Swans: Three Daughters of China.* New York: Anchor Books.

CHEN, DA. 1999. *Colors of the Mountains.* New York: Random House.

———. 2001. *China's Son.* New York: Dell Laurel-Leaf.

ENG, PHOEBE. 1999. *Warrior Lessons: An Asian American Woman's Journey into Power.* New York: Pocket Books.

KINGSTON, MAXINE HONG. 1989. *The Warrior Woman.* New York: Vintage International.

LEE, LI-YOUNG. 1995. *The Winged Seed.* New York: Simon and Schuster.

LIU, ERIC. 1998. *The Accidental Asian: Notes of a Native Speaker.* New York: Random House.

MAH, ADELINE YEN. 1997. *Falling Leaves: The Memoir of an Unwanted Chinese Daughter.* New York: Broadway Books.

MIN, ANCHEE. 1994. *Red Azalea: Life and Love in China.* New York: Pantheon.

TAN, AMY. 2003. *The Opposite of Fate: Memories of a Writing Life.* New York: Penguin Books.

MEMOIRS BY JEWISH AUTHORS AND CENTERING ON JEWISH CULTURAL ISSUES

As you might expect, many Jewish authors write of the Holocaust and of the exile experienced by Jews in many cultural settings. Many of these books do cover that theme, but there is also a book about the struggle of a half-Jewish, half-Christian woman to find her spiritual home. We have not featured here books by Jewish authors such as Mitch Albom's *Tuesdays with Morrie* (see the complete bibliography earlier in this chapter for bibliographic information) that do not seem to center on issues of Jewish culture. Naturally, such books are legion and offer writings about human experiences that we all share, such as watching the slow, agonizing death of a beloved friend as does Albom's best seller. Rather, we have listed here titles that offer particular insights on uniquely Jewish experiences with the aim of using these titles as windows into discussions of that culture and its interlacing with all cultures.

ACIMAN, ANDRE. 2000. *False Papers: Essays on Exile and Memory.* New York: Farrar, Straus, and Giroux.

FREEMONT, HELEN. 1999. *After Long Silence.* New York: Delta Trade Paperback.

KEHOE, LOUISE. 1995. *In This Dark House.* New York: Schocken Books.

SETH, VIKRAM. 2005. *Two Lives.* New York: HarperCollins Publishers.

WIESEL, ELIE. 1995. *Memoirs: All Rivers Run to the Sea.* New York: Schocken Books.

———. 1999. *And the Sea Is Never Full: Memoirs, 1969–.* New York: Alfred Knopf.

WINNER, LAUREN F. 2002. *Girl Meets God: On the Path to a Spiritual Life.* Chapel Hill, NC: Algonquin Books of Chapel Hill.

MEMOIRS BY HISPANIC, CHICANO/A, LATINO/A, CUBAN, AND PUERTO RICAN AUTHORS

This group of authors offers insights on several related cultures. They write of the ways in which their cultures and ethnicities have both hindered and helped them. With our students, we look for commonalities in the authors' experiences and our own, regardless of our ethnicity. Our Hispanic, Chicano, Latino, Cuban, and Puerto Rican students find issues of assimilation, association, and disparity to discuss as they read these works or excerpts from them; and our students of other ethnicities find that they, too, relate to the experiences and themes presented by these authors. We also find it particularly relevant to select works and excerpts on a theme such as coping with a divorce or with feelings of isolation by authors of various ethnicities, looking for ways in which culture influences the authors' perceptions on these themes.

Baca, Jimmy Santiago. 2001. *A Place to Stand*. New York: Grove Press.

Barrios, Flor Fernández. 1999. *Blessed by Thunder: Memoir of a Cuban Girlhood*. Seattle: Seal Press.

Cisneros, Sandra. 1989. *The House on Mango Street*. New York: Vintage Books.

Lopez, Tiffany Ana. 1995. *Growing Up Chicano*. New York: Avon Books.

O'Hearn, Claudine Chiawei. 1998. *Half and Half: Writers on Growing Up Biracial and Bicultural*. New York: Pantheon.

Santiago, Esmeralda. 1998. *When I Was Puerto Rican*. New York: Vintage Books.

Bibliography of Memoirs Clustered by Themes of Interest

Memoirs can be clustered around almost any theme that is of interest to you and your students. Here are a few themes that appeal to us.

MEMOIRS ABOUT SPIRITUAL QUESTS

The authors of the books we've listed in this section are searching for, and often finding, answers to questions larger than themselves. They are seeking their spiritual homes, their spiritual identities, and their spiritual roots. Some discuss their journeys and interactions with a specific religion. Others discuss spirituality in more global terms. Some touch on issues of deliverance from drug use, on Catholicism, on Judaism, on finding spirituality through study of the natural order, and on the role of an encompassing force in human life. All offer views on mortality and on our moral and spiritual conduct during this life. These books work best with sophisticated readers who can juggle viewpoints that may differ from their own on the issues of religion, God, spirituality, and the place of all people in a spiritual setting.

Davis, Heather Choate. 1998. *Baptism by Fire*. New York: Bantam Books.

Dillard, Annie. 1999. *For the Time Being*. New York: Alfred Knopf.

Fox, Matthew. 1996. *Confessions: The Making of a Post-Denominational Priest*. San Francisco: Harper Collins.

FREEMONT, HELEN. 1999. *After Long Silence*. New York: Delta Trade Paperback.

GOODALL, JANE. 1999. *Reason for Hope: A Spiritual Journey*. New York: Warner Books.

HAMPL, PATRICIA. 1992. *Virgin Time*. New York: Ballantine Books.

KÜBLER-ROSS, ELISABETH. 1997. *The Wheel of Life: A Memoir of Living and Dying*. New York: Scribners.

LAMOTT, ANNE. 1999. *Traveling Mercies: Some Thoughts on Faith*. New York: Pantheon.

NORRIS, KATHLEEN. 1993. *Dakota: A Spiritual Geography*. Boston: Houghton Mifflin.

———. 1996. *The Cloister Walk*. New York: Riverhead Books.

———. 1999. *Amazing Grace: A Vocabulary of Faith*. New York: Riverhead Books.

———. 2001. *The Virgin of Bennington*. New York: Riverhead Books.

SWANDER, MARY. 2004. *The Desert Pilgrim: In Route to Mysticism and Miracles*. New York. Penguin Compass.

WIESEL, ELIE. 1995. *Memoirs: All Rivers Run to the Sea*. New York: Schocken Books.

———. 1999. *And the Sea Is Never Full: Memoirs, 1969–*. New York: Alfred Knopf.

WINNER, LAUREN F. 2002. *Girl Meets God: On the Path to a Spiritual Life*. Chapel Hill, NC: Algonquin Books of Chapel Hill.

MEMOIRS ABOUT PHYSICAL AND EMOTIONAL CHALLENGES

Although all memoirs conceivably involve the author's emotions, some memoirs focus on particularly challenging emotional and physical issues: the challenges of having a brother dying from AIDS or of having a husband die at the dinner table, the emotions associated with being born a female in China during a time when only males were valued, the challenges of being blind or bipolar, and other such extraordinary human trials. Far from being sentimental tearjerkers, these titles are frank looks at the issues faced by the authors. Nonetheless, they resonate with our emotions and sympathies, so that yes, for one or two of these, you may require a tissue box by your side.

ASHWORTH, ANDREA. 1998. *Once in a House on Fire*. New York: Holt and Company.

BARRIOS, FLOR FERNÁNDEZ. 1999. *Blessed by Thunder: Memoir of a Cuban Girlhood*. Seattle: Seal Press.

CHANG, JUNG. 1992. *Wild Swans: Three Daughters of China*. New York: Anchor Books.

DAVIS, HEATHER CHOATE. 1998. *Baptism by Fire*. New York: Bantam Books.

DIDION, JOAN. 2005. *The Year of Magical Thinking*. New York: Alfred A. Knopf.

DODSON, JAMES. 1996. *Final Rounds: A Father, a Son, the Golf Journey of a Lifetime*. New York: Bantam Books.

FIFFER, STEVE. 1999. *Three Quarters, Two Dimes, and a Nickel: A Memoir of Becoming Whole*. New York: The Free Press.

FREEMONT, HELEN. 1999. *After Long Silence*. New York: Delta Trade Paperback.

JAMISON, KAY REDFIELD. 1996. *An Unquiet Mind: A Memoir of Moods and Madness*. New York: Vintage Books.

JOHNSON, FENTON. 1996. *Geography of the Heart*. New York: Scribners.

Kehoe, Louise. 1995. *In This Dark House*. New York: Schocken Books.

Kincaid, Jamaica. 1998. *My Brother*. New York: Farrar, Straus, and Giroux.

Kübler-Ross, Elisabeth. 1997. *The Wheel of Life: A Memoir of Living and Dying*. New York: Scribners.

Kuusisto, Stephen. 1998. *Planet of the Blind*. New York: The Dial Press.

London, Joan. 1995. *Jack London and His Daughters*. Berkeley, CA: Heyday Books.

Mah, Adeline Yen. 1997. *Falling Leaves: The Memoir of an Unwanted Chinese Daughter*. New York: Broadway Books.

Min, Anchee. 1994. *Red Azalea: Life and Love in China*. New York: Pantheon.

Snyder, Don J. 1998. *The Cliff Walk: A Job Lost and a Life Found*. Boston: Little, Brown and Co.

Wiesel, Elie. 1995. *Memoirs: All Rivers Run to the Sea*. New York: Schocken Books.

———. 1999. *And the Sea Is Never Full: Memoirs, 1969–*. New York: Alfred Knopf.

Williams, Terry Tempest. 1991. *Refuge: An Unnatural History of Family and Place*. New York: Pantheon Books.

———. 2000. *Leap*. New York: Pantheon Books.

MEMOIRS ABOUT MEN'S LIVES AND ISSUES

Men's issues are as diverse as the males who live their individual lives. These titles offer a male author's perspective on subjects as diverse as basketball, golf, and fishing; physical abuse of a son by a father; restoring a ranch; and running the Iditarod race. Yet, these are not just books for boys; on the contrary, memoirs speak to the common experiences that we all share, so that many females will also enjoy these reads. And yes, some males may not find every title here to their liking. Taste in reading, after all, is an individual choice.

Bragg, Rick. 2001. *Ava's Man*. New York: Vintage Books.

Buck, Rinker. 1997. *Flight of Passage*. New York: Hyperion.

Conroy, Pat. 2003. *My Losing Season*. New York: Bantam.

Diskin, Saul. 2001. *The End of the Twins: A Memoir of Losing a Brother*. Woodstock and New York: The Overlook Press.

Dodson, James. 1996. *Final Rounds: A Father, a Son, the Golf Journey of a Lifetime*. New York: Bantam Books.

Gantos, Jack. 2002. *Hole in my Life*. New York: Farrar, Straus and Giroux.

Johnson, John. 2002. *Only Son*. New York: Warner Books.

LaRose, Lawrence. 2004. *Gutted: Down to the Studs in My House, My Marriage, My Entire Life*. New York: Bloomsbury.

Matousek, Mark. 2000. *The Boy He Left Behind: A Man's Search for His Lost Father*. New York: Riverhead Books.

McGahern, John. 2006. *All Will Be Well: A Memoir*. New York: Alfred A. Knopf.

McMurtry, Larry. 1999. *Walter Benjamin at the Dairy Queen: Reflections at Sixty and Beyond*. New York: Simon and Schuster.

O'BRIEN, DAN. 2001. *Buffalo for the Broken Heart: Restoring Life to a Black Hills Ranch*. New York: Random House.

OFFULT, CHRIS. 1994. *The Same River Twice*. New York: Penguin.

PAULSEN, GARY. 1997. *Pilgrimage on a Steel Ride*. New York: Harcourt Brace.

RAINES, HOWELL. 1993. *Fly Fishing Through the Midlife Crisis*. New York: Doubleday.

SETH, VIKRAM. 2005. *Two Lives*. New York: HarperCollins Publishers.

SNYDER, DON J. 1998. *The Cliff Walk: A Job Lost and a Life Found*. Boston: Little, Brown and Co.

WIWA, KEN. 2001. *In the Shadow of a Saint: A Son's Journey to Understand His Father's Legacy*. South Royalton, VT: Steerforth Press.

WOLFF, TOBIAS. 1989. *This Boy's Life*. New York: The Atlantic Monthly Press.

MEMOIRS ABOUT WOMEN'S LIVES AND ISSUES

Women's issues are also as diverse as the individual women who live their individual lives. These titles offer perspectives on successful women in several arenas of life, on what happens to a girl who develops a reputation for being fast and loose, on what it's like to be the daughter of a famous person, on the challenges of battling breast cancer, on the struggle of coming to terms with one's sexual identity, and on other issues often related to women's lives. Again, not all women will enjoy these titles, and these are not just girl books. There's not a frilly book in the lot; rather, these books offer insightful and enlightening explorations of various lives and challenges faced by the women who wrote them.

ANGELOU, MAYA. 1997. *The Heart of a Woman*. New York: Bantam.

BATESON, MARY CATHERINE. 1990. *Composing a Life*. New York: Plume Books.

CONWAY, JILL KER. 1992. *The Road from Coorain*. New York: Vintage Books.

———. 1995. *True North*. New York: Vintage Books.

———. 2001. *A Woman's Education*. New York: Alfred Knopf.

DOBIE, KATHY. 2004. *The Only Girl in the Car*. New York: Delta Trade Books.

ENG, PHOEBE. 1999. *Warrior Lessons: An Asian American Woman's Journey into Power*. New York: Pocket Books.

FRASER, JOELLE. 2003. *The Territory of Men: A Memoir*. New York: Random House Trade Paperbacks.

GILCHRIST, ELLEN. 1987. *Falling Through Space*. Boston: Little Brown.

HAKAKIAN, ROYA. 2004. *Journey from the Land of No: A Girlhood Caught in Revolutionary Iran*. New York: Crown Publishers.

HARRISON, KATHRYN. 1998. *The Kiss: A Memoir*. New York: Bard and Avon Book.

———. 2004. *The Mother Knot: A Memoir*. New York: Random House.

KINGSTON, MAXINE HONG. 1989. *The Warrior Woman*. New York: Vintage International.

LONDON, JOAN. 1995. *Jack London and His Daughters*. Berkeley: Heyday Books.

LYDEN, JACKI. 1997. *Daughter of the Queen of Sheba: A Memoir*. New York: Houghton Mifflin.

McCALL, CATHERINE. 2006. *Lifeguarding: A Memoir of Secrets, Swimming, and the South*. New York: Harmony Books.

NAFISI, AZAR. 2004. *Reading Lolita in Tehran: A Memoir in Books*. New York: Random House.

O'FAOLAIN, NUALA. 1996. *Are You Somebody? The Accidental Memoir of a Dublin Woman*. New York: Holt and Company.

RAY, JANISSE. 1999. *Ecology of a Cracker Childhood*. Minneapolis, MN: Milkweed Editions.

———. 2003. *Wildcard Quilt: Taking a Chance on Home*. Minneapolis, MN: Milkweed Editions.

SARTOR, MARGARET. 2006. *Miss American Pie: A Diary of Love, Secrets, and Growing Up in the 1970s*. New York: Bloomsbury.

SCHREIBER, LE ANNE. 1996. *Light Years*. New York: Anchor Books.

SCULLY, JULIA. 1998. *Outside Passage: A Memoir of an Alaskan Childhood*. New York: Random House.

SHULMAN, ALIX KATES. 1995. *Drinking the Rain*. New York: Farrar, Straus, Giroux.

———. 1999. *A Good Enough Daughter*. New York: Schocken Books.

WILLIAMS, TERRY TEMPEST. 1991. *Refuge: An Unnatural History of Family and Place*. New York: Pantheon Books.

MEMOIRS OF PLACE

To some extent, all memoirs honor place; and in many memoirs, setting plays such a powerful role in the telling of the memoirist's story that it may assume a significance similar to that of a character. As the memoirist tells us the stories associated with a place, we see how that place shaped, limited, enhanced, and otherwise affected the author. The author can't tell the story of his or her life without telling the story of place. These are some memoirs in that category.

AL-WINDAWI, THURA. 2004. *Thura's Diary: My Life in Wartime Iraq*. New York: Viking.

BARRIOS, FLOR FERNÁNDEZ. 1999. *Blessed by Thunder: Memoir of a Cuban Girlhood*. Seattle: Seal Press.

CAMPBELL, BEBE MOORE. 1989. *Sweet Summer: Growing Up With and Without My Dad*. New York: Putnam's Sons.

CARTER, JIMMY. 2001. *An Hour Before Daylight: Memories of a Rural Boyhood*. New York: Simon and Schuster.

DILLARD, ANNIE. 1987. *An American Childhood*. New York: Harper and Row.

FULLER, ALEXANDRA. 2003. *Don't Let's Go to the Dogs Tonight: An African Childhood*. New York: Random House.

GILCHRIST, ELLEN. 1987. *Falling Through Space*. Boston: Little Brown.

MASON, BOBBIE ANN. 1999. *Clear Springs: A Memoir*. New York: Random House.

MAYES, FRANCES. 1996. *Under the Tuscan Sun: At Home in Italy*. New York: Broadway Books.

McMURTY, LARRY. 1999. *Walter Benjamin at the Dairy Queen: Reflections at Sixty and Beyond*. New York: Simon and Schuster.

MOMADAY, N. SCOTT. 1976. *The Names*. Tucson: University of Arizona Press.

NORRIS, KATHLEEN. 1993. *Dakota: A Spiritual Geography*. Boston: Houghton Mifflin.

Norton, Lisa Dale. 1996. *Hawk Flies Above*. New York: Picador USA.

Offult, Chris. 1994. *The Same River Twice*. New York: Penguin.

Pamuk, Orhan. 2006. *Istanbul—Memories and the City*. New York: Alfred A. Knopf.

Perry, Michael. 2003. *Population: 485—Meeting Your Neighbors One Siren at a Time*. New York: Perennial.

Pham, Andrew X. 1999. *Catfish and Mandala: A Two-Wheeled Voyage Through the Landscape and Memory of Vietnam*. New York: Picador.

Raines, Howell. 1993. *Fly Fishing Through the Midlife Crisis*. New York: Doubleday.

Ray, Janisse. 1999. *Ecology of a Cracker Childhood*. Minneapolis, MN: Milkweed Editions.

———. 2003. *Wildcard Quilt: Taking a Chance on Home*. Minneapolis, MN: Milkweed Editions.

Schreiber, Le Anne. 1996. *Light Years*. New York: Anchor Books.

Scully, Julia. 1998. *Outside Passage: A Memoir of an Alaskan Childhood*. New York: Random House.

Shah, Saira. 2003. *The Storyteller's Daughter*. New York: Alfred A. Knopf.

Shulman, Alix Kates. 1995. *Drinking the Rain*. New York: Farrar, Straus, Giroux.

Thwe, Pascal Khoo. 2003. *From the Land of Green Ghosts: A Burmese Odyssey*. New York: Perennial.

Tucker, Neely. 2004. *Love in the Driest Season: A Family Memoir*. New York: Crown Publishers.

Williams, Terry Tempest. 1991. *Refuge: An Unnatural History of Family and Place*. New York: Pantheon Books.

MEMOIRS BY POETS

We have found it fascinating to read the memoirs of authors whose poetry we love. We notice that the lyrical imagery, figurative language, and development of metaphor that enliven the poetry of these authors also enhance their prose writings. Sometimes, we notice that similar themes in a particular poem or collection of poems are also developed in sections of the same author's memoir. Noticing how language and figurative devices impact both prose and poetry is one of our favorite topics for discussion with our students who are learning how to manipulate their writing for the most impact with an audience. These titles feature memoirs by poets whom we like.

Angelou, Maya. 1997. *The Heart of a Woman*. New York: Bantam.

Baca, Jimmy Santiago. 2001. *A Place to Stand*. New York: Grove Press.

Green, Melissa. 1995. *Color Is the Suffering of Light*. New York: W. W. Norton.

Hall, Donald. 1993. *Life Work*. Boston: Beacon Press.

Heller, Michael. 2000. *Living Root: A Memoir*. Albany, NY: SUNY Press.

Lee, Li-Young. 1995. *The Winged Seed*. New York: Simon and Schuster.

Orr, Gregory. 2002. *The Blessing*. San Francisco: Council Oak Books.

MEMOIRS BY CHILDREN'S AND YOUNG ADULT AUTHORS

Although these books are authored by those who typically write for children and young adults, these titles are not necessarily aimed at an audience of young adults and children, so be sure to preview the books before using them with your students. Titles here cover aspects of the author's life that he or she found noteworthy: a prison experience, becoming a writer, and running the Iditarod, to name a few. As readers mature, they often find that they want to know more about a favorite author. One way to learn more is to read that author's memoir, not just a biography of the author. These memoirs often portray a voice that fans of the author will recognize; at other times, the reader will enjoy hearing a different voice than the ones featured in beloved books for younger audiences.

DAHL, ROALD. 1986. *Boy: Tales of Childhood*. New York: Puffin Books.

———. 1988. *Going Solo*. New York: Puffin Books.

GANTOS, JACK. 2002. *Hole in My Life*. New York: Farrar, Straus, and Giroux.

NIXON, JOAN LOWERY. 2002. *The Making of a Writer*. New York: Delacorte Press.

PAULSEN, GARY. 1997. *Pilgrimage on a Steel Ride*. New York: Harcourt Brace

Author Studies: Memoirs Plus

In addition to approaching the study of memoirs according to shared themes, we also find it useful to group memoirs in several additional ways for in-depth examination of the genre and of certain authors. The following bibliographies illustrate some of these additional groupings.

Bibliography of Multiple Memoirs by the Same Author

You might think that each life is worthy of only one memoir, but you'd be wrong. Several authors have written multiple memoirs about their lives, memoirs in which they examine their lives through a variety of lenses to suit various time periods in their lives. The memoirs may explore differing chronological ages in the lives of the authors, various themes important to the authors at certain stages of their lives, or multiple significant, interrelated events. Following are some of these multiple memoirs.

CONWAY, JILL KER. 1992. *The Road from Coorain*. New York: Vintage Books.

———. 1995. *True North*. New York: Vintage Books.

———. 2001. *A Woman's Education*. New York: Alfred Knopf.

DAHL, ROALD. 1986. *Boy: Tales of Childhood*. New York: Puffin Books.

———. 1988. *Going Solo*. New York: Puffin Books.

DILLARD, ANNIE. 1987. *An American Childhood*. New York: Harper and Row.

———. 1989. *The Writing Life*. New York: Harper and Row.

———. 1999. *For the Time Being*. New York: Alfred Knopf.

FULLER, ALEXANDRA. 2003. *Don't Let's Go to the Dogs Tonight: An African Childhood*. New York: Random House.

———. 2004. *Scribbling the Cat: Travels with an African Soldier*. New York: The Penguin Press.

Hampl, Patricia. 1983. *A Romantic Education*. Boston: Houghton Mifflin.

———. 1992. *Virgin Time*. New York: Ballantine Books.

———. 1999. *I Could Tell You Stories: Sojourns in the Land of Memory*. New York: Norton.

Harrison, Kathryn. 1998. *The Kiss: A Memoir*. New York: Bard and Avon Book.

———. 2004. *The Mother Knot: A Memoir*. New York: Random House.

Karr, Mary. 1995. *Liar's Club*. New York: Viking Books.

———. 2000. *Cherry*. New York: Viking Books.

Norris, Kathleen. 1993. *Dakota: A Spiritual Geography*. Boston: Houghton Mifflin.

———. 1996. *The Cloister Walk*. New York: Riverhead Books.

———. 1999. *Amazing Grace: A Vocabulary of Faith*. New York: Riverhead Books.

———. 2001. *The Virgin of Bennington*. New York: Riverhead Books.

Ray, Janisse. 1999. *Ecology of a Cracker Childhood*. Minneapolis, MN: Milkweed Editions.

———. 2003. *Wildcard Quilt: Taking a Chance on Home*. Minneapolis, MN: Milkweed Editions.

Wiesel, Elie. 1995. *Memoirs: All Rivers Run to the Sea*. New York: Schocken Books.

———. 1999. *And the Sea Is Never Full: Memoirs, 1969–*. New York: Alfred Knopf.

Bibliography of Collections of Short Memoirs

Like collected biographies, some memoirs consist of collected shorter essays about life stories in themed books. These volumes are often edited by one versed in memoir. Readings within and among such titles make for interesting comparisons.

Dillard, Annie, and Cort Conley, Eds. *Modern American Memoirs*. 1995. New York: Harper Collins.

Edelman, Marian Wright. 2003. *Dream Me Home Safely: Writers on Growing Up in America*. Boston: Houghton-Mifflin.

Gates, Henry Louis, Jr. 1997. *Thirteen Ways of Looking at a Black Man*. New York: Random House.

O'Hearn, Claudine Chiawei. 1998. *Half and Half: Writers on Growing Up Biracial and Bicultural*. New York: Pantheon.

Sewell, Marilyn, Ed. 2001. *Resurrecting Grace: Remembering Catholic Childhoods*. Boston: Beacon Press.

Bibliography of Memoirs and Other Works by One Author

We like to explore the writings of one author who has written memoir plus at least one additional genre. We find discussions about voice, theme, writing style, metaphor, and language use are enriched when we examine the interplay of genre and author. Sometimes an author clearly excels in one genre and is only mediocre in another genre; some writers are brilliant in any genre in which they publish. These works allow readers to examine one author in-depth, making comparisons across genres, thus adding a new perspective to discussions within the pedagogical approach of genre studies.

Baca, Jimmy Santiago. 1989. *Black Mesa Poems*. New York: New Directions Publishing Corp. (poetry)

———. 1990. *Immigrants in Our Own Land & Selected Early Poems*. New York: New Directions Publishing Corp. (poetry)

———. 2001. *A Place to Stand*. New York: Grove Press. (memoir)

Dahl, Roald. 1986. *Boy: Tales of Childhood*. New York: Puffin Books. (memoir)

———. 1988. *Going Solo*. New York: Puffin Books. (memoir)

———. 2004. *Charlie and the Chocolate Factory*. New York: Alfred A. Knopf. (novel for children)

———. 1996. *James and the Giant Peach*. New York: Puffin. (novel for children)

Dillard, Annie. 1974. *Pilgrim at Tinker Creek*. New York: Perennial Library. (nonfiction nature writing)

———. 1983. *Teaching a Stone to Talk*. New York: Harper Colophon Books. (nonfiction nature writing)

———. 1987. *An American Childhood*. New York: Harper and Row. (memoir)

———. 1989. *The Writing Life*. New York: Harper and Row. (memoir on being a writer; advice to writers)

———. 1999. *For the Time Being*. New York: Alfred Knopf. (spiritual journey)

Goldberg, Natalie. 1993. *Long Quiet Highway: Waking up in America*. New York: Bantam. (memoir)

———. 1996. *Writing Down the Bones: Freeing the Writer Within*. Boston: Shambala Press. (writing instruction)

———. 2004. *The Great Failure: A Bartender, a Monk, and My Unlikely Path to the Truth*. New York: HarperCollins Publishers. (memoir)

Lamott, Anne. 1995. *Bird by Bird: Some Instructions on Writing and Life*. New York: Knopf Publishing Group. (nonfiction essays on being a writer; advice for writers)

———. 1999. *Traveling Mercies: Some Thoughts on Faith*. New York: Pantheon. (spiritual journey)

———. 2002. *Blue Shoe*. New York: Riverhead Books. (fiction)

———. 2005. *Plan B: Further Thoughts on Faith*. New York: Riverhead Books. (spiritual journey)

Lee, Li-Young. 1992. *The City in Which I Love You*. Rochester, NY: BOA Editions, Ltd. (poetry)

———. 1992, *Rose*. Rochester, NY: BOA Editions, Ltd. (poetry)

———. 1995. *The Winged Seed*. New York: Simon and Schuster. (memoir)

———. 2001. *Book of My Nights*. Rochester, NY: BOA Editions, Ltd. (poetry)

———. 2001. *Paper Cathedrals*. Kent, OH: Kent State University Press. (poetry)

Lopez, Barry. 1978. *Of Wolves and Men*. New York: Scribner's. (nonfiction nature writing)

———. 1980. *River Notes: The Dance of Herons*. New York: Avon Books. (nonfiction nature writing)

———. 1980. *Desert Notes*. New York: HarperCollins Publishers. (nonfiction nature writing)

———. 1986. *Arctic Dreams: Imagination and Desire in a Northern Landscape*. New York: Scribner's. (nonfiction nature writing)

———. 1989. *Crossing Open Ground*. New York: Vintage Books. (nonfiction nature writing)

———. 1995. *Field Notes: The Grace Note of the Canyon Wren.* New York: Avon Books. (nonfiction nature writing)

———. 1998. *About This Life: Journeys on the Threshold of Memory.* New York: Alfred Knopf. (memoir)

MASON, BOBBIE ANN. 1986. *In Country.* New York: Harper Perennial. (novel)

———. 1999. *Clear Springs: A Memoir.* New York: Random House. (memoir)

———. 2001. *Zigzagging Down a Wild Trail.* New York: Random House. (short story collection)

ONDAATJE, MICHAEL. 1987. *In the Skin of a Lion.* New York: Alfred A. Knopf, Inc. (fiction)

———. 1992. *The English Patient.* New York: Alfred A. Knopf, Inc. (fiction)

———. 1993. *Running in the Family.* New York: Vintage Books. (memoir)

———. 1996. *The Cinnamon Peeler: Selected Poems.* New York: Random House, Inc. (poetry)

———. 1996. *Collected Works of Billy the Kid.* New York: Vintage Books. (multigenre fiction)

ORR, GREGORY. 2002. *The Blessing.* San Francisco: Council Oak Books. (memoir)

———. 2002. *The Caged Owl: New and Selected Poems.* Port Townsend, WA: Copper Canyon Press. (poetry)

PAULSEN, GARY. 1992. *The River.* New York: Bantam Doubleday Dell Books for Young Readers. (novel for young adults)

———. 1996. *Hatchet.* New York: Simon & Schuster Children's. (novel for young adults)

———. 1997. *Pilgrimage on a Steel Ride.* New York: Harcourt Brace. (memoir of running the Iditarod)

SACKS, OLIVER. 1988. *The Man Who Mistook His Wife for a Hat and Other Clinical Tales.* New York: Simon & Schuster Adult Publishing Group. (nonfiction clinical case studies)

———. 2001. *Uncle Tungsten: Memories of a Chemical Boyhood.* New York: Alfred Knopf. (memoir)

WIESEL, ELIE. 1982. *Dawn.* New York: Bantam Doubleday Dell Publishing Group. (nonfiction account of his Holocaust experiences)

———. 1982. *Night.* New York: Bantam Doubleday Dell Publishing Group. (nonfiction account of his Holocaust experiences)

———. 1995. *Memoirs: All Rivers Run to the Sea.* New York: Schocken Books. (memoir)

———. 1999. *And the Sea Is Never Full: Memoirs, 1969–.* New York: Alfred Knopf. (memoir)

Memoir Blends

Memoir blends are memoirs that also tie in to another topic, such as one book on cooking and memoir, one on nature and memoir, or one on music and memoir. These blends are fascinating to us because of the ways in which they expand the boundaries of the genre. Some topics in the memoir blend area are expanding, with several authors writing such blends; others are quite narrow with only one or two authors writing in that field. We think that this is a memoir category to watch for future development.

Memoir and Nature

Askins, Renée. 2003. *Shadow Mountain: A Memoir of Wolves, a Woman, and the Wild*. New York: Anchor Books.

Batterson, Anne. 2001. *The Black Swan: Memory, Midlife, and Migration*. New York: Scribner.

Carroll, David. 2004. *Self-Portrait with Turtles: A Memoir*. Boston: Houghton Mifflin.

Meloy, Ellen. 2002. *The Anthropology of Turquoise: Meditations on Landscape, Art, and Spirit*. New York: Pantheon.

Norton, Lisa Dale. 1996. *Hawk Flies Above*. New York: Picador USA.

Ray, Janisse. 1999. *Ecology of a Cracker Childhood*. Minneapolis, MN: Milkweed Editions.

———. 2003. *Wildcard Quilt: Taking a Chance on Home*. Minneapolis, MN: Milkweed Editions.

Shulman, Alix Kates. 1995. *Drinking the Rain*. New York: Farrar, Straus, Giroux.

Williams, Terry Tempest. 1991. *Refuge: An Unnatural History of Family and Place*. New York: Pantheon Books.

Memoir and Medical Issues

Cohen, Elizabeth. 2003. *The House on Beartown Road: A Memoir of Learning and Forgetting*. New York: Random House.

Davis, Heather Choate. 1998. *Baptism by Fire*. New York: Bantam Books.

Jamison, Kay Redfield. 1996. *An Unquiet Mind: A Memoir of Moods and Madness*. New York: Vintage Books.

Kübler-Ross, Elisabeth. 1997. *The Wheel of Life: A Memoir of Living and Dying*. New York: Scribners.

Lauck, Jennifer. 2000. *Blackbird: A Childhood Lost and Found*. New York: Pocket Books.

Styron, William. 1992. *Darkness Visible: A Memoir of Madness*. New York: Vintage Books.

Memoir and Family History

Arana, Marie. 2001. *American Chica: Two Worlds, One Childhood*. The New York: Dial Press.

Baker, Russell. 1982. *Growing Up*. New York: Plume Books.

Bragg, Rick. 2001. *Ava's Man*. New York: Vintage Books.

Campbell, Bebe Moore. 1989. *Sweet Summer: Growing Up With and Without My Dad*. New York: Putnam's Sons.

Carter, Jimmy. 2001. *An Hour Before Daylight: Memories of a Rural Boyhood*. New York: Simon and Schuster.

Delaney, Sarah, and A. Elizabeth Delaney with Amy Hill Hearth. 1993. *Having Our Say: The Delaney Sisters' First 100 Years*. New York: Kodansha International.

Fuller, Alexandra. 2003. *Don't Let's Go to the Dogs Tonight: An African Childhood*. New York: Random House.

Gray, Francine du Plessix. 2005. *Them: A Memoir of Parents*. New York: The Penguin Press.

HAIZLIP, SHIRLEE TAYLOR. 1995. *The Sweeter the Juice: A Family Memoir in Black and White*. New York: A Touchstone Book.

KEHOE, LOUISE. 1995. *In This Dark House*. New York: Schocken Books.

MASON, BOBBIE ANN. 1999. *Clear Springs: A Memoir*. New York: Random House.

McCALL, CATHERINE. 2006. *Lifeguarding: A Memoir of Secrets, Swimming, and the South*. New York: Harmony Books.

McGAHERN, JOHN. 2006. *All Will Be Well: A Memoir*. New York: Alfred A. Knopf.

PAMUK, ORHAN. 2006. *Istanbul—Memories and the City*. New York: Alfred A. Knopf.

SACKS, OLIVER. 2001. *Uncle Tungsten: Memories of a Chemical Boyhood*. New York: Alfred Knopf.

SETH, VIKRAM. 2005. *Two Lives*. New York: HarperCollins Publishers.

THWE, PASCAL KHOO. 2003. *From the Land of Green Ghosts: A Burmese Odyssey*. New York: Perennial.

Memoir and Cooking

CONROY, PAT. 2004. *The Pat Conroy Cookbook*. New York: Doubleday.

MAYES, FRANCES. 1996. *Under the Tuscan Sun: At Home in Italy*. New York: Broadway Books.

Memoir and Music

MARSALIS, WYNTON, AND CARL VIGELAND. 2001. *Jazz in the Bittersweet Blues of Life*. Cambridge: De Capo Books.

Memoir and Sports

Please note that although many books are written about sports stars, coaches, and the like, few are true memoirs as we have defined the genre here, and few are written by the sports figures themselves; they are, instead, written "with" someone or ghost written. Below is a true sports memoir, the one about which we know to date.

Conroy, Pat. 2003. *My Losing Season*. New York: Bantam.

Memoiresque Books for Use with Younger Writers

We have found success using the Memoir Framework with all ages of writers, from first grade to college. For those of you who work specifically with younger students, we include this category. For those of you working with older students, you may find books here that will serve as a helpful introduction to the genre or as a source to illustrate a particular writing technique. Many of the memoir-related books that we think are appropriate for use with younger student writers who are working on a Memoir Framework are not true memoirs. Many are fiction, but their content is that of life experiences closely related to memoir content. Following are some of our favorite books in this category. As always, we encourage you to seek out additional titles that will work well for your students.

ALIKI. 1998. *Painted Words* and *Spoken Memories*. New York: Greenwillow. (two books published under the same cover)

BOWEN, ANNE. 2001. *I Loved You Before You Were Born*. New York: HarperCollins Publishers.

BRADMAN, TONY. 2002. *Daddy's Lullaby*. New York: Margaret K. McElderry Books.

CHAMBERS, VERONICA. 1998. *Marisol and Magdalena: Celebrating Our Sisterhood*. New York: Hyperion.

CHOCOLATE, DEBBI. 1995. *On the Day I Was Born*. New York: Scholastic.

CURTIS, JAMIE LEE. 1996. *Tell Me Again About the Night I Was Born*. New York: Joanna Cotler Books.

FOX, MEM. 1985. *Wilfred Gordon McDonald Partridge*. Brooklyn, NY: A Cranky Nell Book.

FRASIER, DEBRA. 1991. *On the Day You Were Born*. San Diego: Harcourt Brace & Company.

GUY, ROSA. 1996. *The Friends*. New York: Bantam.

HAVILL, JUANITA. 1986. *Jamaica's Find*. New York: Houghton Mifflin.

HOLIDAY, BILLIE, AND ARTHUR HERZOG, JR. 2004. *God Bless the Child*. New York: HarperCollins Publishers.

LANGSTON, LAURA. 2004. *Remember Grandma?* New York: Viking.

RYLANT, CYNTHIA. 1982. *When I Was Young in the Mountains*. New York: Puffin Unicorn.

———. 1985. *The Relatives Came*. New York: Aladdin.

STEPTOE, JAVAKA. 1997. *In Daddy's Arms I Am Tall: African Americans Celebrating Fathers*. New York: Lee & Low.

STEVENSON, JAMES. 1987. *Higher on the Door*. New York: Greenwillow Books.

YUMOTO, KAZUMI. 1998. *The Friends*. New York: Yearling.

In short, there is a multitude of ways to approach the study of memoir as a framework for writing and as a unique genre. These are some of our favorite categories and titles. As you explore the genre and its implications for your student writers, come see us at conferences and workshops; we'll sit down together and chat about your new discoveries in the genre—and about ours.

Index

56 Ford, (Kirby), 91

About This Life: Journeys on the Threshold of Memory, (Lopez), 162, 177
Accidental Asian, The: Notes of a Native Speaker, (Liu), 97, 162, 167
accountability, for teachers, 141
Aciman, André, *False Papers: Essays on Exile and Memory*, 159, 167
acknowledgments, forms and formats, 94
activities, time budgeting and frequency, 61
adding more, Revision through, 67–70
Advice to Writers, (Collins), 60
Afghani American memoir writers, 4
African American authors' memoirs, bibliography, 166
African and African American memoir writers, 4
After Long Silence, (Freemont), 160, 167, 169
After the Fact: Two Countries, Four Decades, One Anthropologist, (Geertz), 161
"Ah ha!" Crafting Options for memoir, 74
Al-Windawi, Thura, *Thura's Diary: My Life in Wartime Iraq*, 159, 172
Albom, Mitch, *Tuesdays with Morrie: An Old Man, a Young Man, and Life's Greatest Lessons*, 159
Aliki, *Painted Words and Spoken Memories*, 180
All Over But the Shoutin', (Bragg), 159
All Will Be Well: A Memoir, (McGahern), 163, 170, 179
altar pieces (triptych), 106
alternate forms of memoir, how to write them

memoir blends, 120–21
multigenre memoirs, 117–19
overview, 105–6
"So What?" stories, 117
triptych, 106–16
Amazing Grace: A Vocabulary of Faith, (Norris), 163, 169, 175
American Chica: Two Worlds, One Childhood, (Arana), 159, 178
American Childhood, An, (Dillard), 54, 160, 172, 174, 176
American Story, An, (Dickerson), 160
anchor piece, 33, 34
And the Sea is Never Full: Memoirs, 1969–, (Wiesel), 96, 165, 167, 170, 175, 177
Angela's Ashes, (McCourt), 163
Angelou, Maya, *Heart of a Woman, The*, 159, 166, 171, 173
"Angstomometer," 125
Anthropology of Turquoise, The: Meditations on Landscape, Art and Spirit, (Meloy), 163, 178
apprenticeships, as authentic work in a context of making and doing, 22
Arana, Marie, 4
Arana, Marie, *American Chica: Two Worlds, One Childhood*, 159, 178
Are You Somebody? The Accidental Memoir of a Dublin Woman, (O'Faolain), 164, 172
Arctic Dreams: Imagination and Desire in a Northern Landscape, (Lopez), 176
Artifacts Piece, 35

Ashworth, Andrea, 4–5

Ashworth, Andrea, *Once in a House on Fire*, 159, 166, 169

Askins, Renée, *Shadow Mountain: A Memoir of Wolves, a Woman, and the Wild*, 159, 178

assembling the memoir, 98–104

Assessment, definition of, 144

Atlas, James, 2

Audit,
    Final Class, 147
    Report for the memoir piece, 131

Audits (reflective logs), 26

Audits, use during writing, 130–32, 143, 154

authentic revision, environment for, 33–34

authentic work
    in writing memoir pieces, 59–60
    value of in studio teaching, 18

authors, multiple memoirs by the same, bibliography, 174–75

author's note, forms and formats, 94

autobiography,
    conventions of, 1
    as different from memoir, 29

Ava's Man, (Bragg), 96, 159, 170, 178

Baca, Jimmy, 4

Baca, Jimmy, *Black Mesa Poems*, 176

Baca, Jimmy, *Immigrants in Our Land & Selected Early Poems*, 176

Baca, Jimmy, *Place to Stand, A*, 159, 168, 173, 176

Baker, Russell, *Growing Up*, 2, 29, 30–31, 103, 159, 178

Baptism by Fire, (Davis), 160, 168, 169, 178

Barrios, Flor Fernandez, 4

Barrios, Flor Fernandez, *Blessed by Thunder: Memoir of a Cuban Girlhood*, 159, 168, 169, 172

Bateson, Mary Catherine, *Composing a Life*, 159, 171

Batterson, Anne, *Black Swan, The: Memory, Midlife, and Migration*, 159, 178

Bayley, John, *Iris and Her Friends*, 159

Beals, Melba Pattillo, *Warriors Don't Cry*, 159

Beals, Melba Pattillo, *White Is a State of Mind: A Memoir*, 159

Beard, Jo Ann, *Boys from My Youth, The*, 159

bedroom, floor plan of, for Boundaries or Map Piece Exploration, 52

beginnings minilesson, Revision through Crafting, 70–75

Bend for Home, The, (Healy), 95, 161

bibliographies in memoir

author studies: memoirs plus, 174–77
    memoir blends, 177–79
    memoiresque books for use with younger writers, 179–80
    overview, 158
    suggested memoirs, 159–65
    themed memoirs and memoir pairings, 165–74

binding
    creating an effective, 103–4
    presentational aspect of, 101

biography, as a memoir, 4

Bird by Bird: Some Instructions on Writing and Life, 176

Black Mesa Poems, (Baca), 176

Black Swan, The: Memory, Midlife, and Migration, (Batterson), 159, 178

Blackbird: A Childhood Lost and Found, (Lauck), 162, 178

Blending Genre, Altering Style, (Romano), 117

Blessed by Thunder, Memoir of a Cuban Girlhood, (Barrios), 159, 168, 169, 172

Blessing, The, (Orr), 83, 164, 173, 177

Blood Runs like a River Through My Dreams, The, (Nasdijj), 163

Blue Shoe, (Lamott), 176

Blunt, Judy, *Breaking Clean*, 94–95, 159

blurred genre memoirs, 5

Bone Black: Memories of Girlhood, (Hooks), 162, 166

book examination, 8, 9

Book of My Nights, (Lee), 176

books, presentational aspects of, 98

bookstores, memoirs in, 4

boundaries, exploring figurative and literal, 53

Boundaries Piece, 35, 51–56

Boundaries Piece excerpts, 54–55

Bowen, Anne, *I Loved You Before You Were Born*, 180

Boy He Left Behind, The: A Man's Search for His Lost Father, (Matousek), 162, 170

Boy: Tales of Childhood, (Dahl), 160, 174, 176

Boy with a Loaded Gun: A Memoir, (Nordan), 163

Boys from My Youth, The, (Beard), 159

Boy's Life, This, (Tobias), 38, 165, 171

Bradman, Tony, *Daddy's Lullaby*, 180

Bragg, Rick, *All Over But the Shoutin'*, 159

Bragg, Rick, *Ava's Man*, 96, 159, 170, 178

brainstorm list, 49

Breaking Clean, (Blunt), 94–95, 159

Bronx Remembered, El, (Mohr), 163

Buck, Rinker, *Flight of Passage*, 159, 170

Buechner, Frederick, 5

Buechner, Frederick, *Eyes of the Heart, The: A Memoir of Lost and Found*, 159

Buffalo for the Broken Heart: Restoring Life to a Black Hills Ranch, (O'Brien), 163, 171

business model for teaching, 14

Caged Owl, The: New and Selected Poems, (Orr), 177

Cahill, Rick, 154

Cambodian American memoir writers, 4

Campbell, Bebe Moore, *Sweet Summer*, 117, 159, 166, 172, 178

Cantwell, Mary, *Speaking with Strangers*, 159

Carroll, David M., *Self-Portrait with Turtles*, 103, 159, 178

Carter, Jimmy, *Hour Before Daylight, An: Memories of a Rural Boyhood*, 159, 172, 178

Catfish and Mandala: A Two-Wheeled Voyage Through the Landscape and Memory of Vietnam, (Pham), 164, 173

Chambers, Veronica, *Marisol and Magdalena: Celebrating Our Sisterhood*, 180

Chang, Jung, *Wild Swans: Three Daughters of China*, 159, 167, 169

character stuffing, Revision Options for the Place Spider Piece, 68

character throwing
  beginning minilesson, 71
  Crafting Options for memoir, 74

Charlie and the Chocolate Factory, (Dahl), 176

chart, creating to instantiate rituals and routines, 61

Checklist Evaluation, Writer's Group, 151

checklist, Revision features, 66–68

Chen, Da, 4

Chen, Da, *China's Son*, 159, 167

Chen, Da, *Colors of the Mountains*, 159, 167

Cherry: A Memoir, (Karr), 48, 162, 175

Chicano/a authors' memoirs, bibliography, 168

childhood, literal and figurative boundaries of, 51

childhoods, troubling and chaotic, in memoirs, 5

children authors, memoirs by, bibliography, 173–74

China's Son, (Chen), 159, 167

Chinese American memoir writers, 4

Chinese authors' memoirs, bibliography, 166–67

Chocolate, Debbi, *On the Day I Was Born*, 180

choices, student decision making with memoirs, 24–25

Cinnamon Peeler, The: Selected Poems, (Ondaatje), 177

circle, Crafting Options for memoir, 74

Cisneros, Sandra, 42, 43

Cisneros, Sandra, *House on Mango Street, The*, 38, 159, 168

City in Which I Love You, The, (Lee), 176

Class Reflection. *see* Final Reflection

Clear Springs: A Memoir, (Mason), 55, 96, 162, 172, 177, 179

Cliff Walk, The: A Job Lost and a Life Found, (Snyder), 164, 170, 171

Clinton, Bill and Hillary Rodham, 5

Cloister Walk, The, (Norris), 163, 169, 175

closing remarks, forms and formats, 97

Cohen, Elizabeth, *House on Beartown Road, The*, 83, 160, 178

Collected Works of Billy the Kid, (Ondaatje), 177

collections
  of memoirs, 5
  of short memoirs, bibliography, 175

Collins, Billy, *Advice to Writers*, 60

Color is the Suffering of Light, (Green), 161, 173

Color of Water, The, (McBride), 83–84, 102, 105, 163, 166

color,
  presentational aspect of, 101
  using effectively in layout, 102–3

Colored People, (Gates), 95, 117, 161, 166

Colors of the Mountains, (Chen), 159, 167

community of learners, definition of, 25

Composing a Life, (Bateson), 159, 171

compositional studies, 17, 23–24

concealing and revealing in memoirs, 2–3

"confessional genre," memoir as, 2

Confessions: The Making of a Post-Denominational Priest, (Fox), 160, 168

connections and commonalities, searching for potential Schemes, 85–86

Conroy, Pat, *My Losing Season*, 95, 121, 160, 170, 179

Conroy, Pat, *Pat Conroy Cookbook, The*, 120, 160, 179

Constructivism, an overview of, 20–21

Contemporary Memoir and studio pedagogy, case for marriage of, 11

Contemporary Memoir (CM)
  definition of, 1–2
  diving into, 7–8
  forms and formats, exploring, 93
  origin of, 2–4
  teaching students to read and write, 5–7
  tenets of teaching, 11–13
  types of, 4–5

conversations, Elaboration strategies, 69

Conway, Jill Ker, 5

Conway, Jill Ker, *Road from Coorain, The*, 160, 171, 174

Conway, Jill Ker, *True North*, 160, 171, 174

Conway, Jill Ker, *Woman's Education, A*, 95, 160, 171, 174

cooking
  and memoir, 120–21
  memoirs about, bibliography, 179

cover
  creating an effective, 103
  presentational aspect of, 101

Crafting Options, 66, 70, 72

Crafting Options for memoir, 74

Critical Assessments, 134

cross-cultural memoirs, 4

Crossing Open Ground, (Lopez), 176

Cruikshank, Julie, *Life Lived Like a Story*, 160

Cuban authors' memoirs, bibliography, 168

cultivation of experimentation, at the heart of studio instruction, 16

culture memoirs bibliography, 166–68

Curtis, Jamie Lee, *Tell Me Again About the Night I Was Born*, 180

Daddy's Lullaby, (Bradman), 180

Dahl, Roald, *Boy: Tales of Childhood*, 160, 174, 176

Dahl, Roald, *Charlie and the Chocolate Factory*, 176

Dahl, Roald, *Going Solo*, 160, 174, 176

Dahl, Roald, *James and the Giant Peach*, 176

daily writing activities, 61

Dakota: A Spiritual Geography, (Norris), 163, 169, 172, 175

Dancing with Cuba, (Guillermoprieto), 95, 161

Darkness Visible: A Memoir of Madness, (Styron), 164, 178

Daughter of the Queen of Sheba, (Lyden), 162, 171

Davis, Heather Choate, *Baptism by Fire*, 160, 168, 169, 178

Dawn, (Wiesel), 177

Debriefings, 136

decision making about options and choices, as a studio value, 24–25

dedications, forms and formats, 94

Delaney, Sarah, Delaney, A. Elizabeth, & Hearty, Amy Hill, *Having Our Say: The Delaney Sisters' First 100 Years*, 103, 160, 166, 178

deleting chunks, Crafting Options for memoir, 75

Desert Notes, (Lopez), 176

Desert Pilgrim, The: In Route to Mysticism and Miracles, (Swander), 165, 169

Dewey, John, 15

dialogue,
  beginning minilesson, 72
  Crafting Options for memoir, 74

Dickerson, Debra, *American Story, An*, 160

Dictionary, Researcher's, 133

Didion, Joan, 94–95

Didion, Joan, *Year of Magical Thinking, The*, 160, 169

Dillard, Annie, 3, 5, 19, 59

Dillard, Annie, & Conley, Cort, *Modern American Memoirs*, 160, 175

Dillard, Annie, *American Childhood, An*, 54, 160, 172, 174, 176

Dillard, Annie, *For the Time Being*, 94, 160, 168, 174, 176

Dillard, Annie, *Inventing the Truth: The Art and Craft of Memoir*, 30

Dillard, Annie, *Pilgrim at Tinker Creek*, 176

Dillard, Annie, *Teaching a Stone to Talk*, 176

Dillard, Annie, *Writing Life, The*, 160, 174, 176

Discovery Tales, 134–35

discussion guidelines for Writer's Group Responses, 78

Diskin, Saul, *End of the Twins, The: A Memoir of Losing a Brother*, 160, 170

Dispatches, use during writing, 129–30, 143

diving into memoir, 7–8

Dobie, Kathy, *Only Girl in the Car, The*, 160, 171

Dodson, James, *Final Rounds: A Father, a Son, the Golf Journey of a Lifetime*, 160, 169, 170

Don't Let's Go to the Dogs Tonight, (Fuller), 97, 160, 172, 174, 178

Doty, Mark, *Firebird: A Memoir*, 160

drawstring, Crafting Options for memoir, 74

Dream House, (Nekola), 163

Dream Me Home Safely, (Edelman), 160, 175

Drinking the Rain, (Shulman), 164, 172, 173, 178

Ecology of a Cracker Childhood, (Ray), 164, 172, 173, 175, 178

ecosystem, as a metaphor for teaching, 14

Edelman, Marian Wright, *Dream Me Home Safely*, 160, 175

editing, as a Revision Behavior, 65

Educating the Reflective Practitioner: Toward a New Design for Teaching and Learning in the Professions, (Schön), 14–15

Edwards, John & Elizabeth, 117

elaborating, as a Revision Behavior, 65

Elaboration
  Revision through, 67–70
  Strategies, 69, 70

Elizabeth Stories, The, (Huggan), 47–48, 66, 67, 162

emotional challenges, memoirs about, bibliography, 169–70

emotional holds, Revision Options for the Place Spider Piece, 68

emotional state in the writing of memoirs, correlating with presentational aspects, 99

end material, how to examine a Contemporary Memoir, 9

End of the Twins, The: A Memoir of Losing a Brother, (Diskin), 160, 170

endings, Crafting Options for memoir, 74

Eng, Phoebe, *Warrior Lessons: An Asian American Woman's Journey into Power,* 160, 167, 171

English Patient, The, (Ondaatje), 177

epilogues, forms and formats, 97

Epistemology, a brief overview of, 19–20

ethnicity memoirs, bibliography, 166–68

evaluating memoir writing
assessing, evaluating and grading work, 146–49
evaluation and grading, 142–43
mapping the assessment territory, 144–46
overview, 140–41
testing, what it is not, 141–42

Evaluation
definition of, 143
as a ritual and routine, 61
Writer's Group, 149
Writer's Group Checklist, 151

Evaluation Rubric
for the Memoir Piece, 152–54
for the Memoir Writer's Portfolio, 155

Every Good-Bye Ain't Gone: Family Portraits and Personal Escapades, (Njeri), 163, 166

examining contemporary memoir texts. *see* book examination

experimentation, as a studio value, 22–23

Explorations, 20, 22, 34–36, 46–47, 51–52, 56, 57, 58, 68–69. *See also* Spider Pieces (short Explorations)

exploring difficult times and personal struggles through memoirs, 6

exploring memoir in the studio classroom, 32

exploring the territory of memoir as genre, 28–29

Eyes of the Heart, The: A Memoir of Lost and Found, (Buechner), 159

factory model for teaching, 14

Falling Leaves: The Memoir of an Unwanted Chinese Daughter, (Mah), 162, 167, 170

Falling Through Space, (Gilchrist), 54, 103, 161, 171, 172

False Papers: Essays on Exile and Memory, (Aciman), 159, 167

familiar patterns, establishing in the studio classroom, 60–62

family history, memoirs about, bibliography, 178

family trees, forms and formats, 96

Favre, Brett, 117

feeling, Crafting Options for memoir, 74

Feels Like Far: A Rancher's Life on the Great Plains, (Hasselstrom), 161

Field Notes: The Grace Note of the Canyon Wren, (Lopez), 177

Fields without Dreams: Defending the Agrarian Idea, (Hanson), 161

Fiffer, Steve, 5

Fiffer, Steve, *Three Quarters, Two Dimes, and a Nickel: A Memoir of Becoming Whole,* 94, 160, 169

Final Class Audit. *see* Final Reflection

Final Memoir Product, grading and evaluating, 149

Final Reflection, 136–38, 146–49, 154

Final Rounds: A Father, a Son, the Golf Journey of a Lifetime, (Dodson), 160, 169, 170

Finding Fish, (Fisher), 160, 166

finding things to like, Writer's Groups, 76

finished piece, 92, 98–104

Firebird: A Memoir, (Doty), 160

first draft, memoir pieces, 62–63

first steps, establishing routines and rituals in the studio classroom, 60–62

Firsts Piece, 35

fish bowl methodology, the, 77

Fisher, Antwone, *Finding Fish,* 160, 166

five-paragraph theme, limitations of, 19

Flight of Passage, (Rinker), 159, 170

Fly Fishing Through the Midlife Crisis, (Raines), 164, 171, 173

focus on piece, not the writer, Writer's Groups, 77

fonts
presentational aspect of, 100
using effectively in layout, 102

For the Time Being, (Dillard), 94, 160, 168, 174, 176

forming and finding, as a Revision Behavior, 65

forms and formats, exploring, 92–97

Fox, Matthew, *Confessions: The Making of a Post-Denominational Priest,* 160, 168

Fox, Matthew, *Reinvention of Work, The: A New Vision of Livelihood for our Time,* 17–18

Fox, Mem, *Wilfred Gordon McDonald Partridge,* 180

frame, as part of the finished piece, 98

Framework, Memoir
  exploring (overview), 29–33
  key points and the pieces, 34–36
  Name Piece, 36–45
  Spider Pieces and environment for authentic revision, 33–34
Francis, Connie, Who's Sorry Now?, 47–48
Fraser, Debra, On the Day You Were Born, 180
Fraser, Joelle, Territory of Men, The: A Memoir, 160, 171
Freemont, Helen, After Long Silence, 160, 167, 169
freewriting, memoir pieces, 62–63
Friends, The, (Guy), 180
Friends, The, (Yumoto), 180
From the Land of Green Ghosts, (Thwe), 95, 165, 173, 179
front material, how to examine a Contemporary Memoir, 9
Fuller, Alexandra, Don't Let's Go to the Dogs Tonight, 97, 160, 172, 174, 178
Fuller, Alexandra, Scribbling the Cat: Travels with an African Soldier, 97, 161, 175

Galileo's Daughter: A Historical Memoir of Science, Faith and Love, (Sobel), 164
Gantos, Jack, Hole in My Life, 161, 170, 174
Gates, Henry Louis, Jr., 4, 5, 59
Gates, Henry Louis, Jr., Colored People, 95, 117, 161, 166
Gates, Henry Louis, Jr., Thirteen Ways of Looking at a Black Man, 161, 166, 175
Geertz, Clifford, After the Fact: Two Countries, Four Decades, One Anthropologist, 161
geneology charts, forms and formats, 96
genres, student narrow understandings of, 28
Geography of the Heart, (Johnson), 162, 169
Geronimo's Bones: A Memoir of My Brother and Me, (Nasdijj), 163
getting started, memoir pieces, 62–63
Ghost Light, (Rich), 164
Gilchrist, Ellen, Falling Through Space, 54, 103, 161, 171, 172
Girl Meets God, (Winner), 97, 165, 167, 169
giving the writer the chance to ask questions, Writer's Groups, 77
God Bless the Child, (Holiday & Herzog), 180
God Speaks to Each of Us, (Rilke), 95
Going Solo, (Dahl), 160, 174, 176
Goldberg, Natalie, Great Failure, The: A Bartender, a Monk, and My Unlikely Path to the Truth, 161, 176
Goldberg, Natalie, Long Quiet Highway: Waking up in America, 161, 176

Goldberg, Natalie, Writing Down the Bones: Freeing the Writer Within, 161, 176
Goldman, William, Temple of Gold, The, 72
Good Enough Daughter, A, (Shulman), 164, 172
Goodall, Jane, 5
Goodall, Jane, & Berman, Phillip, Reason for Hope: A Spiritual Journey, 102, 161, 169
Goodwin, Doris Kearns, Wait Till Next Year, 161
grading and testing, 141–43
grading (evaluation) as a ritual and routine, 61
graphics, forms and formats, 96
Gray, Francine du Plessix, Them: A Memoir of Parents, 161, 166
Great Failure, The: A Bartender, a Monk, and My Unlikely Path to the Truth, (Goldberg), 161, 176
Green, Melissa, Color Is the Suffering of Light, 161, 173
Greenlaw, Linda, Hungry Ocean, The: A Swordboat Captain's Journey, 161
Greenlaw, Linda, Lobster Chronicles, The: Life on a Very Small Island, 161
Growing Up, (Baker), 2, 29, 30–31, 103, 159, 178
Growing Up Chicano, (Lopez), 162, 168
Guillermoprieto, Alma, Dancing with Cuba, 95, 161
Gutted: Down to the Studs in My House, My Marriage, and My Entire Life, (LaRose), 103, 162, 170
Guy, Rosa, Friends, The, 180

Haizlip, Shirlee Taylor, Sweeter the Juice, The: A Family Memoir in Black and White, 161, 166, 179
Hakakian, Roya, Journey from the Land of No: A Childhood Caught in Revolutionary Iran, 103, 161, 171
Half and Half: Writers on Growing Up Biracial and Bicultural, (O'Hearn), 164, 168, 175
Hall, Donald, Life's Work, 60, 161, 173
Halpin, Brendan, Losing My Faculties: A Teacher's Story, 161
Hampl, Patricia, 1, 2, 5, 120
Hampl, Patricia, I Could Tell You Stories: Sojourns in the Land of Memory, 161, 175
Hampl, Patricia, Memory and Imagination, 3–4
Hampl, Patricia, Romantic Education, A, 161, 175
Hampl, Patricia, Virgin Time, 55, 161, 169, 175
Hanson, Victor Davis, Fields Without Dreams: Defending the Agrarian Idea, 161
Harris, Alex, 5
Harris, Alex, Portraits of Southern Childhood, 161
Harrison, Kathryn, Kiss, The, 95, 161, 171, 175

Harrison, Kathryn, *Mother Knot, The: A Memoir*, 161, 171, 175

Hasselstrom, Linda, *Feels like Far: A Rancher's Life on the Great Plains*, 161

Hatchet, (Paulsen), 177

Havill, Juanita, *Jamaica's Find*, 180

Having Our Say: The Delaney Sisters' First 100 Years, (Delaney, Delaney, & Hearty), 103, 160, 166, 178

Hawk Flies Above, (Norton), 163, 173, 178

Healy, Dermot, *Bend for Home, The*, 95, 161

Heart of a Woman, The, (Angelou), 159, 166, 171, 173

Helga exhibit, (Wyeth), 17, 24

Heller, Michael, 4

Heller, Michael, *Living Root: A Memoir*, 102, 161, 173

Here and Nows, 132

Hickam, Homer, 5

Hickam, Homer, *Sky of Stone*, 97, 161

high-stakes testing, 141

Higher on the Door, (Stevenson), 180

Hillerman, Tony, *Seldom Disappointed*, 94, 162

Him, Chanrithy, 4, 59

Him, Chanrithy, *When Broken Glass Floats*, 94, 117, 162

Hinchman, Hannah, *Little Things in a Big Country: An Artist & Her Dog on the Rocky Mountain Front*, 102–103

Hispanic American memoir writers, 4

Hispanic authors' memoirs, bibliography, 168

histories, taking past memoirs into account, 125

history and memoir, 120

Hole in My Life, (Gantos), 161, 170, 174

Holiday, Billie, & Herzog, Arthur Jr., *God Bless the Child*, 180

"home" Exploration, Boundaries or Map Piece, 51–52

hook, 33, 34
beginning minilesson, 71
Crafting Options for memoir, 74

Hooks, Bell, *Bone Black: Memories of Girlhood*, 162, 166

Hour before Daylight, An: Memories of a Rural Boyhood, (Carter), 159, 172, 178

House on Beartown Road, (Cohen), 83, 160, 178

House on Mango Street, The, (Cisneros), 38, 159, 168

Huggan, Isabel, *Elizabeth Stories, The*, 47–48, 66, 67, 162

Hungry Ocean, The: A Swordboat Captain's Journey, (Greenlaw), 161

I Could Tell You Stories: Sojourns in the Land of Memory, (Hampl), 161, 175

I Loved You Before You Were Born, (Bowen), 180

Idea Notebook, 8, 10

Immigrants in Our Land & Selected Early Poems, (Baca), 176

In Country, (Mason), 177

In Daddy's Arms I Am Tall: African Americans Celebrating Fathers, (Steptoe), 180

In the Shadow of a Saint, (Wiwa), 94, 165, 171

In the Skin of a Lion, (Ondaatje), 177

In This Dark House, (Kehoe), 162, 167, 170, 179

individual knowledge, through constructs, 20

individual visions and versions, as a studio value, 23–24

Inside Out: Strategies for Teaching Writing, (Kirby, Kirby, & Liner), 62–63

inside/outside information, Elaboration strategies, 69

intensified images, Revision Options for the Place Spider Piece, 68

interest, themes of, bibliography, 168–74

Inventing the Truth: The Art and Craft of Memoir, (Dillard), 30

Inventing the Truth: The Art and Craft of Memoir, (Zinsser), 3, 30, 64, 165

invention, importance in writing memoirs, 3

inventory of materials needed to write memoir, 128

Iris and Her Friends, (Bayley), 159

Istanbul—Memories and the City, (Pamuk), 164, 173, 179

Jack London and His Daughters, (London), 162, 170, 171

Jaleo, El, exhibit, (Sargent), 17, 82

Jamaica's Find, (Havill), 180

James and the Giant Peach, (Dahl), 176

Jamison, Kay Redfield, 5, 120

Jamison, Kay Redfield, *Unquiet Mind, An: A Memoir of Moods and Madness*, 162, 169, 178

Jazz in the Bittersweet Blues of Life, (Marsalis & Vigeland), 121, 162, 166, 179

Jewish authors' memoirs, bibliography, 167

Jewish memoir writers, 4

Johnson, Fenton, *Geography of the Heart*, 162, 169

Johnson, John, *Only Son*, 162, 166, 170

Journals, 133–134

Journey from the Land of No: A Childhood Caught in Revolutionary Iran, (Hakakian), 103, 161, 171

journey, goals for the, 128

Kaplan, Cynthia, *Why I'm Like This: True Stories*, 96, 162

Karr, Mary, 5

Karr, Mary, *Cherry: A Memoir*, 48, 162, 175

Karr, Mary, *Liar's Club*, 162, 175

Kehoe, Louise, 4

Kehoe, Louise, *In This Dark House*, 162, 167, 169, 179

Kerry, John, 117

Kincaid, Jamaica, 4

Kincaid, Jamaica, *My Brother*, 95–96, 162, 166, 170

King, Stephen, *On Writing: A Memoir of the Craft of Writing*, 162

Kingston, Maxine Hong, 4

Kingston, Maxine Hong, *Warrior Woman, The*, 162, 167, 171

Kiowa folk tale, 38–39

Kirby, Dan, 56 Ford, 91

Kirby, Dan, Kirby, Dawn Latta, & Liner, Tom, *Inside Out: Strategies for Teaching Writing*, 62–63

Kiss, The, (Harrison), 95, 161, 171, 175

Kübler-Ross, Elizabeth, *Wheel of Life, The: A Memoir of Living and Dying*, 162, 169, 170, 178

Kuusisto, Stephen, 5, 59

Kuusisto, Stephen, *Planet of the Blind*, 96–97, 162, 170

Lahiri, Jhumpa, *Namesake, The: A Novel*, 39

Lamott, Annie, 5

Lamott, Annie, *Bird by Bird: Some Instructions on Writing and Life*, 176

Lamott, Annie, *Blue Shoe*, 176

Lamott, Annie, *Plan B: Further Thoughts on Faith*, 162, 176

Lamott, Annie, *Traveling Mercies: Some Thoughts on Faith*, 162, 169, 176

landscape as character, in memoirs, 5

Langston, Laura, *Remember Grandma?*, 180

Language of Blood, The: A Memoir, (Tenka), 94, 102, 165

LaRose, Lawrence, *Gutted: Down to the Studs in My House, My Marriage, and My Entire Life*, 103, 162, 170

Latino/a authors' memoirs, bibliography, 168

Latino memoir writers, 4

Lauck, Jennifer, *Blackbird: A Childhood Lost and Found*, 162, 178

layout options for the final memoir, 102–4

Leap, (Williams), 165, 170

Learning Reports, 135

learning through active engagement, 20

Learning to Love Africa: My Journey from Africa to Harvard Business School and Back, (Maddy), 103

Lee, Li-Young, 4

Lee, Li-Young, *Book of My Nights*, 176

Lee, Li-Young, *City in Which I Love You, The*, 176

Lee, Li-Young, *Paper Cathedrals*, 176

Lee, Li-Young, *Rose*, 176

Lee, Li-Young, *Winged Seed, The*, 162, 167, 173, 176

lens changing, Revision Options for the Place Spider Piece, 68

Lewis and Clark, 133

Liar's Club, (Karr), 162, 175

Life As We Know It: A Collection of Personal Essays from Salon.com, (Sweeney), 165

Life Lived Like a Story, (Cruikshank), 160

Lifeguarding: A Memoir of Secrets, Swimming, and the South, 163, 172, 179

Life's Work, (Hall), 60, 161, 173

Light Years, (Schreiber), 164, 172, 173

linking Explorations, purpose, and professional examples, 57

literature study, memoirs as, 7

Little Things in a Big Country: An Artist & Her Dog on the Rocky Mountain Front, (Hinchman), 102–3

Liu, Eric, *Accidental Asian, The: Notes of a Native Speaker*, 97, 162, 167

Living Root: A Memoir, (Heller), 102, 161, 173

living the life, learning a field of study through, 19

Lobster Chronicles, The: Life on a Very Small Island, (Greenlaw), 161

Logs, 133, 143

London, Joan, 5

London, Joan, *Jack London and His Daughters*, 162, 170, 171

Long Quiet Highway: Waking up in America, (Goldberg), 161, 176

Longest Silence, The, (McGuane), 95, 163

looping, 41

Lopez, Barry, 5

Lopez, Barry, *About This Life: Journeys on the Threshold of Memory*, 162, 177

Lopez, Barry, *Arctic Dreams: Imagination and Desire in a Northern Landscape*, 176

Lopez, Barry, *Crossing Open Ground*, 176

Lopez, Barry, *Desert Notes*, 176

Lopez, Barry, *Field Notes: The Grace Note of the Canyon Wren*, 177

Lopez, Barry, *Of Wolves and Men*, 176

Lopez, Barry, *River Notes: The Dance of Herons*, 176

Lopez, Tiffany Ana, 4

Lopez, Tiffany Ana, *Growing Up Chicano*, 162, 168

Losing My Faculties: A Teacher's Story, (Halpin), 161

Love in the Driest Season, (Tucker), 95, 102, 165, 173

Lucky, (Sebold), 164

Lyden, Jacki, *Daughter of the Queen of Sheba*, 162, 171

Maddy, Monique, *Learning to Love Africa: My Journey from Africa to Harvard Business School and Back*, 103

Mah, Adeline Yen, *Falling Leaves: The Memoir of an Unwanted Chinese Daughter*, 162, 167, 170

Mairs, Nancy, *Voice Lessons: On Becoming a (Woman) Writer*, 162

Making of a Writer, The, (Nixon), 163, 174

Man Who Mistook His Wife for a Hat and Other Clinical Tales, The, (Sacks), 177

Map of My Heart Activity, 53

Map of the Piece (MOP), 32, 89–90, 125, 128, 133

Map Piece, 35, 51–56

Map Piece excerpts, 54–55

maps, forms and formats, 96

Marisol and Magdalena: Celebrating Our Sisterhood, (Chambers), 180

Marsalis, Winton, & Vigeland, Carl, *Jazz in the Bittersweet Blues of Life*, 121, 162, 166, 179

Mason, Bobbie Ann, *Clear Springs: A Memoir*, 55, 96, 162, 172, 177, 179

Mason, Bobbie Ann, *In Country*, 177

Mason, Bobbie Ann, *Zigzagging Down a Wild Trail*, 177

Matousek, Mark, *Boy He Left Behind, The: A Man's Search for His Lost Father*, 162, 170

Mayes, Frances, *Under the Tuscan Sun*, 120, 163, 172, 179

McBride, James, 4

McBride, James, *Color of Water, The*, 83–84, 102, 105, 163, 166

McCall, Catherine, *Lifeguarding: A Memoir of Secrets, Swimming, and the South*, 163, 172, 179

McCourt, Frank, 4–5

McCourt, Frank, *Angela's Ashes*, 163

McCourt, Malachy, *Monk Swimming, A*, 163

McGahern, John, *All Will Be Well: A Memoir*, 163, 170, 179

McGuane, Thomas, 5

McGuane, Thomas, *Longest Silence, The*, 95, 163

McMurty, Larry, *Walter Benjamin at the Dairy Queen: Reflections at Sixty and Beyond*, 163, 170, 172

meaningful work, definition of, 12–13

medical issues, memoirs about, 178

medical metaphor in teaching, 14

Meloy, Ellen, *Anthropology of Turquoise, The: Meditations on Landscape, Art, and Spirit*, 163, 178

memoir

    alternate forms. *See* alternate forms of memoir, how to write them

    assembling the. *See* assembling the memoir

    as different from autobiography, 29

    history of, 1

    as a partial story of a life, 3

    as a unique genre, 4

memoir blends, bibliography, 177–80

Memoir Blueprint, 125–28

Memoir Exploration, Name Piece, 40

Memoir Framework, 32, 34–45, 56, 58, 59, 60

memoir pieces. *See* pieces, of the Memoir Framework

Memoir Portfolio, 154

memoir writing

    additional Explorations in, 57

    evaluating. *See* evaluating memoir writing

memoiresque books for use with younger writers, bibliography, 179–80

memoirists

    definition of, 20

    not limited by responsibility to scholarly accuracy, 3–4

Memoirs: All Rivers Run to the Sea, (Wiesel), 165, 167, 169, 170, 175, 177

memoirs and other works by one author, bibliography, 175–77

memoirs, presentational aspects of finished, 99–101

Memory and Imagination, (Hampl), 3–4

Memory Observed: Remembering in Natural Contexts, (Neisser), 163

men's lives, memoirs about, bibliography, 170–71

Merridale, Catherine, *Night of Stone: Death and Memory in Twentieth-Century Russia*, 163

message of format in writing, the, 93

Miller, Susan J., *Never Let Me Down*, 163

Min, Anchee, 4

Min, Anchee, *Red Azalea: Life and Love in China*, 163, 167, 170

ministories, use of in Contemporary Memoirs, 2

Miss American Pie: A Diary of Love, Secrets, and Growing Up in the 1970s, (Sartor), 164, 172

modeling activities for students as a teaching method, 21

Modern American Memoirs, (Dillard & Conley), 160, 175

Mohr, Nicholasa, *Bronx Remembered, El*, 163

Momaday, Scott, *Names, The: A Memoir*, 38–39, 96, 163, 172

Monk Swimming, A, (McCourt), 163

Mother Knot, The: A Memoir, (Harrison), 161, 171, 175

movement, Crafting Options for memoir, 74

moving chunks, Crafting Options for memoir, 74

Muir, John, 133

multiple memoirs, 5

Murray, Donald, *My Twice Lived Life: A Memoir*, 163

music and memoir, 121

music, memoirs about, bibliography, 179

musing aloud, Writer's Groups, 76–77

My Brother, (Kincaid), 95–96, 162, 166, 170

My Losing Season, (Conroy), 95, 121, 160, 170, 179

My Twice Lived Life: A Memoir, (Murray), 163

Nafisi, Azar, *Reading Lolita in Tehran: A Memoir in Books*, 163, 172

Name Charts, 37, 40

Name Piece, 35–37

    excerpts, 38–39

    student examples of, 42–45

Names, The: A Memoir, (Momaday), 38–39, 96, 163, 172

Namesake, The: A Novel, (Lahiri), 39

narration and reflection, importance in memoirs, 3

Nasdijj, 5

Nasdijj, *Blood Runs like a River Through My Dreams, The*, 163

Nasdijj, *Geronimo's Bones: A Memoir of My Brother and Me*, 163

nature

    and memoir, 120

    memoirs about, bibliography, 178

neighborhood, map of, for Boundaries or Map Piece Exploration, 52

Neisser, Ulrich, *Memory Observed: Remembering in Natural Contexts*, 163

Nekola, Charlotte, *Dream House*, 163

Never Let Me Down, (Miller), 163

Nguyen, Kien, 4

Nguyen, Kien, *Unwanted, The: A Memoir of Childhood*, 97, 163

Night of Stone: Death and Memory in Twentieth-Century Russia, (Merridale), 163

Night, (Wiesel), 177

Nixon, Joan Lowery, *Making of a Writer, The*, 163, 174

Njeri, Itabari, *Every Good-Bye Ain't Gone: Family Portraits and Personal Escapades*, 163, 166

"no hunting" rule, Writer's Groups, 76

Noiseless Patient Spider, The, (Whitman), 33

Nordan, Lewis, *Boy with a Loaded Gun: A Memoir*, 163

Norris, Kathleen, 5

Norris, Kathleen, *Amazing Grace: A Vocabulary of Faith*, 163, 169, 175

Norris, Kathleen, *Cloister Walk, The*, 163, 169, 175

Norris, Kathleen, *Dakota: A Spiritual Geography*, 163, 169, 172, 175

Norris, Kathleen, *Virgin of Bennington, The*, 163, 169, 175

Norton, Lisa Dale, *Hawk Flies Above*, 163, 173, 178

Notes to Self, 135–36

novels, memoirs read like, 2

Oates, Joyce Carol, 94

O'Brien, Dan, *Buffalo for the Broken Heart: Restoring Life to a Black Hills Ranch*, 163, 171

O'Brien, Tim, *Things They Carried, The*, 163

observations on memoir as genre, 30–31

Of Wolves and Men, (Lopez), 176

O'Faolain, Nuala, *Are You Somebody? The Accidental Memoir of a Dublin Woman*, 164, 172

Offult, Chris, *Same River Twice, The*, 164, 171, 173

O'Hearn, Claudine, 5

O'Hearn, Claudine, *Half and Half: Writers on Growing Up Biracial and Bicultural*, 164, 168, 175

On the Day I was Born, (Chocolate), 180

On the Day You Were Born, (Fraser), 180

On the Wing: A Young American Abroad, (Sayre), 164

On Writing: A Memoir of the Craft of Writing, (King), 162

Once in a House on Fire, (Ashworth), 159, 166, 169

Ondaatje, Michael, *Cinnamon Peeler, The: Selected Poems*, 177

Ondaatje, Michael, *Collected Works of Billy the Kid*, 177
Ondaatje, Michael, *English Patient, The*, 177
Ondaatje, Michael, *In the Skin of a Lion*, 177
Ondaatje, Michael, *Running in the Family*, 164, 177
One Writer's Beginnings, (Welty), 3, 29, 31, 165
Only Girl in the Car, The, (Dobie), 160, 171
Only Son, (Johnson), 162, 166, 170
opening remarks, forms and formats, 94–95
Opposite of Fate, The: Memories of a Writing Life, (Tan), 165, 167
options
    for presenting final memoir product, 99–101
    student decision making with memoirs, 24–25
Orr, Greg, *Blessing, The*, 83, 164, 173, 177
Orr, Greg, *Caged Owl, The: New and Selected Poems*, 177
Outside Passage, (Scully), 164, 172, 173
Over the Moat: Love Among the Ruins of Imperial Vietnam, (Sullivan), 164
overcoming handicap or physical disability, chronicling through memoirs, 5

Painted Words and Spoken Memories, (Aliki), 180
Pamuk, Orhan, *Istanbul—Memories and the City*, 164, 173, 179
Paper Cathedrals, (Lee), 176
paragraphs, Crafting Options for memoir, 74
Parent Piece, 47
Paris, studios and salons of, 15
Pat Conroy Cookbook, The, (Conroy), 120, 160, 179
Path, The, (Raymo), 94
pattern for connecting shorter memory pieces, 81
Paulsen, Gary, *Hatchet*, 177
Paulsen, Gary, *Pilgrimage on a Steel Ride*, 164, 171, 174, 177
Paulsen, Gary, *River, The*, 177
people details, Elaboration strategies, 69
Perry, Michael, *Population: 485—Meeting Your Neighbors One Siren at a Time*, 164, 173
personal assessment, for writing a memoir, 128
personal journeys as memoirs, 4–5
Pham, Andrew X., 4
Pham, Andrew X., *Catfish and Mandala: A Two-Wheeled Voyage Through the Landscape and Memory of Vietnam*, 164, 173
Phenomenology, a brief overview of, 19
photographs
    forms and formats, 96
    use in a Snapshot Piece, 49

physical challenges, memoirs about, bibliography, 169–70
pieces, of the Memoir Framework
    adding to on your own, 56
    overview of the, 34–36
Pilgrim at Tinker Creek, (Dillard), 176
Pilgrimage on a Steel Ride, (Paulsen), 164, 171, 174, 177
place
    details, Elaboration strategies, 69
    memoirs about, bibliography, 172–73
Place Spider Piece, 68
Place to Stand, A, (Baca), 159, 168, 173, 176
Plan B: Further Thoughts on Faith, (Lamott), 162, 176
plan for connecting shorter memory pieces, 81
plan, self-assessments of, 136–38
Planet of the Blind, (Kuusisto), 96–97, 162, 170
Planning Documents, 125–128, 133
poets, memoirs by, bibliography, 173
Population: 485—Meeting Your Neighbors One Siren at a Time, (Perry), 164, 173
portfolio's, information about, 152–54
Portraits of Southern Childhood, (Harris), 161
practice, as a studio value, 22–23
preludes, prefaces and prologues, 95
present and present progressive tenses, telling memories in, 47
presentational elements of the finished piece, 92
preserving stories of the past through memoirs, 4–5
principles for developing effective Writing Response Groups, 76
private memoirs, issues with revealing, 6–7
process and product, self-assessments of, 136–38
professional authors' drafting and revising efforts, 64
professional examples, for Spider Pieces, 57
proofreading, as a Revision Behavior, 65
published memoirs, as a source for presentational ideas, 99
Puerto Rican authors' memoirs, bibliography, 168
purpose, territory to explore, of Spider Pieces, 57

Quality Based Education, 14
questioning the writer about next step, Writer's Groups, 77
questions about writing memoirs, 6
Quezada, Juan, 154
quotations, forms and formats, 94–95

Raines, Howell, *Fly Fishing Through the Midlife Crisis*, 164, 171, 173
Ray, Janisse, 5

Ray, Janisse, *Ecology of a Cracker Childhood*, 164, 172, 173, 175, 178

Ray, Janisse, *Wild Card Quilt*, 95, 96, 164, 172, 173, 175, 178

Raymo, Chet, *Path, The*, 94

reading like a writer, 33, 56–58

Reading Lolita in Tehran: A Memoir in Books, (Nafisi), 163, 172

readings
  Boundaries or Map Piece, 51–52
  Name Piece, 36–37
  Snapshot Piece, 47–48

Reality Check, 144

Reason for Hope: A Spiritual Journey, (Goodall & Berman), 102, 161, 169

Red Azalea: Life and Love in China, (Min), 163, 167, 170

Reflection, as a studio value, 25–26

Reflection, Final, 136–38

Refuge: An Unnatural History of Family and Place, (Williams), 165, 170, 172, 173, 178

Reinvention of Work, The: A New Vision of Livelihood for our Time, (Fox), 17–18

Remember Grandma?, (Langston), 180

representational talk, definition of, 23

Researcher's Dictionary, 133

Resurrecting Grace: Remembering Catholic Childhoods, (Sewell), 5, 164, 175

revising and drafting the Scheme, 87

revising memoir, strategies for, 66–67

Revision
  Behaviors, 64, 65, 72–73
  Options, 67
  through Crafting, 70–75

reworking writing work and workshops, 12–13

Rich, Frank, *Ghost Light*, 164

Rilke, Rainer Maria, *God Speaks to Each of Us*, 95

Rinker, Buck, *Flight of Passage*, 159, 170

River Notes: The Dance of Herons, (Lopez), 176

River, The, (Paulsen), 177

Road from Coorain, The, (Conway), 160, 171, 174

role of format in writing, the, 93

Romano, Tom, *Blending Genre, Altering Style*, 117

Romano, Tom, *Writing with Passion*, 117

Romantic Education, A, (Hampl), 161, 175

Rose, (Lee), 176

Rose, Phyllis, *Year of Reading Proust, The: A Memoir in Real Time*, 164

rought draft, memoir pieces, 62–63

routines and rituals, establishing in the studio classroom, 60–62

Running in the Family, (Ondaatje), 164, 177

Rylant, Cynthia, *When I Was Young in the Mountains*, 180

Sacks, Oliver, *Man Who Mistook His Wife for a Hat and Other Clinical Tales, The*, 177

Sacks, Oliver, *Uncle Tungsten: Memories of a Chemical Boyhood*, 164, 177, 179

Same River Twice, The, (Offult), 164, 171, 173

Santiago, Esmeralda, *When I Was Puerto Rican*, 164, 168

Sargent, John Singer, 22, 24

Sargent, John Singer, *Jaleo, El*, exhibit, 17, 82

Sartor, Margaret, *Miss American Pie: A Diary of Love, Secrets, and Growing Up in the 1970s*, 164, 172

Sayre, Nora, *On the Wing: A Young American Abroad*, 164

scene-setting
  beginning minilesson, 71
  Crafting Options for memoir, 74

Schemes
  answering the "So What?" question, 82–84
  applying to Studio Writing Classroom, 82
  definition of, 81–82
  determining a personally relevant Scheme, 84–87
  overview, 80
  samples, 91
  scheming the piece, 88
  using to earn a daily grade, 143

Schön, Donald, 18

Schön, Donald, *Educating the Reflective Practitioner: Toward a New Design for Teaching and Learning in the Professions*, 14–15

Schreiber, Le Anne, *Light Years*, 164, 172, 173

Scribbling the Cat: Travels with an African Soldier, (Fuller), 97, 161, 175

Scully, Julia, *Outside Passage*, 164, 172, 173

Sebold, Alice, *Lucky*, 164

Seldom Disappointed, (Hillerman), 94, 162

selectivity, as a hallmark of Contemporary Memoirs, 3

self-assessments of product, plan or process, 136–38

self-awareness, as a studio value, 25–26

Self-Portrait with Turtles, (Carroll), 103, 159, 178

sentence level, Crafting Options for memoir, 75

Seth, Vikram, *Two Lives*, 164, 167, 171, 179

Sewell, Marilyn, *Resurrecting Grace: Remembering Catholic Childhoods*, 5, 164, 175

Shadow Mountain: A Memoir of Wolves, a Woman, and the Wild, (Askins), 159, 178
Shah, Saira, 4
Shah, Saira, *Storyteller's Daughter, The,* 164, 173
shifting and changing genre, memoirs as, 7
short memoirs, collections of, bibliography, 175
Shulman, Alix Kates, 5
Shulman, Alix Kates, *Drinking the Rain,* 164, 172, 173, 178
Shulman, Alix Kates, *Good Enough Daughter, A,* 164, 172
Siporin, Ona, *Stories to Gather,* 164
Sky of Stone, (Hickam), 97, 161
Sleepaway School, (Stringer), 102, 164
Snapshot excerpts, 48
Snapshot Piece, 35, 46–51, 66, 118
Snyder, Don J., *Cliff Walk, The: A Job Lost and a Life Found,* 164, 170, 171
"So What?"
    asking to capture student writers' intentions, 11
    aspects of finished memoir, 128
    with Debriefings, 136
    idea, 118
    stories, 117
Sobel, Dava, *Galileo's Daughter: A Historical Memoir of Science, Faith and Love,* 164
Solomon's Song, (Wilson), 95
Song of Myself, (Whitman), 2
Speaking with Strangers, (Cantwell), 159
Spider Pieces (short Explorations), 29, 33, 37, 41–42, 56, 57, 66–67, 68, 72, 84, 85, 87, 88, 91. *See also* Explorations
spiritual journeys, pursuing through memoirs, 5, 120
spiritual quest memoirs, bibliography, 168–69
sports
    and memoir, 121
    memoirs about, bibliography, 179
stance of expertise, importance of to writing memoirs, 18
standards
    for conduct, studio-based classroom, 25–26
    for rituals and routines, 61
    for teachers, 141
Status Reports, 133
Steps in the Writing Process posters, 123
Steptoe, Javaka, *In Daddy's Arms I Am Tall: African Americans Celebrating Fathers,* 180
Stevenson, James, *Higher on the Door,* 180
Stories to Gather, (Siporin), 164
Storyteller's Daughter, The, (Shah), 164, 173
Stringer, Lee, *Sleepaway School,* 102, 164

Student Press Conference, 87, 99
students
    asking what they know about memoirs, 7–8
    assuming more responsibility for their writing, 13
    as best judges of revealing personal details in memoirs, 6
studio master, role of, 16
studio-style teaching, 11–13
    applying to memoir, 18
    a brief history of, 15–16
    establishing classroom values, 21–26
    observing contemporary classrooms, 16–17
    observing products and processes, 17
    redefining work, the final piece in, 17–18
    theoretical grounding for working with, 18–21
    using metaphors to redefine pedagogy, 13–15
stylistic elements
    considering in forms and formats, 93
    of the finished piece, 92
Styron, William, *Darkness Visible: A Memoir of Madness,* 164, 178
suggested memoirs bibliography, 159–165
suggestions for Elaboration, Writer's Groups, 76
Sullivan, James, *Over the Moat: Love Among the Ruins of Imperial Vietnam,* 164
surprise, Crafting Options for memoir, 74
Swander, Mary, *Desert Pilgrim, The: In Route to Mysticism and Miracles,* 165, 169
Sweeney, Jennifer Foote, *Life As We Know It: A Collection of Personal Essays from Salon.com,* 165
Sweet Summer, (Campbell), 117, 159, 166, 172, 178
Sweeter the Juice, The: A Family Memoir in Black and White, (Haizlip), 161, 166, 179

table of contents, how to examine a Contemporary Memoir, 9
Tales of Childhood, (Dahl), 174
Tan, Amy, *Opposite of Fate, The: Memories of a Writing Life,* 165, 167
teachers
    learning how to mentor and coach students, 13
    learning through teaching, 20
Teacher's Reflective Log, 154–57
teacher's response establishes the ground rules, Writer's Groups, 76
teaching
    as artistry, Schön's idea, 15
    and grading, 141–43
    memoir from a interactive, shared, communal stance, 12
    students to read and write memoirs, 5–7

Teaching a Stone to Talk, (Dillard), 176
tell it all, Elaboration strategies, 69
Tell Me Again about the Night I was Born, (Curtis), 180
telling detail
    beginning minilesson, 71
    Crafting Options for memoir, 74
telling stories, Revision Options for the Place Spider Piece, 68
Temple of Gold, The, (Goldman), 72
Tenka, Jane Jeong, *Language of Blood, The: A Memoir,* 94, 102, 165
"tense game," the, 51
Territory of Men, The: A Memoir, (Fraser), 160, 171
testing (state and/or district), as a part of ritual and routine, 62
text, dividing in forms and formats, 95–96
textual material, how to examine a Contemporary Memoir, 9
Them: A Memoir of Parents, (Gray), 161, 178
themed memoirs and memoir pairings, 165–74
themes in memoirs, correlating with presentational aspects, 99
Things They Carried, The, (O'Brien), 163
Thirteen Ways of Looking at a Black Man, (Gates), 161, 166, 175
Three Quarters, Two Dimes, and a Nickel: A Memoir of Becoming Whole,(Fiffer), 94, 160, 169
Thura's Diary: My Life in Wartime Iraq, (Al-Windawi), 159, 172
Thwe, Pascal Khoo, *From the Land of Green Ghosts,* 95, 165, 173, 179
time period in memoirs, correlating with presentational aspects, 99
Time Sheets, 148–50
title, how to examine a Contemporary Memoir, 9
town, map of, for Boundaries or Map Piece Exploration, 52
tracking memoir-writing processes
    overview, 123–24
    reflections after writing, 134–38
    reflections before writing, 124–29
    reflections during writing, 129–34
traditional writing workshops, not key to effective instruction, 12
translating and transcribing, as a Revision Behavior, 65
Traveling Mercies: Some Thoughts on Faith, (Lamott), 162, 169, 176
triptych, alternate memoir form
    getting started, ideas for pieces, 107–10

history of, 106
    sample pieces, 110–16
True North, (Conway), 160, 171, 174
Tucker, Neely, *Love in the Driest Season,* 95, 102, 165, 173
Tuesdays with Morrie: An Old Man, a Young Man, and Life's Greatest Lessons, (Albom), 159
Two Lives, (Seth), 164, 167, 171, 179
types of memoir, 4–5

Uncle Tungsten: Memories of a Chemical Boyhood, (Sacks), 164, 177, 179
Under the Tuscan Sun, (Mayes), 120, 163, 172, 179
understanding the writer, Writer's Groups, 76
Unquiet Mind, An: A Memoir of Moods and Madness, (Jamison), 162, 169, 178
Unwanted, The: A Memoir of Childhood, (Nguyen), 97, 163
Updates, 133, 154

values, studio, 22–26, 60–61
versions, presenting multiple for final memoir product, 99–101
Vietnamese American memoir writers, 4
Virgin of Bennington, The, (Norris), 163, 169, 175
Virgin Time, (Hampl), 55, 161, 169, 175
visual material, how to examine a Contemporary Memoir, 9
Voice Lessons: On Becoming a (Woman) Writer, (Mairs), 162
Vygotsky, Lev, 13–14

Wait Till Next Year, (Goodwin), 161
walking
    beginning minilesson, 71
    Crafting Options for memoir, 74
Walter Benjamin at the Dairy Queen: Reflections at Sixty and Beyond, (McMurty), 163, 170, 172
Warrior Lessons: An Asian American Woman's Journey into Power, (Eng), 160, 167, 171
Warrior Woman, The, (Kingston), 162, 167, 171
Warriors Don't Cry, (Beals), 159
Welty, Eudora, *One Writer's Beginnings,* 3, 29, 31, 165
What I Think I Did: A Season of Survival in Two Acts, (Woiwode), 165
"What I Think I Did" reports, 135
Wheel of Life, The: A Memoir of Living and Dying, (Kübler Ross), 162, 169, 170, 178
When Broken Glass Floats, (Him), 94, 117, 162
When I Was Puerto Rican, (Santiago), 164, 168
When I Was Young in the Mountains, (Rylant), 180

White is a State of Mind: A Memoir, (Beals), 159
white space
    presentational aspect of, 100
    using effectively in layout, 103
Whitman, Walt, *Noiseless Patient Spider, The,* 33
Whitman, Walt, *Song of Myself,* 2
Who's Sorry Now?, (Francis), 47–48
Why I'm Like This: True Stories, (Kaplan), 96, 162
Wiesel, Elie, 5
Wiesel, Elie, *And the Sea Is Never Full: Memoirs, 1969–,* 96, 165, 167, 170, 175, 177
Wiesel, Elie, *Dawn,* 177
Wiesel, Elie, *Memoirs: All Rivers Run to the Sea,* 165, 167, 169, 170, 175, 177
Wiesel, Elie, *Night,* 177
Wild Card Quilt, (Ray), 95, 96, 164, 172, 173, 175, 178
Wild Swans: Three Daughters of China, (Chang), 159, 167, 169
Wilfred Gordon McDonald Partridge, (Fox), 180
Williams, Terry Tempest, 5, 120
Williams, Terry Tempest, *Leap,* 165, 170
Williams, Terry Tempest, *Refuge: An Unnatural History of Family and Place,* 165, 170, 172, 173, 178
Wilson, Cassandra, *Solomon's Song,* 95
Winged Seed, The, (Lee), 162, 167, 173, 176
Winner, Lauren F., 5
Winner, Lauren F., *Girl Meets God,* 97, 165, 167, 169
Wiwa, Ken, 4
Wiwa, Ken, *In the Shadow of a Saint,* 94, 165, 171
Woiwode, Larry, *What I Think I Did: A Season of Survival in Two Acts,* 165
Wolff, Tobias, 4–5
Wolff, Tobias, *Boy's Life, This,* 38, 165, 171
Woman's Education, A, (Conway), 95, 160, 171, 174
women's lives, memoirs about, bibliography, 171–72
work, as a studio value, 21–22
workers, work and works, valuing in the Studio Classroom, 145–146
working and writing within a community of learners, as a studio value, 25

working plan, for writing a memoir, 128–29
Working Plans, 133
Writer's Groups, 49, 64, 66, 67, 73, 80, 85, 99, 124, 129
    Checklist Evaluation, 151
    Evaluation, 149
    using effectively, 75–79
writer's insights, Schemes, 85
Writer's Notebooks, 23, 26, 44, 59, 77, 80, 85–86, 88, 107, 130, 133, 143
writer's reflections. *See* tracking memoir-writing processes
Writing Down the Bones: Freeing the Writer Within, (Goldberg), 161, 176
writing in practice and experimentation stages, value of, 23
Writing Life, The, (Dillard), 160, 174, 176
writing like a reader, 33, 56–58
writing memoir pieces
    drafting, 62–63
    first steps, establishing routines and rituals, 60–62
    overview, 59–60
    revising, 63–73
writing, teaching through modeling, 21
Writing with Passion, (Romano), 117
writing workshops, problems and solutions, 12–13
writings
    Boundaries or Map Piece, 52–56
    Name Piece, 37
    Snapshot Piece, 49–51
Wyeth, Andrew, 22, 25
Wyeth, Andrew, *Helga* exhibit, 17, 24

Year of Magical Thinking, The, (Didion), 160, 169
Year of Reading Proust, The: A Memoir in Real Time, (Rose), 164
young adult authors, memoirs by, bibliography, 173–74
Yumoto, Kazumi, *Friends, The,* 180

zero draft, memoir pieces, 62–63
Zigzagging Down a Wild Trail, (Mason), 177
Zinsser, William, *Inventing the Truth: The Art and Craft of Memoir,* 3, 30, 64, 165